WHAT IS A THING?

by Martin Heidegger

translated by W. B. Barton, Jr. and Vera Deutsch
with an analysis by Eugene T. Gendlin

HENRY REGNERY COMPANY
Chicago, Illinois

First published in German as *Die Frage nach dem Ding*
by Max Niemeyer Verlag, Tübingen

Contents

Translators' Note   v
Preface   vii

A. Various Ways of Questioning About
   the Thing
   1. Philosophical and scientific questioning   1
   2. Ambiguous talk about the thing   4
   3. The difference in kind between the question
      of thingness and scientific and technical
      methods   7
   4. The everyday and scientific experiences of
      the thing   11
   5. Particularity and being-this-one   14
   6. The thing as just this one   24
   7. Subjective-objective; the question of truth   26
   8. The thing as the bearer of properties   32
   9. The essential construction of the truth,
      the thing, and the proposition   35
   10. The historicity of the definition of the thing   39
   11. Truth—proposition (assertion)—thing   44
   12. Historicity and decision   49
   13. Summary   52

B. Kant's Manner of Asking About the Thing
   I. The Historical Basis on Which Kant's *Critique
      of Pure Reason* Rests   55
   1. The reception of Kants' work in his lifetime   57
   2. The title of Kant's major work   61
   3. The categories as modes of assertion   62
   4. Λόγος—ratio—reason   64
   5. The modern mathematical science of nature
      and the origin of a critique of pure reason   65

6. The history of the question about
the thing: summary   108
7. Rational metaphysics (Wolff, Baumgarten)   112
II. The Question About the Thing in
Kant's Main Work   119
1. What does "critique" mean in Kant   119
2. The relation of the "critique" of pure reason
to the "system of all principles of the pure
understanding"   121
3. Interpretation of the second main section
of the transcendental analytic   124
4. The highest principle of all analytic
judgments   132
5. Kant's essential definition of the judgment   153
6. On the highest principle of all synthetic
judgments   181
7. Systematic representation of all the
synthetic principles of pure understanding   184

Analysis   245

Indices   297

TRANSLATORS' NOTE

Translating Heidegger always presents difficulties. We have attempted to be as accurate as possible, while holding the invention of cumbersome terms to a minimum. *Dasein* has been retained wherever possible. This key word, translated literally as "Being-there," is Heidegger's unique term for man's own way of Being over against other entities in the world. In a few instances, however, it seemed best to translate it as "existence," according to the accepted mode. In these cases the German word is retained in parentheses.

We take this opportunity to acknowledge the valuable assistance of Waltraut J. Stein in translating some knotty sentences, Marsha Lynn Ballew, who helped with proofing and the indices, and Elizabeth Barton, who worked indefatigably in typing the manuscript.

W. B. Barton, Jr.
Vera Deutsch (*Emeritus*)

Memphis State University

PREFACE

This work presents the text of a lecture which was held in the winter semester, 1935–36, at the University of Freiburg. The lecture was entitled "Basic Questions of Metaphysics."

Martin Heidegger

Freiburg
April, 1962

WHAT IS A THING?

A. Various Ways of Questioning About the Thing[1]

1. Philosophical and Scientific Questioning

From the range of the basic questions of metaphysics we shall here ask this *one* question: What is a thing? The question is quite old. What remains ever new about it is merely that it must be asked again and again.

We could immediately begin a lengthy discussion *about* the question "What is a thing?" before we have really posed it. In one respect this would even be justified, since philosophy always starts from an unfavorable position. This is not so with the sciences (*Wissenschaften*), for there is always a direct transition and entrance to them starting out from everyday representations, beliefs, and thinking. If one takes the everyday representation as the sole standard of all things, then philosophy is always

---

[1] The following footnote appears on the first page of the authorized German text from which this translation is made: "A transcript of this lecture was reproduced without the knowledge of the author and was put on the market outside Germany without mentioning the source." *Trans.*

something deranged (*verrücktes*). This shifting (*Verrückung*) of the attitude of thought can be accomplished only after a jolt (*Ruck*). Scientific lectures, on the other hand, can immediately begin with the presentation of their subject. The plane of questioning thus chosen will not be abandoned again when the questions become more difficult and complex.

Philosophy, on the other hand, executes a continuous shifting of standpoint and level. Therefore, one does not know for a time which way to turn in it. However, in order that this unavoidable and often beneficial entanglement does not go to excess, there is a need for a preliminary reflection about what should be asked. Otherwise there is the danger of one's speaking long-windedly about philosophy without considering its meaning. We shall use the first hour, and only it, to reflect on our intention (*Vorhaben*).

When the question "What is a thing?" arises, a doubt immediately announces itself. One may say that it makes sense to use and enjoy things in our reach, to eliminate objectionable things, to provide for necessary ones, but that one can really do nothing with the question "What is a thing?" This is true. One can start to do nothing with it. It would be a great misunderstanding of the question itself if we tried to prove that one can start to do something with it. No one can start to do anything with it. This assertion about our question is so true that we must even understand it as a determination of its essence. The question "What is a thing?" is one with which nothing can be started. More than this need not be said *about* it.

Since the question is already very old (as old, in fact, as the beginning of Western philosophy in Greece in the seventh century B.C.), it is therefore advisable that this question also be outlined from its historical point of view. Regarding this question, a little story is handed down which Plato has preserved in the *Theaetetus* (174 a.f.):

Ὥσπερ καὶ Θαλῆν 'αστρονομοῦντα . . . καὶ ἄνω βλέποντα, πεσόντα εἰς φρέαρ, θρᾷττά τις ἐμμελὴς καὶ χαρίεσσα θεραπαινὶς ἀποσκῶψαι λέγεται ὡς τὰ μὲν ἐν οὐρανῷ προθυμοῖτο εἰδέναι, τὰ δ'ἔμπροσθεν αὐτοῦ καὶ παρὰ πόδας λανθάνοι αὐτόν. "The story is that Thales, while occupied in studying the heavens above and looking up, fell into a well. A good-looking and whimsical maid from Thrace laughed at him and told him that while he might passionately want to know all things in the universe, the things in front of his very nose and feet were unseen by him." Plato added to this story the remark: ταὐτὸν δὲ ἀρκεῖ σκῶμμα ἐπὶ πάντας ὅσοι 'εν φιλοσοφίᾳ διάγουσι. "This jest also fits all those who become involved in philosophy." Therefore, the question "What is a thing?" must always be rated as one which causes housemaids to laugh. And genuine housemaids must have something to laugh about.

Through the attempt to determine the question of the thing we have unintentionally arrived at a suggestion about the characteristic of philosophy which poses that question. Philosophy, then, is that thinking with which one can start nothing and about which housemaids necessarily laugh. Such a definition of philosophy is not a mere joke but is something to think over. We shall do well to remember occasionally that by our strolling we can fall into a well whereby we may not reach ground for quite some time.

There remains the question as to why we talk about the fundamental questions of metaphysics. The term "metaphysics" here should indicate only that the questions dealt with stand at the *core* and *center* of philosophy. However, by "metaphysics" we do not mean a special field or branch within philosophy in contrast to logic and ethics. There are no fields in philosophy because philosophy itself is not a field. Something like a division of labor is senseless in philosophy; scholastic learning is to a certain extent indispensable to it but is never its essence. We therefore want to keep the term metaphysics free from all that historically adheres to it. For us it signifies only that procedure during which one runs the danger of falling into a well. Now, after this general preparation, we can more closely delineate the question "What is a thing?"

2. Ambiguous Talk About the Thing

First, what are we thinking about when we say "a thing"? We mean a piece of wood, a rock, a knife, a watch, a ball, a javelin, perhaps a screw or a piece of wire. But also a huge building, or a depot, or a giant spruce are referred to as "huge things." In the summertime we speak of many things in the meadow: grasses, herbs, the butterflies and the bugs. The thing there on the wall—the painting—we also call it a thing, and the sculptor has many different finished and unfinished things in his workshop.

By contrast, we hesitate to call the number five a thing, because one cannot reach for the number—one cannot hear it or see it. In the same way a sentence "The weather is bad" is not a thing any more than is a single word "house." We distinguish precisely the thing "house" and the word which names this thing. Also, an attitude or disposition which we maintain or lose on some occasion is not considered as a thing.

If, however, a betrayal is in the air we say, "There are uncanny things going on." Here we do not refer to pieces of wood, utensils, or similar items. When, in making a decision, it depends "above all things" on this or that consideration, the other things which have been omitted are not rocks or similar items but other considerations and decisions. Also, when we say "things aren't right," "thing" is used in a much broader sense than at the start of our inventory. Now it has the sense which our German word had from the very beginning, namely a court trial or an affair.[2] Similarly, we "clear things up somewhere," or as the proverb states, "Good things take time." Also that which is not wood or stone, but every task and enterprise needs time. And someone for whom "things are going well" is a man whose affairs, wishes, and works are in good order.

It now becomes clear that we understand the term "thing" in both a narrower and a broader sense. The *narrower* or limited meaning of "thing" is that which can be touched, reached, or seen, i.e., what is present-at-hand (*das Vorhandene*). In the *wider* meaning of the term, the "thing" is every affair or transaction, something that is in this or that condition, the things that happen in the world —occurrences, events. Finally, there is still another use of this word in the *widest* possible sense; this use was introduced within the philosophy of the eighteenth century and was long in preparation. With respect to this, Kant speaks of the "thing-in-itself" (*Ding an sich*) in order to distinguish it from the "thing-for-us" (*Ding für uns*), that is, as a "phenomenon." A thing-in-itself is that which is <u>not</u> approachable through experience as are the rocks, plants, and animals. Every thing-for-us is as a thing and also a thing-in-itself, which means that it is recognized absolutely within the absolute knowledge of God. But not every thing-in-itself is also a thing-for-us: God, for instance, is a thing-in-itself, as Kant uses the word, according to the meaning of Christian theology. Whenever Kant calls God a thing, he does not mean a giant gaslike formation that acts somewhere in hidden depths. According to strict usage, "thing" here means only "something" (*etwas*), that which is not nothing. We can think *some-*

---

[2] *Das Ding:* From Germanic legal language, originally designating the tribunal, or assembly of free men. The *thing*[(OHG)] was a cause one negotiated or reconciled in the assembly of judges. Heidegger in a later work refers to this in setting forth the notion of *thing* as what *assembles* a world. *See* the lecture on *Das Ding* in Martin Heidegger, *Vorträge und Aufsätze* (*VA*) (Pfullingen: Verlag Neske, 1954), pp. 172-74. *Trans.*

thing by the term and concept of "God," but we cannot experience God as we do this piece of chalk, about which we can make and prove such statements as: If we drop this piece of chalk it will fall with a certain velocity.

God is a thing insofar as He is something at all, an X. Similarly, number is a thing, faith and faithfulness are things. In like manner the signs > < are "something," and similarly "and" and "either/or."

If we again ask our question "What is a thing?" we realize that this question is not in good order, because what should be put into question, that is, the "thing," is ambiguous in its meaning. What is to be put into question must be sufficiently defined to become questionable in the right way. "Where is the dog?" "The dog" cannot be searched for if I do not know whether it is our own dog or the neighbor's. "What is a thing?" Thing in what sense— in the limited, the wider, or the widest? We have to distinguish three different meanings even if the means of distinction is still uncertain:

1. A thing in the sense of being present-at-hand: a rock, a piece of wood, a pair of pliers, a watch, an apple, and a piece of bread. All inanimate and all animate things such as a rose, shrub, beech tree, spruce, lizard, and wasp....

2. Thing in the sense in which it means whatever is named but which includes also plans, decisions, reflections, loyalties, actions, historical things....

3. All these and anything else that is a something (*ein Etwas*) and not nothing.

Within what boundaries we determine the meanings of the term "thing" always remains arbitrary. With respect to this the scope and direction of our questions will change.

It is closer to our linguistic usage of today to understand the term "thing" in the first (narrower) signification. Then each of these things (rock, rose, apple, watch) is also something (*etwas*), but not every something (the number five, fortune, bravery) is a thing.

In asking "What is a thing?" we shall adhere to the *first* meaning; not only because we want to stay close to the usage of language but also because the question concerning the thing, even where it is understood in its wider and widest meanings, mostly aims at this narrower field and begins from it. As we ask "What is a thing?" we now mean the things around us. We take in view what is most immediate, most capable of being grasped by the hand. By observing such, we reveal that we have learned something from the laughter of the housemaid. She thinks we should first look around thoroughly in this round-about-us (*Um-uns-herum*).

3. *The Difference in Kind Between the Question of Thingness (*Dingheit*) and Scientific and Technical Methods*

As soon as we begin to define these things, however, we run into an embarrassment. All these things have really been settled long ago, and, if not, there are proven scientific procedures and methods of production in which they can be settled. What a stone is can best and most quickly be told by mineralogy and chemistry; what a rose or a bush is, botany teaches reliably; what a frog or a falcon is, zoology; as to what a shoe is, or a horseshoe, or a watch, the shoemaker, the blacksmith, and the watchmaker, respectively, give the best technical information.

It turns out that we are always too slow with our question, and we are immediately referred to quarters which already have a far better answer ready or, at least, experiences and methods to give such answers quickly. This only confirms what we have already admitted, namely, that we cannot start to do anything with the question "What is a thing?" But since we intend (*vorhaben*) to clarify this question, especially with regard to immediate things, it will be necessary to make clear what else we want to know in contradistinction to the sciences.

With our question "What is a thing?" it obviously is
not our purpose to discover what granite, a pebble, lime-
stone, or sandstone is but rather what the rock is as a
thing. We do not care to know how to distinguish at any
time mosses, ferns, grasses, shrubs, and trees, but what
the plant is as a thing, and similarly in respect to animals.
We do not care to know what pliers are in comparison
with a hammer, what a watch is in comparison with a
key; but we want to know what these implements and
tools are as things. What this means, of course, must be
further clarified. But if one once admits that we can ask
the question in this way, then obviously one demand remains: namely, that we stick to the facts and their exact
observations in order to discover *what* things are. What
things are cannot be contrived at a desk or prescribed by
generalized talk. It can be determined only in workshops
and in the research laboratories. And if we do not confine
ourselves to this then we will be exposed to the laughter
of housemaids. We are inquiring about things, and yet we
pass over (*überspringen*) all the givens and the opportu-
nities which, according to general opinion, give us adequate information about all these things.

This is how it actually looks. With our question "What
is a thing?" we not only pass over the particular rocks
and stones, particular plants and their species, animals
and their species, implements and tools, we also pass over
whole realms of the inanimate, the animate, and tools,
and desire to know only "What is a thing?" In inquiring
this way, we seek what makes the thing a thing and not
what makes it a stone or wood; what conditions
(*be-dingt*)[3] the thing. We do not ask concerning a thing of
some species but after the thingness of a thing. For the

---

[3] *Be-dingt;* verb *bedingen:* "conditioned"; "to condition." As
already suggested, Heidegger wants to connect *dingen* with the
notion of "assembling." Thus he writes: *"Das Ding dingt. Das
Dingen versammelt."* "The thing things. The thinging assembles"
(*VA*, p. 172). Here he seems to want to call our attention to the
original significance of *bedingen*. The original legal connotation

condition of being a thing, which conditions the thing as a thing, cannot itself again be a thing, i.e., something conditioned. The thingness must be something un-conditioned (*un-bedingtes*). With the question "What is a thing?" we are asking for something unconditioned. We ask about what is all around us and can be grasped by the hand, and yet we alienate ourselves from those immediate things very much more than did Thales, who could see only as far as the stars. But we want to pass beyond even these things to the unconditioned, where there are no more things that provide a basis and ground.

And, nevertheless, we pose this question only in order to know what a rock is, and a lizard taking a sunbath on it, a blade of grass that grows beside it, and a knife which perhaps we hold in our hands while we lie in the meadow. We want to know just that, something that the mineralogist, botanist, zoologist, and metallurgist perhaps don't want to know at all, something that they only think they want to know while actually wanting something else: to promote the progress of science, or to satisfy the joy of discovery, or to show the technical usage of things, or to make a livelihood. We, however, desire to know what these men not only do not want to know but perhaps what they never can know in spite of their science and technical skill. This sounds presumptuous. It doesn't only *sound* so, it *is*. Naturally this is not the presumptuousness of a single person any more than our doubt about the desire and ability of the sciences to know passes sentence on the attitude and conviction of particular persons or even against the utility and the necessity of science.

The demand for knowledge in our question is a presumption of the kind found in every essential decision (*Entscheidung*). Although we are already familiar with this decision, that does not mean that we have already passed through it. It is the decision whether we want to

---

of these words must not be overlooked. An "assembly" does condition something. *Trans.*

know those things with which one can start to do nothing
—in the sense of this figure of speech. If we forego this
knowledge and don't ask this question, then all remains
as it is. We shall pass our examinations, perhaps even better, without asking this question. Even if we ask this
question, we shall not overnight become better botanists,
zoologists, historians, jurists, or physicians. But perhaps better or more cautiously put—certainly different
teachers, different physicians and judges, although even
then we can start to do nothing with this question in our
professions.

*With our question, we want neither to replace the sci-
ences nor to reform* (verbessern) *them.* On the other
hand, we want to participate in the preparation of a decision; the decision: Is science the measure of knowledge,
or is there a knowledge in which the ground and limit of
science and thus its genuine effectiveness are determined?
Is this genuine knowledge necessary for a historical people, or is it dispensable or replaceable by something
else?

However, decisions are not worked out by merely talking about them but by creating situations and taking positions in which the decision is unavoidable, in which it
becomes the most essential decision when one does not
make it but rather avoids it.

The uniqueness of such decisions remains that they are
prepared for only by questions with which one cannot
start to do anything insofar as common opinion and the
horizon of housemaids are concerned. Furthermore, this
questioning always looks like a pretense to know better
than the sciences. The term "better" always means a
difference of degree in one and the same realm. However,
with our question we stand outside the sciences, and the
knowledge for which our question strives is neither better nor worse but totally different. Different from science
but also different from what one calls a "Weltan-
schauung."

4. *The Everyday and Scientific Experiences of the Thing; The Question Concerning Their Truth*

The question "What is a thing?" seems now to be in order. It is at least roughly determined: (1) *What* is put in question, and (2) That whereafter we ask regarding what is put in question. Put in question is the "thing" in its narrower meaning, which refers us to the present-at-hand (*Vorhanden*). That whereafter the thing is asked and interrogated, as it were, is thingness, what determines a thing as such to be a thing.

Yet when we start to ascertain this thingness of a thing we are immediately helpless in spite of our well-ordered question. *Where* should we grasp the thing? And besides: we nowhere find "the thing," but only particular things, these and those things. What makes this so? Is it only we, because, first and foremost, we strike only the particular and then only afterward, as it seems, extract and pull off (abstract) the general, in this case the thingness, from the particular? Or is the fact that we always meet only particular things inherent in the things themselves? And if it is in the things, is it then only their somehow basic or accidental caprice to meet us in this way, or do they meet us as particulars because they are within themselves particular, as the things which they are?

In any case, this is where our everyday experience and opinion about things is directed. But before we continue this line of our questioning, it is necessary to insert an intervening examination of our everyday experience. There is not at first, nor later on, any valid reason to doubt our everyday experiences. Of course, it is not sufficient simply to claim that that which everyday experience shows of the things is true, any more than it is sufficient to maintain in a seemingly more critical and cautious way: after all, as individual humans we are individual subjects and egos, and what we represent and

mean are only subjective pictures which we carry around
in us; we never reach the things themselves. This view, in
turn, will not be overcome, in case it is not true, by talking about "we" instead of "I" and by taking into account
the community rather than the individual. There always
remains the possibility that we only exchange subjective
pictures of things with one another, which may not
thereby become any truer because we have exchanged
them communally.

We now set aside these different interpretations of our
relation to the things as well as the truth of this relation.
But, on the other hand, we do not want to forget that it is
not at all sufficient to appeal only to the truth and certainty of everyday experience. Precisely if everyday experience carries in itself a truth, and a superior truth at
that, this truth must be founded, i.e., its foundation must
be laid, admitted, and accepted. This will become even
more necessary when it turns out that the everyday things
show still another face. That they have long done, and
they do it for us today to an extent and in a way that we
have hardly comprehended, let alone mastered.

Take the common example: The sun's diameter is at
most half a meter to one meter wide when it sets behind
the mountains in the form of a glowing disk. All that the
sun is for the shepherd coming home with his flock does
not now need to be described, but it is the real sun, the
same one the shepherd awaits the next morning. But the
real sun has already set a few minutes before. What we
see is only a semblance (*Schein*) caused by certain processes of rays. But even this semblance is only a semblance,
for "in reality," we say, the sun never sets at all. It does
not wander over the earth and around it but the reverse.
The earth turns around the sun, and this sun, furthermore, is not the ultimate center of the universe. The sun
belongs to larger systems which we know today as the
Milky Way and the spiral nebula, which are of an order
of magnitude compared to which our solar system must

be characterized as diminutive. And the sun, which daily rises and sets and dispenses light, is ever growing colder; our earth, in order to maintain the same degree of warmth, would have to come always closer to the sun. However, it is moving away from the sun. This means it rushes toward a catastrophe, albeit in "time spans" in comparison with which the few thousand years of human history on earth amount to not even one second.

Now which of these is the true sun? Which thing is the true one, the sun of the shepherd or the sun of the astrophysicist? Or is the question wrongly put, and if so, why? How should this be decided? For that, obviously, it is necessary to know what a thing is, what it means to-be-a-thing, and how the truth of a thing is determined. On these questions neither the shepherd nor the astrophysicist informs us. Neither can or needs to pose these questions in order to be immediately who they are.

Another example: The English physicist and astronomer Eddington once said of his table that every thing of this kind—the table, the chair, etc.—has a double. Table number one is the table known since his childhood; table number two is the "scientific table." This scientific table, that is, the table which science defines in its thingness, consists, according to the atomic physics of today, not of wood but mostly of empty space; in this emptiness electrical charges are distributed here and there, which are rushing back and forth at great velocity. Which one now is the true table, number one or number two? Or are both true? In the sense of what truth? What truth mediates between the two? There must be still a third one according to which number one and number two are true in their way and represent a variation of this truth. We cannot save ourselves by the favored road of saying: whatever is asserted about the scientific table number two, the spiral nebula, and the dying sun are but viewpoints and theories of physics. To that the retort is: on this physics are founded all our giant power stations, our airplanes, radio and television, the whole of technology which has altered the earth and man with it more than he suspects. These are realities, not viewpoints which some investigators "distant from life" defend. Does one want science even "closer to life"? I think that it is already so close that it suffocates us. Rather, we need the right distance from life in order to attain a perspective in which we measure what is going on with us human beings.

No one knows this today. For this reason we must ask everyone and ask again and again, in order to know it, or at least in order to know why and in what respects we do not know it. Have man and the nations only stumbled into the universe to be similarly slung out of it again, or is it otherwise? We must ask. For a long time there is first something much more preliminary: we must first again *learn* how to ask. That can only happen by asking questions—of course, not just any questions. We chose the question "What is a thing?" It now turns out: the things stand in different truths. What is the thing such that it is like this? From what point of view should we decide the being-a-thing of things? We take our standpoint in everyday experience with the reservation that its truth, too, will eventually require a foundation (*eine Begründung*).[4]

5. *Particularity and Being-This-One (*Jediesheit*).*
Space and Time as Determinations of Things

In everyday experience we always meet particular things. With this suggestion we resume the pursuit of our question after the above digression.

---

[4] *Begründung:* "A foundation," "establishment," "argument," "reasons for," "explanation," "proof." The English "ground" is equivalent to *Grund;* but the German includes the idea of a foundation of a building. Heidegger seems to emphasize this aspect of its meaning. Therefore, in the related words this sense will be adhered to where possible. *Kant and the Problem of Metaphysics,* James S. Churchill, trans. (Bloomington: Indiana University Press, 1962), p. 3, n. 1. *Trans.*

The things are particular. That means first: the stone, the lizard, the blade of grass, and the knife are each-for-itself (*je für sich*). Moreover, the stone is a completely definite one, exactly this one; the lizard is not a lizard in general, but just this one, and so it is with the blade of grass and the knife. There is no thing in general, only particular things; and the particulars, moreover, are just these (*je diese*). Each thing is one such this one (*ein je dieses*) and no other.

Unexpectedly, we meet with something which belongs to the thing as a thing. This is a determination that is disregarded by the sciences which, with their thrust toward facts, apparently come closest to things. For a botanist, when he examines the labiate flower, will never be concerned about the single flower as a single one: it always remains an exemplar only. That is also true of the animals, for example, the countless frogs and salamanders which are killed in a laboratory. The "this one" (*je dieses*) which distinguishes every thing, is passed over by science. Should we now consider the things in this way? With the countlessness of things we would never come to an end, and we would continually establish nothing but irrelevancies. However, we are not directing ourselves exclusively at the particulars, always these things (*je diese Dinge*) one after another, but are after every thing's general characteristic of being "this one": the being-this-one (*Jediesheit*), if such a word formation is acceptable.

But is the sentence "Every thing is a this one (*ein je dieses*) and not another one" at all applicable? There are things which do not differ at all from one another, things which are exactly alike, as two buckets or two pine needles which we cannot distinguish from each other in any respect. The fact, one could say, that we cannot distinguish between the two exactly alike things does not prove that, in the end, they are not different. However, even assuming that two single things are simply alike, each is still this thing because each of these two pine needles is in another place (*Ort*); and if they are to occupy the same place, they can do so only at a different time point. Place and time point make even absolutely alike things be these very ones (*je diesen*), i.e., different ones. Insofar as each thing has its place, its time, and its time duration, there are never two same things. The particularity (*Jeweiligkeit*) of the places and their manifoldness are grounded in space, and the particularity of the time points is grounded in time. That basic characteristic of the thing, i.e., that essential determination of the thingness of the thing to be this one (*je dieses*), is grounded in the essence of space and time.

Our question "What is a thing?" includes, therefore, the questions "What is space?" and "What is time?" It is customary for us to speak of them both together. But how and why are space and time conjoined? Are they conjoined at all, as though externally thrust onto one another and into one another, or are they primordially at one? Do they stem from a common root, from some third, or better, some first which is neither space nor time because more primordially it is both? These and other related questions will occupy us, i.e., we will not set our minds at rest that there is space and time and that we place them next to each other—space *and* time—by use of the patient little word "and," as in "dog and cat." In order to keep hold of these questions by means of a title, we call them the question of the time-span (*Zeitraum*). We understand by time-span a certain length of time, and say: within the time-span of a hundred years. By this expression we really mean only something temporal. In contrast to this very common usage, which is very instructive for further thought, we will give the composite "*Zeitraum*" a meaning that is designed to indicate the inner unity of space and time. Thereby, the real question applies to the "and." That we name time first, that we say *Zeitraum* and not *Raumzeit*, should indicate that time plays a special role in this question. But that should not mean at all that space can be deduced from time or that it is something secondary to it.

The question "What is a thing?" includes in itself the question: "What is *Zeitraum* (time-span)?", the puzzling unity of space and time within which, as it seems, the basic character of things, to be only this one, is determined.

We will not escape the question about the essence of space and time, because immediately so many doubts arise regarding the distinguishing mark we gave of the thingness of the thing. We said: Place and time point make even absolutely identical things just these (*je diesen*), i.e., different ones. But are space and time at all determinations of the thing itself? The things, as we say, are indeed within space and time. Space and time are a frame, an ordering realm, with the help of which we establish and indicate the place and time point of the particular things. It might be, therefore, that each thing, if it is determined with respect to place and time, is now just this (*je dieses*), not mistakable for any other. However, these are only determinations which are externally brought to and at a thing through the space-time relation. As yet, nothing is said about the thing itself or what makes it to be this one. We easily see that behind these difficulties hides the principal question: Are space and time only a frame for the things, a system of co-ordinates which we lay out in order to reach sufficiently exact statements about things, or are space and time something else? Is the relation to them of the thing not this external one? (Compare Descartes.)[5]

---

[5] Descartes identifies space or internal place with the body which occupies it: "For, in truth, the same extension in length, breadth, and depth, which constitutes space, constitutes body." The distinction we make is only a conceptual one; extension being the common factor, individualized in the case of body, but given a generic unity in the case of space. For this reason Descartes rejects the notion of the vacuum. (*The Principles of Philosophy,*

According to the everyday manner we are used to, we look at what is around us. We can notice: this chalk is white; this wood is hard; the door is closed. But such statements do not carry us to the goal. We want to look at the things with respect to their *thingness*, therefore for *what* presumably characterizes *all* things and *each* thing. When we look at them with respect to this we find that things are singular: *one* door, *one* piece of chalk, *one* blackboard, etc. Being singular is obviously a general, universally applicable characteristic (*Zug*) of things. If we look more closely, we even discover that these single things are just these (*je diese*): this door, this chalk, this now and here, not those of classroom six and not the ones from last semester.

Thus, we already have an answer to our question "What is a thing?" A thing is always a this one (*je dieses*). We now seek to understand more precisely wherein this essential characteristic of the thing consists. The above named characteristic of the things, that they are always these (*je diese*), stands in conjunction with space and time. Through its particular space and time point, each thing is unmistakably this one and not another. However, some doubts arise as to whether with such a reference to space and time we are saying anything about the thing itself. Such statements about the place and time point after all concern only the frame within which things stand

---

Part II, Principles X–XVI, E. S. Haldane and G. R. T. Ross, trans., *The Philosophical Works of Descartes* [N. Y.: Dover Publications, 1955], 2 vols., 1, 259–62.)

In *Meditation III* and in his reply to P. Gassendi's objections, Descartes asserts the doctrine of continual creation, based on his belief that the moments of time are discrete. Thus he asserts: ". . . that the single moments of this time can be separated from their neighbours, i.e., that a thing which endures through individual moments may cease to exist." (*Ibid.*, II, 219; 1, 163, 164.)

Descartes, therefore, identifies both space and time with the existent thing. Both are considered as external in their relation to the thing only because of the way we conceptually give them generic unity. *Trans.*

and how, that is to say where and when, they happen to stand within it. One could point out that each thing—as far as we know things—has its space-time-position (*Raum-Zeit-Stelle*), and that this relation of the thing to space and time is not something arbitrary. Do things necessarily stand within this space-time-relation (*Raum-Zeit-Bezug*), and what is the basis for this necessity? Does this basis lie in the things themselves? If this were the case, then the aforementioned characteristic would have to assert something about things themselves, about the being-a-thing (*Dingsein*).

First, however, we have the impression that space and time are something outside of things. Or does this impression deceive us? Let us look more closely: this piece of chalk, the room—better, the space of the classroom— lies around this thing, if we must speak of a "lying" around. We say that this piece of chalk takes up a certain space. This space is delimited by the surface of the piece of chalk. Surface? Plane? The piece of chalk itself is extended. The space is not only around it, but directly in it, even within it; but this space is occupied, filled up. The chalk itself consists inwardly of space. After all, we say the chalk takes *up* this space, encloses this space by its surface, in itself, as its interior. Therefore, for the chalk, this space is not a mere exterior frame. But what does interior mean here? What does the interior of the chalk look like? Let us see. We break it into two pieces. Are we now at the interior? Exactly as before we are again outside. Nothing has changed. The pieces of chalk are smaller, but bigger or smaller does not matter now. The surfaces where it is broken are less smooth than the rest of the surface, but that does not matter. The moment we wanted to open the chalk by breaking it, to grasp the interior, it had enclosed itself again. And we could continue this action until the piece of chalk had become a little pile of powder. Under a magnifying glass and a microscope we could still break up these tiny grains. Where this limit of such a "mechanical" division lies cannot be clearly determined. In any case, such breaking up never yields anything but what was already here, from which it started. Whether this piece of chalk is four centimeters or .004 millimeters only makes a difference in *how much* but not in what (essence).

Following this mechanical division we could carry out a chemical-molecular analysis. We could even go behind that, to the atomic structure of the molecules. But according to the starting point of our question, we want to remain in the realm of the things immediately around us. But even if we go the way of chemistry and physics, we never reach beyond the sphere of mechanics, that is, beyond such a spatial sphere wherein matter moves from place to place or rests in one place. On the basis of the results of our present atomic physics—since Niels Bohr exhibited his model of the atom (1913)—the relations between matter and space are no longer so simple, although fundamentally still the same. What keeps a place occupied, takes up space, must itself be extended. Our question has been what the interior of a physical body looks like; more exactly, the space "there." The result is: this interior is always again an exterior for the smaller and smaller particles.

Meanwhile, our piece of chalk has become a little pile of powder. Even if we assume that nothing of the matter has escaped, that the full amount is still here, it is no longer our chalk, i.e., we can no longer write with it on the blackboard. We could accept that. But we cannot accept that we could not find the space we looked for in the interior of the chalk, the space which belongs to the chalk itself. But, perhaps we did not reach for it fast enough. Let us break the piece of chalk again! The surface where it is broken and the pieces of surface are now the exterior. But this piece of surface which was just previously "interior" is exactly that piece of surface delimiting the grains of chalk, and it was always the exterior of these pieces of chalk. Where does the interior begin and the exterior end? Does the chalk consist of space? Or is the space always a container, something of an enclosure, of which the chalk consists, of that which the chalk itself is? The chalk only fills space; a place is always placed into the thing. This placing in of space tells us exactly that the space remains outside. Whatever occupies space always forms the border between an outside and an inside. But the interior is really only an exterior lying farther back. (Strictly speaking, there is no outside or inside within space itself.) But where in the world would there be an outside and inside, if not in space? Perhaps, however, space is only the possibility of outside and inside but itself neither an interior nor an exterior. The statement "Space is the possibility of inside and outside" might be true. What we call "possibility" (*Möglichkeit*) is still rather indefinite. "Possibility" can mean many things. We are not of the opinion that we have decided with such a statement the question of the relation between the thing and space. Perhaps the question has not yet been sufficiently posed. Up to now we have not considered that space which especially concerns such things as this chalk, as well as writing tools and implements in general, which we call the storeroom (equipment room: *Zeugraum*).

We were concerned to reflect on whether space and time are "exterior" to things or not. Yet it became evident that the space which appears most likely to be within things is something exterior when viewed from the physical thing and its particles.

Still more exterior to things is time. The chalk here also has its times: the time point (*Zeitpunkte*) now in which the chalk is here, and this next now when it is there. With the question concerning space there still appeared some prospects of finding it within the thing itself. But even this is not the case with time. Time runs over things as a brook passes over rocks. Perhaps not even in this way, because, in the movement of the waters, the rocks are pushed and driven so that they rub and polish each other. The movement of time, however, leaves things untouched. That the time now advances from 5:15 to 6:00 does nothing to the chalk. We do say "with" time or "with the passing" of time things are changing. It is even said that the ill-famed "tooth" of time is "nibbling" on things. That things are changing in the passing of time is not to be denied. But did anyone ever observe how time nibbles at things, that is, generally speaking, how time goes to work on things?

But perhaps time is identifiable only with some outstanding things. We know such things: clocks. They show the time. Let us look at this clock. Where is time? We see the figures and the hands which move, but not time. We can open a clock and examine it. Where here is time? But this clock does not give the time immediately. This clock is set according to the German Observatory in Hamburg. If we were to travel there and ask the people where they have the time, we would be just as wise as before our journey.

If, therefore, we cannot even find time on that thing which shows time, then it actually seems to have nothing to do with things themselves. On the other hand, it is after all not merely empty talk when we say that we can tell the time with the help of clocks. If we deny this, where would that lead? Not only the schedule of everyday life would fall to pieces, but every technical calculation would also become impossible; history, every memory, and every decision would be gone.

And yet, in what relation do things stand to time? With every attempt to determine this, the impression is renewed more strongly than before that space and time are only perceptual realms for things, indifferent toward these but useful in assigning every thing to its space-time-position. Where and how these perceptual realms really are remains open. But this much is certain: only on account of this position do particular things become just these (*je diesen*). And there is then, after all, at least the possibility of many same things. Precisely when we look at the question from things themselves and not from their frame of reference, each thing is not unmistakably a single one (*je dieses*); it is that only with respect to space and time.

Now, it is true that one of the greatest German thinkers, Leibniz, has denied that there ever could be two identical things. Leibniz established, with regard to this, a special principle which ruled throughout this philosophy, of which today we hardly have an idea. It is the *principium identitatis indiscernibilium*, the principle of the identity of indiscernible things. The principle states: Two indistinguishable things, i.e., two alike things, cannot be two things but must be the same, i.e., *one* thing. Why, we ask? The reason Leibniz gives is just as essential for the fundamental principle as for his entire basic philosophical system. Two alike things cannot be two, i.e., each is irreplaceably this one (*je dieses*) because two alike things cannot exist at all. Why not? The *being* of things is their creation by God, as understood in the Christian theological interpretation. If there ever were two alike things, then God had twice created the same, i.e., simply repeating something eternal. Such a superficially mechanical deed, however, contradicts the completeness of the absolute Creator, the *perfectio Dei*. Therefore, there can never be two alike things, by reason of the essence of being, in the sense of being created. This principle is based here upon certain more or less explicit principles and basic perceptions of what is in general and the being of that; moreover, upon certain conceptions of the perfection of creation and production in general.

We are not now sufficiently prepared to take our stand with respect to the principle expressed by Leibniz and its foundation. It is necessary always to see again to what lengths the question "What is a thing?" immediately leads. It could be that this theological argument of the principle is impossible for us, even disregarding the question of the dogmatic truth of Christianity. However, one thing remains certain; in fact, it now first comes to light that the question concerning the character of the being of things, to be singular and "this one," is completely and entirely hung up in the question concerning being. Does being still mean to us being created by God? If not, what then? Does being no longer mean anything at all to us, so that we are only staggering around in a confusion? Who can decide how it stands with being and its determination?

But we first ask only about the proximate things around us. They show themselves as singular and as "just these." From our reference to Leibniz, we concluded that the character of the things, to be "just these," could be based on the being of things themselves and not only with reference to their position in space and time.

6. The Thing as Just This One (je dieses)

But we shall let alone the question from where the character of a thing as "just this one" is determined, and pose a still more preliminary question, which is wrapped in the preceding one.

We said that the single things around us are "just these." When we say of something which encounters us that it is *this*, are we saying anything about the thing itself at all? This, namely, the one here, i.e., that which we now point out. In "this" lies a pointing, a referring. We indicate something to the others who are with us, with whom we are together. It is a reference within the range of the "here"—this one here, this here. The "this" means, more precisely, here in our immediate neighborhood; while we always mean something more distant by "that," but still within the range of "the here and there"—this here, that there. The Latin language has in this connection still sharper distinctions. *Hic* means "this here," *iste* means

"that there." *Ille* means "that far away," the Greek ἐκεῖ—
by which the poets intend what is at the periphery—what
we call the ulterior (*Jenseitige*).

In grammar such words as "this" and "that" are called
demonstratives, for these words demonstrate, they point
at. . . . The general verbal character of these reference
words comes to expression in the term demonstrative
pronoun (*Für-wörter*). The Greeks said ἀντωνυμία, which
became the standard for Western grammar ('Αντωνυμίαι
δεικτικαί). In this designation of such words as "this" and
"that" lies a quite definite explanation and interpretation
of their essence. The interpretation is indeed significant
for Western grammar (which, in spite of everything, still
governs us today). Yet it is misleading. The name "pronoun" (*Für-wort*), considering a word as a noun (*nomen*),
a name (*Name*) and substantive, means that such words
as "this" take the place of substantives. It is true that they
do this, yet it is only what they do *also*. We speak of the
chalk but do not always use the name, using instead the
expression "this." However, such a substituting role is
not the original essence of the pronoun; its naming function is more primordial. We grasp it immediately when
we remember that the article "the" is derived from the
demonstrative words. It is customary to place the article
before the substantive. The naming reference of the article always goes beyond the noun. The naming of the substantive itself always occurs on the basis of a pointing-
out. This is a "demonstration," exhibiting the encountered and the present-at-hand. The function of naming,
which is performed in the demonstrative, belongs to the
most primordial way of speaking in general. It is not
merely a substitution, i.e., not a second or later order of
expression.

To consider what has been said is important for the
correct evaluation of the "this." It is somehow included in
every naming as such. Insofar as things confront us, they
come into the character of "this." But thereby we are say-

ing that the "this" is not characteristic of the thing itself. The "this" takes the thing only insofar as it is an object of a demonstration. Those speaking and thinking, however, who use such demonstrative words, i.e., human beings, are always single subjects. The "this," instead of being a character of the thing itself, is only a subjective addition on our part.

7. Subjective-Objective. The Question of Truth

To see how little, indeed, is said by the statement that "this" is only a "subjective" determination of the thing is recognizable from the fact that we are just as justified in calling it "objective," for *objectum* means something thrown against you. The "this" means a thing insofar as it faces us, i.e., it is objective. What a "this" is does not depend upon our caprice and our pleasure. But even if it depends on us, it also equally depends upon the things. This only is clear, that such determinations as the "this," which we use in the everyday experience of the things, are not as self-evident as they may appear to be. It remains absolutely questionable which kind of truth concerning the thing is contained in the determination of it as a "this." It is questionable which kind of truth in general we have of things in our daily experience, whether it is subjective or objective, whether both together or neither.

Up to now we have only seen that beyond the sphere of daily experiences the things also stand in different truths (the sun of the shepherd and of the astrophysicist, the ordinary table and the scientific table). Now it becomes clear that the truth about the sun for the shepherd, the truth about the ordinary table, e.g., the determination "this sun" and "this table"—this truth about the "this" —remains opaque in its essence. How shall we ever say something about the thing without being sufficiently instructed about the kind of truth which is proper to it? At the same time we can state the opposite question: How are we to know something about the essential truth of the thing if we do not know the thing itself to determine what kind of truth can and must be proper to it?

It is now clear: to go straight to the things cannot be carried out, not because we shall be stopped on the way but because those determinations at which we arrive and which we attribute to the things themselves—space, time, and "this"—present themselves as determinations which do not belong to the things themselves.

On the other hand, we cannot invoke the common answer which says that if determinations are not "objective" they are "subjective." It could be that they are neither, that the distinction between subject and object, and with it the subject-object relationship itself, is a highly questionable, though generally favored, sphere of retreat for philosophy.

Hardly a gratifying position—so it seems. There is no information about the thingness of the thing without knowledge of the kind of truth in which the thing stands. But there is no information about this truth of the thing without knowledge of the thingness of the thing whose truth is in question.

Where are we to get a foothold? The ground slips away under us. Perhaps we are already close to falling into the well. At any rate the housemaids are already laughing. And what if only we ourselves are these housemaids, i.e., if we have secretly discovered that all this talk of the "this," as well as similar discussions, is fantasy and empty!

The worst, however (not for our daily livelihood but for philosophy), would be if we wanted to escape from the above bad position by trying to steal away on some clandestine path. We could say: our everyday experiences are still reliable; this chalk is this chalk, and I take it if I need it and leave it aside if I do not. This is as clear as day, certainly, if we are concerned about daily use. But now it is a question of what the thingness of this thing is and whether the "this" is a true characteristic of the thing itself. Perhaps we still have not understood the "this" sufficiently clearly. We renew our question of whence and how the truth of a thing as a "just this" (*je dieses*) is determined. Here we come upon an observation which Hegel has already made in his *Phenomenology of Mind.*[6] To be sure, the approach (*Ansatz*), level (*Ebene*), and intention (*Absicht*) of Hegel's way of thinking are of a different kind.

The suspicion arose that a thing's characteristic as "just this" is only subjective, since this characteristic depends on the standpoint of the experiencing individual and the time point in which, on the part of the subject, the experience of a thing happens to be made.

Why is the chalk "just this" and no other? Only because it is just right here now. The "here" and the "now" make it to be "*this.*" With the demonstrative characteristic "this" we refer to the "here," i.e., to a place, to a space, and, equally, to the now, i.e., time. We already know this, at least in general. Let us now pay special attention to the truth about the chalk: "Here is the chalk." That is a truth; the here and the now hereby characterize the chalk so that we emphasize by saying: *the* chalk, which means "this." However, this is almost too obvious, almost offen-

---

[6] It is interesting to compare Heidegger's analysis of "this" with that of Hegel, whom he apparently has in mind throughout this section. For Hegel, at the level of sensory experience, "pure being" breaks into "thises": "I" on the one hand and "object" on the other. Together they make up "the This." The This exists in the twofold form of the Now and the Here. But Hegel wants to establish that the Now and Here, as well as the This, are Universals. It is not the individual thing that continues to maintain itself but the Now and Here. (G. F. W. Hegel, *Phenomenology of Mind*, J. B. Baillie, trans. [2nd ed.; New York: Macmillan Co., 1949], section A, 1, 151–52.) *Trans.*

sively self-evident. But we want to do something more and elaborate still further the self-evident truth about the chalk. We even want to write down this truth about the chalk to avoid losing this great valuable.

For this purpose we take a scrap of paper and we write the truth down: "Here is the chalk." We lay this written statement beside the thing of which it is the truth. After the lecture is finished both doors are opened, the classroom is aired, there will be a draft, and the scrap of paper, let us suppose, will flutter out into the corridor. A student finds it on his way to the cafeteria, reads the sentence "Here is the chalk," and ascertains that this is not true at all. Through the draft the truth has become an untruth. Strange that a truth should depend on a gust of wind. Usually philosophers tell each other that the truth is something which is valid in itself, which is beyond time and is eternal, and woe to him who says that truth is not eternal. That means relativism, which teaches that everything is only relatively true, only partly true, and that nothing is fixed any longer. Such doctrines are called nihilism. Nihilism, nothingness, philosophy of anxiety, tragedy, unheroic, philosophy of care and woe—the catalog of these cheap titles is inexhaustible. Contemporary man shudders at such titles, and, with the help of the shudder thus evoked, the given philosophy is contradicted. What wonderful times when even in philosophy one need no longer think, but where someone somewhere, occasionally, on higher authority, cares to provide shuddering! And now the truth should even depend on a draft! Should it? I ask whether perhaps it is not so.

But finally, this simply depends upon the fact that we have written only half of the truth and entrusted it to an unstable scrap of paper. "Here is the chalk and right *now*." We want to define this "now" more exactly. So that the written truth will not be exposed to the draft, we intend to put the truth about the "now," and thus about

the chalk, on a blackboard. Now—*when* now? We write
on the blackboard: "Now it is afternoon." All right, just
now, this afternoon. We suppose that after the lecture
the classroom will be locked up so that no one can creep
to the written truth and secretly falsify it. Only early the
next morning the custodian is permitted to enter and to
clean the blackboard. He reads the truth: "Now it is afternoon." And he finds that the statement is untrue and that
this professor has made a mistake. The truth became an
untruth overnight.

What a remarkable truth! All the more remarkable
since every time we want sure information about the
chalk, it itself is here and always now here, a thing present
here and now. What changes is always only the determination of the "here" and "now," and, accordingly, of the
thing. But the chalk remains always a "this." Therefore,
in spite of everything, these determinations belong to the
thing itself. The "this" is a general characteristic of the
thing and belongs to its thingness. But the generality of
the "this" demands generally always to be determined as
particular (*jeweilige*). The chalk could not be for us what
it is, that is, "a" chalk, i.e., "this chalk" and no other,
were it not always a now and here. Of course, we shall say
that *for us* the chalk is always a "this." But we finally
want to know what the chalk is *for itself*. For this purpose
we have made the truth about the chalk independent of us
and have entrusted it to a scrap of paper and the blackboard. And observe: while in truth something about the
chalk itself was to be truly preserved, the truth changed
into untruth.

This gives us a hint for approaching the truth about
the chalk in another way, namely, instead of entrusting
this truth to a scrap of paper or to the blackboard, to
keep it with us, to guard it much more carefully than we
have so far done, whereby we drop our peculiar fear before subjectivism or perhaps even endure it. So it could be
that the more we understand the truth about the chalk as

our truth, the more we come closer to what the chalk itself is. It has been shown to us more than once that the truth about a thing is connected with space and time. Therefore, we also may suspect that we shall come closer to the thing itself if we penetrate into the essence of space and time, although it always again appears as though space and time are only a frame for the thing.

Finally, the question shall arise whether the truth concerning the thing is only something that is carried to the thing and pinned on it with the help of a scrap of paper —or whether, on the contrary, the thing itself hangs within the truth, just as it does in space and time, whether the truth is not such that it neither depends on the thing, nor lies in us, nor stands somewhere in the sky.

All our reflections up to now have presumably led to no other conclusion than that we do not yet know either the ins or outs of the thing and that we only have a great confusion in our heads. Certainly, that was the intention —of course, not to leave us in this confusion, but to let us know that this happy-go-lucky advance toward the things has its special circumstances in *the* moment. Therein we wish to know how it is with the thingness of the thing.

If we now remember our position at the beginning, we can determine, on the basis of our intentional and peculiar questioning back and forth, why we have not come closer to the thing itself. We began with the statement: Things around us are single, and these single things are "just these." With this latter characteristic we reached the realm of reference to the things; seen in reverse: the realm of how things meet us. Reference and encounter— that means generally the realm in which we, the alleged subjects, also reside. When we attempt to grasp this realm we always run into space and time. We called it "time-space," which makes reference and encounter possible. This is the realm which lies around things and manifests itself in the compulsive bringing up of space and time.

8. The Thing as the Bearer of Properties

Perhaps we can never experience anything concerning things and make out anything about them except as we remain in the realm in which they encounter us. Meanwhile, we cannot get loose from the question whether or not we approach the things themselves, at least within this realm, whether in it we aren't always already with them. If this is so, then starting from here we shall make out something about the things themselves, i.e., we shall acquire some conception (*Vorstellung*) of how they themselves are constructed. It is decidedly advisable to disregard the frame around things and look exclusively at their construction. In any case, this way exerts as strong a claim as the previous one.

We again ask: "What is a thing? How does a thing look?" Though we are looking for the thingness of the thing, we now cautiously go to work, stopping first at the single things, looking at them, and holding fast to what is seen. A rock—it is hard, gray, and has a rough surface; it has an irregular form, is heavy, and consists of this and that substance. A plant—it has roots, a stem, foliage. The latter is green and grooved. The stem of the foliage is short, etc. An animal has eyes and ears and can move from place to place; it has, in addition to the sense organs, equipment for digestion and sexual reproduction—organs which it uses, generates, and renews in a certain way. Along with the plant, which also has organs, we call this thing an organism. A watch has gears, a spring, a dial, etc.

In this way we could continue indefinitely. What we ascertain thereby is correct. The statements we make are taken from a faithful fitting to what things themselves show us. We now ask more definitely: As what do the things show themselves to us? We disregard that they are a rock, rose, dog, watch, and other things and only consider what things are in general: a thing is always something that has such and such properties, always something that is constituted in such and such a way. This something is the bearer of the properties; the something, as it were, underlies the qualities. This something is what endures, and we always return to it again as the same when we are in the process of determining the qualities. This is how things themselves are. What accordingly is a thing? It is a nucleus around which many changing qualities are grouped, or a bearer upon which the qualities rest; something that possesses something else in itself (*an sich*). However we twist and turn it, this is how the construction of things shows itself; and around them are space and time, as their frame. This is all so intelligible and self-evident that one almost shuns lecturing expressly on such commonplaces. All is so very plain that one does not understand why we make such a fuss and still talk about "this" and about questionable metaphysical principles, about steps of truth and so forth. We said that the inquiry ought to move within the realm of everyday experience. What is closer than to take things as they are? We could continue the description of the things still further and say: If one thing changes its qualities, this can have an effect upon another thing. Things affect each other and resist one another. From such relations between things further qualities then derive which things also again "have."

This description of things and their interdependence corresponds to what we call the "natural conception of the world." "Naturally"—since here we remain completely "natural" and disregard all the profound metaphysics and extravagant and useless theories about knowledge. We remain "natural" and also leave to things themselves their own "nature."

If we now allow philosophy to join in, and we question it, it becomes clear that philosophy too from ancient times has said nothing else. That the thing is a bearer of many qualities was already said by Plato and above all by

Aristotle. Later on perhaps it was expressed in other words and concepts. However, basically the meaning is always the same, even when the philosophical "positions" are as different as, for instance, those of Aristotle and Kant. Thus, Kant states in the *Critique of Pure Reason* (*A* 182: *N.K.S.*, p. 212)[7] as a principle: "All appearances (i.e., all the things for us) contain the permanent (substance) as the object itself, and the changeable as its mere determination, that is, as a way in which the object exists."

What then is a thing? Answer: A thing is the existing (*vorhanden*) bearer of many existing (*vorhanden*) yet changeable properties.

This answer is so "natural" that it also dominates scientific thought, not only "theoretical" thought but also all intercourse with things, their calculation and evaluation.

We can retain the traditional determination of the essence of the thingness of things in the familiar and usual titles:

1. ὑποκείμενον[8]   —συμβεβηκός
   Foundation (*Unterlage*)—what always already
   (what underlies)   stands along with, and
                             also comes in along with
2. *Substantia*   —*accidens*
3. The bearer (*Träger*)   —properties
                             (*Eigenschaften*)
4. Subject   —predicate

---

[7] References to the *Critique of Pure Reason* accord with Raymund Schmidt, *Philosophische Bibliothek* (Hamburg: Verlag Meiner, 1956). In the Preface to the fourteenth edition, written in 1930, Schmidt expresses his special thanks to E. Franck in Marburg, Norman Kemp Smith in Edinburgh, and M. Heidegger in Freiburg for their valuable suggestions. "A" refers to the first edition and "B" to the second edition of the *Critique of Pure Reason*. "N.K.S." refers to the translation by Norman Kemp Smith (London, 1929).

References to quotations Heidegger utilizes from the *Critique of Pure Reason* remain in the text as they were originally placed. Occasionally we have given translations in footnotes when Heidegger has given only references. *Trans.*

[8] ὑποκείμενον: Derived from ὑπόκειμαι. In ancient philosophy

9. The Essential Construction of the Truth,
the Thing, and the Proposition

The question "What is a thing?" has long been decided with general satisfaction, i.e., the question is obviously no longer a question.

Moreover, the answer to the question, i.e., the definition of the thing as the present-at-hand (*vorhanden*) bearer of properties present-at-hand on it, has been established (and in its truth is at any time capable of being established) in such a way that it cannot be improved upon. For the establishing is also "natural" and, therefore, so familiar that one must especially emphasize it even to notice it.

Wherein lies this basis for the truth of the familiar determination of the essence of the thing? Answer: In nothing less than the essence of truth itself. Truth—what does it mean? The true is what is valid; what is valid corresponds to the facts. Something corresponds to the facts when it is directed to them, i.e., when it fits itself to what the things themselves are. Truth, therefore, is fitting (*Anmessung*) to things. Obviously, not only do single truths have to suit themselves to single things, but the essence of truth must also. If truth is correctness, a directing-to (*Sich-richten*) ... then this must obviously be really valid

---

ὑποκείμενον signified the foundation in which something else could inhere, also what is implied or presupposed by something else. But at least three senses must be distinguished: (1) ὕλη (matter), the substrate that received form. The so-called material cause (Aristotle, *Metaphysics*, 983ᵃ 30); (2) the substance, including matter and form, in which the accidents (συμβεβηκός) inhere (*ibid.*, 983ᵇ 16). It is interesting that Aristotle says of the substance: καί γάρή οὐσία ἕν τι καὶ τόδε τι σημαίνει, ὡς φάμεν (*Metaphysics*, 1037ᵇ 28). "For substance means a 'one' and a 'this,' as we maintain." (*The Basic Works of Aristotle*, Richard McKeon, ed. [New York: Random House, 1941], p. 803.) *See also* the comment of W. D. Ross on this passage in *Aristotle's Metaphysics* (Oxford, 1953), II, 205; (3) the logical subject to which attributes and properties are predicated (*Metaphysics*, 103ᵇ 5).

Heidegger takes account of (2) and (3) only. He uses *Träger*, the "bearer," as the most general term to include all that traditionally was meant by the ὑποκείμενον and *substantia*. *Trans.*

all the more for the essential determination of the truth. It must fit itself to the essence of the thing (its thingness). It is necessary from the essence of truth as fitting that the structure of things be reflected in the structure of truth.

If we thus come upon the same framework (*Gefüge*) in the essential structure (*Wesensbau*) of truth as in the essential structure of the things, then the truth of the familiar determination of the essential structure of the thing is demonstrated from the essence of truth itself.

Truth is a fitting to things, a correspondence (*Überein-stimmung*) with the things. But what is now the character of what fits itself? What does the corresponding? What is this about which we say it may be true or false? Just as it is "natural" to understand truth as correspondence to the things, so we naturally determine what is true or false. The truth which we find, establish, disseminate, and defend we express in words. But a single word—such as door, chalk, large, but, and—is neither true nor false. Only combinations of words are true or false: The door is closed; the chalk is white. Such a combination of words is called a simple assertion. Such an assertion is either true or false. The assertion is thus the place and seat of the truth. Therefore, we likewise simply say: This and that assertion are truths. Assertions are truths and falsities.

What is the structure of such a truth as assertion? What is an assertion? The name "assertion" is ambiguous. We distinguish four meanings, all of which belong together, and only in this unity, as it were, do they give a complete outline of the structure of an assertion:

assertions of (*Aussagen von*)	—proposition (*Satz*)
assertions about (*Aussagen über*)	—information (*Auskunft*)
assertions to (*Aussagen an*)	—communication (*Mitteilung*)
to declare oneself (*Sich-Aussprechen*)	—expression (*Ausdruck*)

Someone called to court as a witness refuses to give a

deposition (*Aussage*), i.e., in the first place, he does not speak out, he keeps what he knows to himself. Here assertion means communicating, speaking out into the open, in contrast to silent concealment (*Verschweigung*). If the assertion is made it does not consist mostly of single incoherent words, but is a report (*Bericht*). The witness who decides to give a deposition tells (*erzählt*). In this report the state of facts is asserted. The assertions set forth the event, e.g., what occurred and the circumstances of a just observed burglary attempt. The witness asserts: The house lay in darkness, the shutters were closed, etc.

The assertion in the wider sense of communication consists of "assertions" in the narrower sense, i.e., of propositions. Asserting something in the narrower sense does not mean speaking out, but it means telling information about the house, its condition, and the entire state of things. To assert now means in view of the situation and circumstances to say something about it from them, as seen from their point of view. Assertion, that is giving information about. . . . This information is given in such a way that assertions are made about what is under consideration, about which information is given. Thirdly, assertion means to talk starting from that which is under consideration, e.g., from the house, to take what belongs to the house, to attribute to it what properly belongs to it, to ascribe it, bespeak it. What is asserted in this sense we call the predicate. Assertion in the third sense is "predicative"; it is the proposition.

Assertion, therefore, is threefold: a proposition giving information and which, when carried out vis-à-vis others, becomes communication.[9] This communication is correct

<hr/>

[9] Compare this summary of the threefold character of assertion with *SZ*, p. 156: "When we take together the three analyzed meanings of 'assertion' in a unified view of the complete phenomenon, we may define assertion as a communicative and determinative pointing out." *Sein und Zeit* (Tubingen: Max Niemeyer, 1957), symbolized by "SZ." *Trans.*

when the information is right, i.e., if the proposition is true. The assertion as a proposition, as an assertion of "a, b of H," is the seat of truth. In the structure of the proposition, i.e., of a simple truth, we distinguish subject, predicate, and copula—object, assertion, and connective (*Satzgegenstand, Satzaussage, und Verbindungswort*). Truth consists in the predicate's belonging to the subject and is posited and asserted in the proposition as belonging. The structure and the structural parts of the truth, i.e., of the true proposition (object and assertion), are exactly fitted to that by which truth as such guides itself to the thing as the bearer and to its properties.

Thus we take from the essence of truth, i.e., of the structure of the true proposition, an unambiguous proof for the truth of the definition which gives the thing's structure.

If we survey again all that characterizes the answer to our question "What is a thing?" then we can establish three aspects:

1. The definition of the thing as the bearer of properties results quite "naturally" out of everyday experience.

2. This definition of thingness was established in ancient philosophy, obviously because it suggests itself quite "naturally."

3. The correctness of this definition of the essence of the thing is finally proved and grounded through the essence of truth itself, which essence of truth is likewise intelligible of itself, i.e., is "natural."

A question which is answered in such a natural way and can be grounded just as naturally at any time is seriously no longer a question. If one still wanted to maintain the question it would be either blind obstinacy or a kind of insanity which ventures to run up against the "natural" and what stands beyond all question. We shall do well to give up this question "What is a thing?" as one that is settled. But before we expressly give up this settled question, let us interject a question.

10. The Historicity (Geschichtlichkeit) of the Definition of the Thing

It was shown that the answer to the question "What is a thing?" is the following: A thing is the bearer of properties, and the corresponding truth has its seat in the assertion, the proposition, which is a connection of subject and predicate. We said that this answer as well as the reason for it is quite natural. We now only ask: What does "natural" mean here?

We call "natural" (*natürlich*) what is understood without further ado and is "self-evident" in the realm of everyday understanding. For instance, the internal construction of a big bomber is by itself understandable for an Italian engineer, but for an Abyssinian from a remote mountain village such a thing is not at all "natural." It is not self-evident, i.e., not understandable in comparison to anything with which such a man and his tribe have everyday familiarity. For the Enlightenment the "natural" was what could be proved and comprehended according to certain determinate principles of reason based upon itself, which was, therefore, appropriate to every human as such and to mankind in general. In the Middle Ages everything was "natural" which obtained its essence, its *natura*, from God and, because of this origin, could then form and preserve itself in a definite mode without further intervention from God. What was natural to a man of the eighteenth century, the rationality of reason as such in general, set free from any other limitation, would have seemed very unnatural to the medieval man. Also the contrary could become the case, as we know from the French Revolution. Therefore, it follows: What is "natural" is *not* "natural" at all, here meaning self-evident for any given ever-existing man. The "natural" is always historical.

A suspicion creeps up from behind us. What if this so "natural" appearing essential definition of the thing were by no means self-evident, were not "natural"? Then there must have been a time when the essence of the thing was not defined in this way. Consequently, there also must have been a time when the essential definition of the thing was first worked out. The formation of this essential definition of the thing did not, then, at some time just fall absolute from heaven, but would have itself been based upon very definite presuppositions.

This is in fact so. We can pursue the origin of this essential definition of the thing in its main outline in Plato and Aristotle. Not only this, but at the same time and in the same connection with the disclosure of the thing, the proposition as such was also first discovered and, similarly, that the truth as correspondence to the thing has its seat in the proposition. The so-called natural determination of the essence of the truth—from which we have drawn a proof for the correctness of the essential definition of the thing, this natural concept of the truth—is, therefore, not "natural" without more ado.

Therefore, the "natural world-view" (natürliche Weltansicht), to which we have constantly referred, is not self-evident. It remains questionable. In an outstanding sense this overworked term "natural" is something historical. So it could be that in our natural world-view we have been dominated by a centuries-old interpretation of the thingness of the thing, while things actually encounter us quite differently. This answer to our interjected question of the meaning of "natural" will prevent us from thoughtlessly taking the question "What is a thing?" as settled. This question seems only now to be becoming more clearly determined. The question itself has become a historical one. As we, apparently untroubled and unprejudiced, encounter things and say that they are the bearers of properties, it is not we who are seeing and speaking but rather an old historical tradition. But why do we not want to leave this history alone? It does not bother us. We can adjust ourselves quite easily with this conception of things. And suppose we acknowledge the history of the disclosure and interpretation of thingness of the thing? This changes nothing in the things: the streetcar goes no differently than before, the chalk is a chalk, the rose is a rose, the cat is a cat.

We emphasized in the first hour that philosophy is that thinking with which we can begin to do nothing immediately. But perhaps mediately we can, i.e., under certain conditions and in ways no longer obviously seen as forged by philosophy and as capable of being forged only by it.

Under certain conditions: if, for example, we undertake the effort to think through the inner state of today's natural sciences, non-biological as well as biological, if we also think through the relation of mechanics and technology to our existence (*Dasein*),[10] then it becomes clear that knowledge and questioning have here reached limits which demonstrate that, in fact, an original reference to things is missing, that it is only simulated by the progress of discoveries and technical successes.[11] We feel that what zoology and botany investigate concerning animals and plants and how they investigate it may be correct. But are they still animals and plants? Are they not machines duly prepared beforehand of which one afterward even admits that they are "cleverer than we"?

We can, of course, spare ourselves the effort of thinking these paths through. We also can, furthermore, stick to what we find "natural," that is, something with which one

---

[10] *Dasein:* Literally, "being-there." It is a common German word applicable to the presence of any thing. It is often transliterated in English. Heidegger's use of the term refers to man's own unique way of existing in contrast to other entities. *Trans.*

[11] In *Die Frage nach der Technik* (Pfullingen: Verlag Neske, 1962), p. 13, Heidegger points out the danger in the progress of modern technology for man to misinterpret the meaning of technology: ". . . endangered man boasts himself as the master of earth." Everything man encounters appears entirely as man-made. However, true thinking leads one to see technology (τεκνή) as that by which the forces of Nature are challenged to the revelation and unconcealedness of the truth (ἀλήθεια). *Trans.*

thinks no further. We can take this thoughtlessness as a standard for the things. The streetcar then goes exactly as before. The decisions which are made or not made do not take place in the streetcar or on the motorcycle, but somewhere else—that is, in the sphere of historical freedom, i.e., where a historical being (*Dasein*) decides its ground, as well as how it decides, what level of freedom of knowledge it will choose and what it will posit as freedom.

These decisions are different at differing periods and among different peoples. They cannot be forced. With the freely chosen level of the actual freedom of knowledge, i.e., with the inexorableness of *questioning*, a people always posits for itself the degree of its being (*Dasein*). The Greeks saw the entire nobility of their existence in the ability to question. Their ability to question was their standard for distinguishing themselves from those who did not have it and did not want it. They called them barbarians.

We can leave alone the question of our knowledge about the things and suppose that someday it will set itself right on its own. We can admire the achievements of today's natural sciences and technology and need not know how they got that way, that, for instance, modern science only became possible by a dialogue carried on (out of the earliest passion for questioning) with ancient knowledge, its concepts, and its principles. We need know nothing and can believe we are such magnificent men that the Lord must have given it to us in our sleep.

But we can also be convinced of the indispensability of questioning, which must exceed everything up to now in significance, depth, and certitude, because only in this way can we master what otherwise races away beyond us in its self-evidence.

Decisions are not made by proverbs but only by work. We decide to question, and in a very detailed and drawn out way, which for centuries remains only a questioning. Meanwhile, others can safely bring home their truths.

Once during his lone walks Nietzsche wrote down the sentence: "Enormous *self-reflection!* To become conscious not as an individual but as mankind. Let us reflect, let us think back: let us go all the small and the great ways!" (*Will to Power* [*Wille zur Macht*], §585).

We go here only a small way, the little way of the little question "What is a thing?" We concluded that the definitions which seem so self-evident are not "natural." The answers we give were already established in ancient times. When we apparently ask about the thing in a natural and unbiased way, the question already expresses a preliminary opinion about the thingness of the thing. History already speaks through the type of question. We therefore say that this question is a historical one. Therein lies a definite direction for our purposes, should we desire to ask the question with sufficient understanding.

What should we do if the question is a historical one? And what does "historical" mean? In the first place we only establish that the common answer to the question about the thing stems from an earlier, past time. We can establish that since that time the treatment of this question has gone through various although not earthshaking changes, so that different theories about the thing, about the proposition, and about the truth regarding the thing have regularly emerged through the centuries. Thereby it can be shown that the question and the answer have, so to speak, their history, i.e., they already have a past. But this is just what we do not mean when we say that the question "What is a thing?" is historical, because every report of the past, that is of the preliminaries to the question about the thing, is concerned with something that is static. This kind of historical reporting (*historischen Berichts*) is an explicit shutting down of history, whereas it is, after all, a happening. We question historically if we ask what is still happening even if it seems to be past. We ask what is still happening and whether we remain equal to this happening so that it can really develop.

Therefore, we do not ask about opinions, viewpoints, and propositions which appeared in earlier times about the thing in order to arrange them one after another, as in a museum of weapons where the javelins are ordered by particular centuries. We do not ask at all about the formula and the definition of the essence of the thing. These formulas are only the residuum and sediment of basic positions taken by historical being (*Dasein*), toward, and in the midst of, things taken as a whole, and which it took itself. However, we ask about these basic positions and about the happening in them and about the basic movements of human beings (*Dasein*) that have occurred, movements which apparently are no longer movements because they are past. But a movement need not be gone just because it cannot be established; it can also be in the state of quiescence (*Ruhe*).

What appears to us as though past, i.e., simply as a happening that is no longer going on, can be quiescence. And this quiescence can contain a fullness of being and reality which, in the end, essentially surpasses the reality of the real, in the sense of the *actual* (*Aktuellen*).

This quiescence of happening is not the absence of history, but a basic form of its presence. What we normally know as past, and first represent, is mostly only the formerly "actual," what once caused a stir or even made the noise which always belongs to history but which is not history proper. What is merely past does not exhaust what has been. This still has being, and its way of being is a peculiar quiescence of a happening of a kind determined in turn by what happens. Quiescence is only a self-contained movement, often more uncanny (*unheimlicher*) than movement itself.

11. Truth—Proposition (Assertion)—Thing

There can be various forms and reasons for the quiescence of the happenings of ancient times. Let us see how it is with our question in this respect. We heard that in the time of Plato and Aristotle the definition of the thing was set forth as the bearer of properties. The discovery of the essence of the proposition was made at the same time. Also simultaneously arose the characterization of the truth as the fitting of the perception to the things, which truth has its place in the proposition. All this can be presented in detail and unequivocally from the discussions and essays of Plato and Aristotle. We also can point out how these teachings about the thing, the truth, and the proposition changed with the Stoics; furthermore, how again differences appeared in medieval Scholasticism, and some others in our modern times, and again, still others in German Idealism. Thus, we would tell a "history" (*Geschichte*) about this question, but not ask historically at all, i.e., we would, thereby, leave the *question* "What is a thing?" completely quiescent. The movement would then consist only in the fact that, with the help of a report about theories, we may contrast these with one another. We bring the question "What is a thing?" out of its quiescence by inserting the Platonic-Aristotelian determinations of the thing, the proposition and the truth into specific possibilities, and by putting these up for decision. We ask: Do the definition of the essence of the thing *and* the definition of the essence of the truth occur at the same time only by accident, or do they all cohere among themselves, perhaps even necessarily? If such proves to be the case, how do these definitions cohere? Obviously, we have already given an answer to this question when we refer to what has been cited to prove the correctness of the essential definition of the thing. Thereby, it is demonstrated that the definition of the essential structure of truth must conform to the essential structure of things on the basis of the essence of truth as correctness (*Richtigkeit*). This establishes a certain interdependence between the essence of the thing, of a proposition, and of truth. This also shows itself externally in the order of the determination of the thing and the proposition according to which the subject-predicate relationship is fourth (cf. p. 34). We should certainly not forget that we cited the reference to the so viewed connection as the opinion of the common and "natural" conception of this question. But this "natural" opinion is absolutely *not* natural. This means that its supposed firmness dissolves itself into a series of questions. These run as follows: Was the essential structure of truth and of the proposition suited to the structure of the things? Or is it the opposite: Was the essential structure of the thing as a bearer of attributes interpreted according to the structure of the proposition, as the unity of "subject" and "predicate"? Has man read off the structure of the proposition from the structure of the things, or has he transferred the structure of the proposition into the things?

If the latter were the case, then the further question would immediately arise: How does the proposition, the interpretation, come to present the measure and model of how things in their thingness are to be determined? Since the proposition, the assertion, the positing, and the telling are human actions, we would conclude that man does not adjust himself to things, but the things to man and to the human subject, as which one usually understands the "I." Such an interpretation of the relation of origin between the determination of the thing and that of the proposition seems improbable, at least among the Greeks. For the "I" standpoint is something modern and, therefore, non-Greek. The *polis* set the standard for the Greeks. Everyone today is talking of the Greek *polis*. Now, among the Greeks, the nation of thinkers, someone coined the sentence: πάντων χρημάτων μέτρον ἐστὶν ἄνθρωπος, τῶν μὲν ὄντων ὡς ἔστιν, τῶν δὲ οὐκ ὄντων ὡς οὐκ ἔστιν ("Man is the measure of all things, of things that are that they are, and of things that are not that they are not.") The man who made this statement, Protagoras, supposedly wrote a work with the simple title ἡ Ἀλήθεια, *The Truth*. The statement of this proposition is temporally not too far from Plato's time.

Perhaps this implies that the structure of the thing adjusts itself to the structure of the proposition, rather than the contrary, not "subjectivism"; only later opinions about the thinking of the Greeks are subjective. If, indeed, the proposition and that truth settled in the proposition, understood as correctness, be the measure for the determination of the thing; if now the facts are different and reversed from what natural opinion holds, then the further question arises: What is the ground and guarantee that we have really hit on the essence of the proposition? Whence is it determined what truth is?

Thus we see that what happened in the determination of the essence of the thing is by no means past and settled, but at most bogged down and therefore to be set in motion anew and so still questionable today. If we do not want simply to repeat opinions but to grasp what we ourselves say and usually mean, then we immediately come into a whole turmoil of questions.

First of all, the question relative to the thing now stands thus: Do the essences of the proposition and of the truth determine themselves from out of the essence of the thing, or does the essence of the thing determine itself from out of the essence of the proposition? The question is posed as an either/or. However (and this becomes the decisive question), does this either/or itself suffice? Are the essence of the thing and the essence of the proposition only built as mirror images because both of them together determine themselves from out of the same but deeper lying root? However, what and where can be this common ground for the essence of the thing *and* of the proposition and of their origin? The unconditioned (*Unbedingt*)? We stated at the beginning that what conditions the essence of the thing in its thingness can no longer itself be thing and conditioned, it must be an unconditioned (*Un-bedingtes*). But also the essence of the unconditioned (*Unbedingt*) is co-determined by what has been established as a thing and as condition (*Be-dingung*). If the thing is taken as *ens*

creatum, a present-at-hand created by God, then the unconditioned is God in the sense of the Old Testament. If
the thing is considered as that which, as object, faces the
"I," i.e., as the "not-I," then the "I" is the unconditioned,
the absolute "I" of German Idealism. Whether the unconditioned is sought beyond, behind, or in things depends
upon what one understands as condition and being conditioned (*als Bedingung und Bedingtsein*).

Only with this question do we advance in the direction
of the possible ground for the determination of the thing
and the proposition *and* its truth. This, however, shatters[12]
the original ways of posing the questions concerning the
thing with which we began. That happening (*Geschehen*)
of the formerly standard determination of the thing, which
seemed long past but was in truth only stuck and since
then rested, is brought out of its quiescence. The question
of the thing again comes into motion from its beginning.

With this reference to the inner questionability of the
question about the thing, we ought now to clarify in
what sense we take the question as historical. To question
historically means to set free and into motion the happening which is quiescent and bound in the question.

To be sure, such a procedure easily succumbs to a mis-
interpretation. One could take this as belatedly attributing
mistakes to the original determination of the thing or at
least insufficiency and incompleteness. This would be a
childish game of an empty and vain superiority and after-
thought which all those latecomers may at any time play
with those of earlier times simply because they have come
later. Insofar as our questioning is concerned with critique
at all, it is not directed against the beginning, but only
against ourselves, insofar as we drag along this beginning

---

[12] Heidegger entitles the section in *SZ* where he calls for a renewal of the question of being from the standpoint of its
historicity, "The Task of the Destruction of the History of
Ontology" (*SZ*, p. 19). *Trans.*

no longer as such, but as something "natural," i.e., in an indifferent falsification.

The conception of the question "What is a thing?" as historical is just as far removed from the intention of merely reporting historically about former opinions about the thing as it is from the mania for criticizing these opinions and, by adding together what is temporarily correct, from figuring out and offering a new opinion from past opinions. Rather it is a question of setting into motion the original inner happening of this question according to its simplest characteristic moves, which have been arrested in a quiescence. This happening does not lie somewhere aloof from us in the dim and distant past but is here in every proposition and in each everyday opinion, in every approach to things.

12. Historicity and Decision

What has been said about the historical character of the question "What is a thing?" is valid for every philosophical question which we put today or in the future, assuming, of course, that philosophy is a questioning that puts itself in question and is therefore always and everywhere moving in a circle.

We noticed at the outset how the thing determined itself for us first as single and as a "this." Aristotle calls it τόδε τι, "this here." However, the determination of the singleness (*Einzelnheit*) inherently depends also on how the universality of the universal is conceived, for which the single is an instance and an example. Also, in this regard, certain decisions set in with Plato and Aristotle which still influence logic and grammar. We further observed that a closer circumscription of the "this" always involves the help of the space-time relationship. Also with regard to the essential determination of space and time, Aristotle and Plato sketched the ways on which we still move today.

In truth, however, our historical being-here (*Dasein*) is

already on the way to a transformation which, if stifled in itself, only experiences this destiny because it does not find its way back to its own self-laid grounds in order to found itself anew out of them.

It is easy to derive from all that has been said what our task must be, if we are to set our question "What is a thing?" into motion as a historical question.

It would first be necessary to set into motion the beginning of the essential determination of the thing and the proposition of the Greeks, not in order to acknowledge how it was before, but to pose for decision how essentially it *still* is today. But in this lecture we must forego carrying out this fundamental task, and this for two reasons. The one is seemingly more external. The task mentioned would not be fulfilled by putting together a few quotations about what Plato and Aristotle said here and there about the thing and the proposition. Rather, we would have to bring into play the whole of Greek *Dasein*, its gods, its art, its polity, its knowledge, in order to experience what it means to discover something like the thing. In the framework of this lecture all the presuppositions are missing for this approach. And even if these were supplied we could not follow this path to the beginning, in regard to the task posed.

It has already been indicated that a mere definition of the thing does not say much, whether we dig it out in the past, or whether we ourselves have the ambition to solder together a so-called new one. The answer to the question "What is a thing?" is different in character. It is not a proposition but a transformed basic position or, better still and more cautiously, the initial transformation of the hitherto existing position toward things, a change of questioning and evaluation, of seeing and deciding; in short, of the being-there (*Da-sein*) in the midst of what is (*inmitten des Seienden*). To determine the changing basic position within the relation to what is, that is the task of an entire historical period. But this requires that we perceive more exactly with clearer eyes what most holds us captive and makes us unfree in the experience and determination of the things. This is modern natural science, insofar as it has become a universal way of thinking along certain basic lines. The Greek origin also governs this, although changed, yet not alone and not predominantly. The question concerning our basic relations to nature, our knowledge of nature as such, our rule over nature, is not a question of natural science, but this question is itself in question in *the* question of whether and how we are still addressed by what is as such within the whole. Such a question is not decided in a lecture, but at most in a century, and this only if the century is not asleep and does not merely *have the opinion* that it is awake. This question is made decisive only through discussion.

In connection with the development of modern science, a definite conception of the thing attains a unique preeminence. According to this, the thing is material, a point of mass in motion in the pure space-time order, or an appropriate combination of such points. The thing so defined is from then on considered as the ground and basis of all things, their determinations and their interrogation. The animate is also here, insofar as one does not believe that some day one will be able to explain it from out of lifeless matter with the help of colloidal chemistry. Even where one permits the animate its own character, it is conceived as an additional structure built upon the inanimate; in the same way, the implement and the tool are considered as material things, only subsequently prepared, so that a special value adheres to them. But this reign of the material thing (*Stoffdinges*), as the genuine substructure of all things, reaches altogether beyond the sphere of the things into the sphere of the "spiritual" (*Geistigen*), as we will quite roughly call it; for example, into the sphere of the signification of language, of history, of the work of art, etc. Why, for example, has the treatment and interpretation of the poets for years been so dreary in our higher schools? Answer: Because the teachers do not know the difference between a thing and a poem; because they treat poems as things, which they do because they have never gone through the question of what a thing is. That today one reads more *Nibelungenlied* and less Homer may have its reasons, but this changes nothing. It always is the same dreariness, before in Greek and now in German. However, the teachers are not to blame for this situation, nor the teachers of these teachers, but an entire period, i.e., we ourselves—if we do not finally open our eyes.

The question "What is a thing?" is a historical question. In its history, the determination of the thing as the material present-at-hand (*Vorhanden*) has an unshattered preeminence. If we really ask this question, i.e., if we pose for decision the possibility of the determination of the thing, then we can as little skip the modern answer as we are permitted to forget the origin of the question.

However, at the same time and before all we should ask the harmless question "What is a thing?" in such a way that we experience it as our own so that it no longer lets go of us even when we have long since had no opportunity to listen to lectures on it, especially since the task of such lectures is not to proclaim great revelations and to calm psychic distress. Rather, they can only perhaps awaken what has fallen asleep, perhaps put back into order what has become mixed up.

13. Summary

We now summarize in order to arrive at the final delineation of our intention. It was emphasized at the outset that in philosophy, in contrast to the sciences, an immediate approach to the questions is never possible. It necessarily always requires an introduction. The introductory reflections on our question "What is a thing?" now come to their conclusion.

The question has been characterized in two essential respects: What is put in question and how it is questioned.

First, with regard to *what* is in question—the thing—with an admittedly very poor light we have searched the horizon in which, according to tradition, the thing and the determination of its thingness stand. We reached a double result: first, the frame of the thing, time-space, and the thing's way of encountering, the "this," and then the structure of the thing itself as being the bearer of properties, entirely general and empty: to form the one for a many.

Second, we tried to characterize the question in regard to the manner in which it must be asked. It turned out that the question is historical. What is meant by that has been explained.

The introductory reflection on our question makes it clear that two leading questions permanently go along with it and, therefore, must be asked with it. The one: Where does something like a thing belong? The other: Whence do we take the determination of its thingness? Only from these as they are asked along with our question result the clue and guideline along which we must go if everything is not to tumble around in mere chance and confusion and if the question concerning the thing is not to get stuck in a dead end.

But would that be a misfortune? This is the same question as the following: Is there, after all, a serious sense in posing such questions? We know that we cannot begin to do anything with its elucidation. The consequences are also accordingly if we do not pose the question and ignore it. If we ignore the warning of a high-power line and touch the wires, we are killed. If we ignore the question "What is a thing?" then "nothing further happens."

If a physician mishandles a number of patients, there is the danger that they will lose their lives. If a teacher interprets a poem to his students in an impossible manner, "nothing further happens." But perhaps it is good if we speak more cautiously here. By ignoring the question concerning the thing and by insufficiently interpreting a poem, it appears as though nothing further happens. One day, perhaps after fifty or one hundred years, nevertheless, something has happened.

The question "What is a thing?" is a historical question. But it is more important to act according to this historical character in the questioning than to talk about the historical character of the question. Herewith, for the purposes and possibilities of the lecture, we must be content with an evasive way out.

We can neither present the great beginning of the question with the Greeks, nor is it possible, in its full context, to display the precise determination of the thing, which has become preeminent through modern science. But, on the other hand, the knowledge of that beginning as well as of the decisive periods of modern science is indispensable if we are to remain equal to the question at all.

B. Kant's Manner of Asking About the Thing

I. The Historical Basis on Which Kant's *Critique of Pure Reason* Rests

How do we, nevertheless, although in an improvised manner, get on the path (*Weg*) to the intrinsic "living" history of our question? We choose a middle section of this way, one in which, in a creative sense, the beginning and a decisive age are joined together in a new manner. This is the philosophical determination of the thingness of the thing which Kant has created. The essential delineation of the thing is not an accidental by-product in the philosophy of Kant; the determination of the thingness of the thing is its metaphysical center. By means of an interpretation of Kant's work we put ourselves on the path of the inherently historical question concerning the thing.

Kant's philosophy shifts for the first time the whole of modern thought and being (*Dasein*) into the clarity and transparency of a foundation (*Begründung*). This determines every attitude toward knowledge since then, as well as the bounds (*Abgrenzungen*) and appraisals of the sciences in the nineteenth century up to the present time. Therein Kant towers so far above all who precede and follow that even those who reject him or go beyond him still remain entirely dependent upon him.

Moreover, in spite of all differences and the extent of the historical interval, Kant has something in common with the great Greek beginning, which at the same time distinguishes him from all German thinkers before and after him. This is the incorruptible clarity of his thinking and speaking, which by no means excludes the questionable and the unbalanced, and does not feign light where there is darkness.

We turn our question "What is a thing?" into Kant's and, vice versa, Kant's question into ours. The further task of the lecture thus becomes very simple. We need not report in broad surveys and general phrases "about" the philosophy of Kant. We put ourselves within it. Henceforth, only Kant shall speak. What we contribute, from time to time, will indicate the sense and the direction so that, en route, we do not deviate from the path of the question. The lecture is thus a kind of signpost. Signposts are indifferent to what happens on the highway itself. They emerge only here and there on the edge of the road to point out and to disappear again in passing.[13]

The way (*Weg*) of our question "What is a thing?" leads to Kant's major work, the *Critique of Pure Reason,* the whole of which we cannot go through in this lecture. We must once more limit the stretch of our way. But we shall try to get to the middle of this stretch (*Strecke*) and thus into the center of this major work in order to understand it in its chief inner directions. If this succeeds, then we have not become acquainted with a book which a professor once wrote in the eighteenth century, but we have entered a few steps into a historical-intellectual basic position which carries and determines us today.

[13] This reference to signposts is not facetious. See *SZ* pp. 76–83, for his enlightening analysis of "signs" (*Zeichen*). *Trans.*

1. The Reception of Kant's Work in His Lifetime; Neo-Kantianism

Kant once said in conversation during the last years of his life: "I have come a century too soon with my writings. After a hundred years, people will first correctly understand me and then study my books anew and admit them!" (Varnhagen von Ense, *Tagebücher*, I, 46.)

Does a vain self-importance speak these words or even the angry hopelessness of being shoved aside? Neither, for both are foreign to Kant's character. What is thus expressed is Kant's deep knowledge about the manner and method by which philosophy realizes itself and takes effect. Philosophy belongs to the most primordial of human efforts. Of these, Kant once remarked: "Man's efforts turn in a perpetual circle, and return to a point where they have already once been; thus materials now lying in the dust can perhaps be worked into a magnificent building" (Kant's answer to Garve, *Prolegomena*, Karl Vorländer, ed. [6th ed.; Leipzig: 1926], p. 194). Here speaks the superior calm of a creator who knows that "contemporary" standards are dust and that what is great has its own law of movement.

When Kant published the *Critique of Pure Reason* in 1781, he was fifty-seven, and, until the time of its publication, he had been silent for more than ten years. During the decade of this silence, 1770–81, Hölderlin, Hegel, and Beethoven lived through their boyhood. Six years after the first appearance of the work, the second edition was published. Isolated passages were worked over, some proofs were sharpened. But the total character of the work remained unchanged.

Contemporaries stood helpless before the work. It went beyond anything customary by the elevation of its question-posing, by the rigor of its concept-formation, by the far-seeing organization of its questioning, and by the novelty of the language and its decisive goal. Kant knew this; he realized that this work in its entire plan and method was against the taste of the time. Kant himself once described the ruling taste of his age as the effort to represent the difficult in philosophical things as easy.[14] Although not understood in its essential purposes, but always apprehended only from an accidental exterior, the work was provocative. An eager tug-of-war developed in writings opposing and defending it. Up to the year of Kant's death, 1804, the number of these had reached two thousand. It is this condition of the argumentation with Kant to which Schiller's famous verse entitled "Kant and His Interpreters" refers.

> *Wie doch ein einziger Reicher so viele*
> *Bettler in Nahrung*
> *Setzt! Wenn die Könige baun, haben die*
> *Kärrner zu tun.*

(How a single rich man
   so many beggars feeds!
When kings build, the
   carters have work.)

This same Schiller first helped Goethe to a conception of Kant's philosophy and to philosophy in general. Goethe later said that reading one page in Kant affected him "like stepping into a brightly lighted room."

During the last decade of Kant's life, 1794–1804, the conception of his work and consequently the effect of his philosophy took a certain direction. This happened through the work of younger thinkers, Fichte, Schelling, and Hegel. Their philosophy developed on the basis of

---

[14] "Allein so gütig und bereitwillig Sie auch in Ansehung dieses meines Gesuchs sein möchten, so bescheide ich doch gerne, dass, nach dem herrschenden Geschmacke dieses Zeitalters, das Schwere in speculativen Dingen als leicht vorzustellen (nicht leicht zu machen), Ihre gefälligste Bermühung in diesem Punkte doch fruchtlos sein würde." *Prolegomena*, p. 193. *Trans.*

Kant's (or, rather, by taking off from it) and formed itself into what is commonly known as "German Idealism." This philosophy leaped over Kant with all due respect but did not overcome him. This could not be done, if for no other reason, because his essential foundation was not attacked but only abandoned. It was not even abandoned, because it was never even taken; it was only skirted. Kant's work remained like an unconquered fortress behind a new front, which, in spite of (or perhaps because of) its vehemence, was already thrust into emptiness a generation later, i.e., it was not capable of generating a truly creative opposition. It seemed as if in German Idealism all philosophy had reached an end and finally and exclusively had entrusted the administration of knowledge to the sciences. Around the middle of the nineteenth century, however, there arose the call, "Back to Kant."[15] This return to Kant sprang from a new historical intellectual situation; at the same time it was determined by a renunciation of German Idealism. This intellectual situation toward the middle of the nineteenth century is essentially characterized by the definite predominance of a particular form of science; it is designated by the catchword "positivism." This is knowledge whose pretention to truth is from beginning to end based on what one calls "facts" (*Tatsachen*); one holds that there can be no argument about facts; they are the highest court of appeal for the decisions concerning truth and untruth. What is proved by experiments in the natural sciences and what is verified by manuscripts and documents in the historical-cultural sciences is true, and is the only scientifically verifiable truth.

The return to Kant was guided by the intention of finding in Kant the philosophical foundation and justification

---

[15] Otto Liebmann (1840–1912) closed each chapter of *Kant und die Epigonen* (1865) with his famous call, *"Also muss auf Kant zurückgegangen werden!"* For reference, *see* Z. Weber, *History of Philosophy*, Frank Thilly, trans., with section "Philosophy since 1860" by Ralph Barton Perry (New York: Scribners, 1925), p. 461, n. 1. *Trans.*

for the positivistic conception of science. But it was simultaneously a conscious renunciation of German Idealism, a
renunciation which understood itself as the renunciation
of metaphysics. This new turn toward Kant, therefore,
took his philosophy as the destruction of metaphysics.
This return to Kant was called Neo-Kantianism, in contrast to the disciples of Kant's lifetime, the former Kant-
ians. When from our present position we survey this return to Kant, it must immediately become questionable
whether it could have regained, or could even *find* at all,
Kant's basic position, which German Idealism had also
simply skirted or leapt over. That was and is indeed not
the case. Nevertheless, the philosophical movement of
Neo-Kantianism has its undeniable merits within the intellectual history of the second half of the nineteenth century. These are above all three:

(1) Although one-sided, the renewal of Kant's philosophy saved positivism from a complete slide into the deifi-
cation of facts. (2) Kant's philosophy itself was made familiar in its entire range through careful interpretation
and elaboration of his writings. (3) The general investigation of the history of philosophy, especially ancient philosophy, was carried out on a higher plane of inquiry under
the guidance of Kant's philosophy.

All this is, of course, little enough when we measure it
by the standard of the intrinsic task of the philosophy,
which, again, also does not mean much as long as it only
remains a counterclaim, instead of a counter achievement.

Meanwhile, we see Kant's philosophy in a wider visual
field than Neo-Kantianism did. Kant's historical position
within Western metaphysics has become clearer. But this
means, at first, only an improved historical recognition in
the usual sense and not the discussion with the basic position he first captured. Here what he predicted must be
made to come true: "People will study my books anew and
admit them." When we are so far, there is no more Kant-
ianism. For every mere "ism" is a misunderstanding and

the death of history. Kant's *Critique of Pure Reason* is among those philosophical works which, as long as there is philosophy on this earth at all, daily become inexhaustible anew. It is one of those works that have already pronounced judgment over every future attempt to "overcome" them by only passing them by.

2. The Title of Kant's Major Work

We are attempting here to put as learners our question "What is a thing?" to Kant's work.

At first it is certainly completely obscure what a work with the title *Critique of Pure Reason* has to do with our question "What is a thing?" We shall only truly experience how that is if we enter into the work, i.e., through the subsequent interpretation. However, in order not to leave everything in complete darkness for too long we shall attempt a preliminary elucidation (*vordeutende Erläuterung*). We attempt to gain a foothold at the center of this work in order to come into the movement of our question at once. First, a preliminary explanation is to be given concerning the extent to which our question is intimately connected with this work—regardless of whether we take over Kant's basic position or not, or how far we do or don't transform it. We give this enlightenment by way of elucidating the title. This is so arranged that we immediately orient ourselves at the spot in Kant's work where our interpretation of it begins, without first knowing the preceding parts of the work. *Critique of Pure Reason*—everyone knows what "critique" and "to criticize" mean; "reason" and what a "reasonable" man or a "reasonable" suggestion is, are also understood by everyone. What "pure" signifies in distinction to impure (e.g., impure water) is clear also. Yet we cannot think anything appropriate to the title, *Critique of Pure Reason*. Above all, one would expect a critique to reject something unsatisfactory, insufficient, and negative; one would expect criticism of something like an impure reason. Finally, it is quite incomprehensible what the *Critique of Pure Reason* can have to do with the question concerning the thing. And yet we are completely justified in asserting that this title expresses nothing else but the question concerning the thing—but as a question. The question is, as we know, historical. The title means this history in a decisive era of its movement. The title means this question, and is a thoroughly historical one. In an external sense this means that Kant, who was thoroughly clear about his work, has given it a title demanded by his age and, at the same time, led beyond it. What history of the question concerning the thing is expressed in this title?

3. The Categories as Modes of Assertion

We remind ourselves of the beginning of the essential determination of the thing. This takes place along the lines of the assertion (*Aussage*). As a proposition the simple assertion is a saying in which something is asserted about something, e.g., "The house is red." Here "red" is said of (*zu-gesagt*) the house. That of which it is said, ὑποκείμενον, is what underlies. Therefore, in the attribution (*Zu-sagen*), as it were, something is said from above down to what underlies. In the Greek language κατά means "from above down to something below." To say means φάναι, the saying is φάσις. The simple assertion is a κατάφασις, a λέγειν τι κατά τινος.

Much can be said down to a thing, about it (Auf ein Ding kann verschiedenes heruntergesagt, über es ausgesagt werden). "The house is red." "The house is high." "The house is smaller" (than that one beside it). "The house is on the creek." "The house is an eighteenth-century one."

Guided by these different assertions, we can follow how the thing itself is determined at any given time. Thereby we do not now pay attention to this particular thing in the

example, the house, but to that which, in every such assertion of this sort, characterizes every thing of this kind in
general, i.e., the thingness. "Red" says in a certain respect,
namely, in respect of color, how the thing is constituted.
Viewed in general, a trait or quality is attributed to
(*zugesagt*) the thing. In the attribution, "large" becomes
size, extension, (quantity). With the "smaller than," there
is asserted what the house is, in relationship to another
(relation); "on the creek": the place; "eighteenth century": the time.

Quality, extension, relation, place, and time are determinations which are said in general of the thing. These determinations name the respects in which things exhibit
themselves to us if we address them in the assertion and
talk about them, the perspectives from which we view
things, in which they show themselves. Insofar as these
determinations are always said down to the thing, the
thing in general is always already co-asserted (*mitgesagt*)
as the already present (*als das schon Anwesende*). What is
said in general about each thing as a thing, this "that is
spoken down to the thing" wherein its thingness and generality determine themselves, is called by the Greeks
κατηγορία (κατα-ἀγορεύειν). But what is thus attributed means
nothing other than the being characterized, being extended, being in relation to, being there, being now, of the
thing as something that is. In the categories the most general determinations of the being of something that is are
said. The thingness of the thing means the being of the
thing as something that is. We cannot lay this state of facts
too often and too emphatically before our eyes—namely,
that those determinations which constitute the being of
something that is, i.e., of the thing itself, have received
their name from assertions about the thing. This name for
the determination of being (*Seinsbestimmungen*) is not
an arbitrary designation. In thus naming the determinations of being modes of assertedness (*Ausgesagtheit*) lies
a unique interpretation of being. That since then in West-

ern thinking the determinations of being are called "categories" is the sharpest expression for what we have already emphasized: that the structure of the thing is connected with the structure of the assertion. If in the past and still today, the Scholastic teaching of the being of what is, "ontology," sets as its proper goal to erect a "theory of categories" (*Kategorienlehre*), it is because therein speaks the beginning interpretation of the being of what is, i.e., the thingness of the thing from out of the assertion.

4. Λόγος—Ratio—Reason

The assertion is a kind of λέγειν—addressing something as something. This implies something taken as something. Considering and expressing something as something in Latin is called *reor, ratio*. Therefore, *ratio* becomes the translation of λόγος. The simple asserting simultaneously gives the basic form in which we mean and think something about the things. The basic form of thinking, and thus of thought, is the guideline for the determination of the thingness of the thing. The categories determine in general the being of what is. To ask about the being of what is, what and how what is, is at all, counts as philosophy's principal task. To ask in this way is first, first-ranking, and proper philosophy, πρώτη φιλοσοφία, *prima philosophia*.

It remains essential that thought as simple assertion, λόγος, *ratio*, is the guideline for the determination of the being of what is, i.e., for the thingness of the thing. "Guideline" (*Leitfaden*) here means that the modes of asserting direct the view in the determining of presence (*Anwesenheit*), i.e., of the being of what is.

Λόγος and *ratio* are translated in German as reason (*Vernunft*). Herein there appears for us, as it were, for the first time a connection between the question about the thing on the one hand, and about "reason" (*Critique of Pure Reason*) on the other. But therewith has not yet been shown how the process of Western metaphysics arrived at a critique of pure reason and what this means. We shall now attempt this in a few rough outlines.

5. *The Modern Mathematical Science of Nature and the Origin of a Critique of Pure Reason*

We have seen that, with the exception of the beginning among the Greeks, the rise of modern natural science became decisive for the essential definition of the thing. The transformation of *Dasein,* which was basic to this event, changed the character of modern thought and thus of metaphysics and prepared the necessity for a critique of pure reason. It is, therefore, necessary for many reasons that we acquire a more defined conception of the character of modern natural science. In this we must forego entering deeply into special questions. Here we cannot even pursue the main periods of its history. Most of the facts of its history are known, and yet our knowledge of the innermost driving connections of this happening is still very poor and dark. It is very clear only that the transformation of science basically took place through centuries of discussion about the fundamental concepts and principles of thought, i.e., the basic attitude toward things and toward what is at all. Such a discussion could be carried through only with complete mastery of the tradition of medieval as well as ancient science of nature. This demanded an unusual breadth and certainty of conceptual thought and finally a mastery of the new experiences and modes of procedure. All this presupposed a unique passion for an authoritative knowledge, which finds its like only among the Greeks, a knowledge which first and constantly questions its own presuppositions and thereby seeks their basis. To hold out in this constant questioning appears as the only human way to preserve things in their inexhaustibility, i.e., without distortion.

The transformation of science is accomplished always

only through itself. But science itself thereby has a two-fold foundation: (1) work experiences, i.e., the direction and the mode of mastering and using what is; (2) metaphysics, i.e., the projection of the fundamental knowledge of being, out of which what is knowledgeably develops. Work experiences and the projection of being are reciprocally related to one another and always meet in a basic feature of attitude and of humanly being there (*Dasein*).

We shall now try to clarify roughly this basic feature of the modern attitude toward knowledge. But we do this with the intention of understanding modern metaphysics and (identical with that) the possibility and necessity of something like Kant's *Critique of Pure Reason*.

a. The Characteristics of Modern Science in Contrast to Ancient and Medieval Science

One commonly characterizes modern science in contradistinction to medieval science by saying that modern science starts from facts while the medieval started from general speculative propositions and concepts. This is true in a certain respect. But it is equally undeniable that the medieval and ancient sciences also observed the facts, and that modern science also works with universal propositions and concepts. This went so far as to criticize Galileo, one of the founders of modern science, with the same reproach that he and his disciples actually made against Scholastic science: They said it was "abstract," i.e., it proceeded with general propositions and principles. Yet in an even more distinct and conscious way the same was the case with Galileo. The contrast between the ancient and the modern attitude toward science cannot, therefore, be established by saying there concepts and principles and here facts. Both ancient and modern science have to do with both facts and concepts. However, the way the facts are conceived and how the concepts are established are decisive.

The greatness and superiority of natural science during the sixteenth and seventeenth centuries is because all the scientists were philosophers. They understood that there are no mere facts, but that a fact is only what it is in the light of the fundamental conception and always depends upon how far that conception reaches. The characteristic of positivism, wherein we have stood for decades and to-day more than ever, is contrary to this in that it thinks it can sufficiently manage with facts or other and new facts, while concepts are merely expedients which one some-how needs but should not get too involved with, since that would be philosophy. Furthermore, the comedy, or rather the tragedy, of the present situation of science is, first, that one thinks to overcome positivism through positivism. To be sure, this attitude only prevails where average and sub-sequent work is done. Where genuine and discovering research is done, the situation is no different from that of three hundred years ago. That age also had its indolence, just as, conversely, the present leaders of atomic physics, Niels Bohr and Heisenberg, think in a thoroughly philo-sophical way, and only therefore create new ways of posing questions and, above all, hold out in the question-able.

Thus, if one tries to distinguish modern from medieval science by calling it the science of facts, this remains basi-cally inadequate. Further, the difference between the old and the new science is often seen in that the latter ex-periments and "experimentally" proves its cognitions. But the experiment, the test, to get information concern-ing the behavior of things through a definite ordering of things and events was also already familiar in ancient times and in the Middle Ages. This kind of experience lies at the basis of all technological contact with things in the crafts and the use of tools. Here, too, it is not the experi-ment as such in the wide sense of testing through observa-tion, but the manner of setting up the test and the intent with which it is undertaken and in which it is grounded.

The manner of experimentation is presumably connected with the kind of conceptual determination of the facts and way of applying concepts, i.e., with the kind of hypothesis about things.

Besides these two constantly cited characteristics of modern science, science of facts and experimental research, one also usually meets a third. This third affirms that modern science is a calculating and measuring investigation. That is true. However, it is also true of ancient science, which also worked with measurement and number. Again it is a question of how and in what sense calculating and measuring were applied and carried out, and what importance they have for the determination of the objects themselves.

With these three characteristics of modern science, that it is a factual, experimental, measuring science, we still miss the fundamental characteristic of modern science. The fundamental feature must consist in what rules and determines the basic movement of science itself. This characteristic is the manner of working with the things and the metaphysical projection of the thingness of the things. How are we to conceive this fundamental feature?

We entitle this fundamental feature of modern science for which we are searching by saying that modern science is *mathematical*. From Kant comes the oft-quoted but still little understood sentence, "However, I maintain that in any particular doctrine of nature only so much *genuine* science can be found as there is mathematics to be found in it." (Preface to *Metaphysical Beginning Principles of Natural Science*.)

The decisive question is: What do "mathematics" and "mathematical" mean here? It seems as though we can only take the answer to this question from mathematics itself. This is a mistake, because mathematics itself is only a particular formation of the mathematical.

The fact that today mathematics in a practical and pedagogical sense is included in the department of natural science has its historical basis, but it is not essentially necessary. Formerly, mathematics belonged to the *septem artes liberales*. Mathematics is as little a natural science as philosophy is one of the humanities. Philosophy in its essence belongs as little in the philosophical faculty as mathematics belongs to natural science. To house philosophy and mathematics in this way today seems to be a blemish or a mistake in the catalog of the universities. But perhaps it is something quite different (and there are people who are even concerned about such things), namely, a sign that there no longer is a fundamental and clarified unity of the sciences and that this unity is no longer either a necessity or a question.

b. The Mathematical, Μάθησις

How do we explain the mathematical if not by mathematics? In such questions we do well to keep to the word itself. Of course, the facts are not always there where the word occurs. But with the Greeks, from whom the word stems, we may safely make this assumption. In its formation the word "mathematical" stems from the Greek expression τὰ μαθήματα, which means what can be learned and thus, at the same time, what can be taught; μανθάνειν means to learn, μάθησις the teaching, and this in a twofold sense. First, it means studying and learning; then it means the doctrine taught. To teach and to learn are here intended in a wide and at the same time essential sense, and not in the later narrow and trite sense of school and scholars. However, this is not sufficient to grasp the proper sense of the "mathematical." To do this we must inquire in what further connection the Greeks employ the mathematical and from what they distinguish it.

We experience what the mathematical properly is when we inquire *under what* the Greeks classify the mathematical and *against what* they distinguish it within this classification. The Greeks identify the mathematical, τὰ μαθήματα, with the following determinations:

1. Τὰ φυσικά: The things insofar as they originate and come forth from themselves.

2. Τὰ ποιούμενα: The things insofar as they are produced by the human hand and stand as such.

3. Τὰ χρήματα: The things insofar as they are in use and therefore stand at our constant disposal—they may be either φυσικά, rocks and so on, or ποιούμενα, something specially made.

4. Τα πράγματα: The things insofar as we have to do with them at all, whether we work on them, use them, transform them, *or* we only look at and examine them—πράλματα, with regard to πρᾶξις: here πράξις is taken in a truly wide sense, neither in the narrow meaning of practical use (χρῆσθαι), nor in the sense of πρᾶξις as moral action: πρᾶξις is all doing, pursuing, and enduring, which also includes ποίησις; finally:

5. Τὰ μαθήματα: According to the characterization running through these four, we must also say here of μαθήματα: The things insofar as they . . . but the question is: In what respect?

In every case we realize that the mathematical concerns things, and in a definite respect. With the question concerning the mathematical we move within our original question "What is a thing?" In what respect are things taken when they are viewed and spoken of mathematically?

We are long used to thinking of numbers when we think of the mathematical. The mathematical and numbers are obviously connected. Only the question remains: Is this connection because the mathematical is numerical in character, or, on the contrary, is the numerical something mathematical? The second is the case. But insofar as numbers are in a way connected with the mathematical there still remains the question: Why precisely are the numbers something mathematical? What is the mathematical itself that something like numbers must be conceived as something mathematical and are primarily brought forward as the mathematical? Μάθησις means learning; μαθήματα, what is learnable. In accord with what has been said, this denomination is intended of things insofar as they are learnable. Learning is a kind of grasping and appropriating. But not every taking is a learning. We can take a thing, for instance, a rock, take it with us and put it in a collection of rocks. We can do the same with plants. It says in our cookbook that one "takes," i.e., uses. To take means in some way to take possession of a thing and have disposal over it. Now, what kind of taking is learning? Μαθήματα—things, insofar as we learn them. But strictly speaking, we cannot learn a thing, e.g., a weapon; we can learn only its use. Learning is therefore a way of taking and appropriating in which the use is appropriated. Such appropriation occurs through the using itself. We call it practicing. However, practicing is again only a kind of learning. Not every learning is a practicing. What is now the essential aspect of learning in the sense of μάθησις? Why is learning a taking? What of the things is taken, and how is it taken?

Let us again consider practicing as a kind of learning. In practicing we take the use of the weapon, i.e., we take how to handle it into our possession. We master the way to handle the weapon. This means that our way of handling the weapon is focused upon what the weapon itself demands; "weapon" does not mean just this individual rifle of a particular serial number, but perhaps the model "98." During the practice we not only learn to load the rifle, handle the trigger and aim it, not only the manual skill, but, at the same time, and only through all this, we become familiar with the thing. Learning is always also becoming familiar. Learning has different directions: learning to use and learning to become familiar. Becoming familiar also has different levels. We become familiar with a certain individual rifle, which is one of a certain model and also a rifle in general. With practice, which is a learning of its use, the becoming familiar involved in it remains within a certain limit. Generally, the thing becomes known in general only in that the learner becomes a good marksman. But there is "more" to become familiar with about the thing—the rifle—i.e., to learn in general, for example, ballistics, mechanics, and the chemical reaction of certain materials. Furthermore, one can learn on it what a weapon is, what this particular piece of equipment is. But is there much else still to learn? There is: How does such a thing work? (*Welche Bewandtnis es . . . hat.*) But to use the thing, to shoot it, we need not know that. Certainly not. But this does not deny that how it works belongs to the thing. When a thing we are practicing to use must be produced, in order to provide it so that it can be at one's disposal, the producer must have become familiar beforehand with how the thing works (*Bewandtnis*). With respect to the thing there is a still more basic familiarity, whatever must be learned before, so that there can be such models and their corresponding parts at all; this is a familiarity with what belongs to a gun as such and what a weapon is.

This must be known in advance, and must be learned, and must be teachable. This becoming familiar is what makes it possible to produce the thing; and the thing produced, in turn, makes its practice and use possible. What we learn by practice is only a limited part of what can be learned of the thing. The original basic learning takes into cognition what a thing is, what a weapon is, and what a thing to be used is. But we already know that. We do not first learn what a weapon is when we become familiar with this rifle or with a certain model of rifle. We already know that in advance and must know it; otherwise we could not perceive the rifle as such at all. Because we know in advance what a weapon is, and only in this way, does what we see laid out before us become visible as what it is. Of course, we know what a weapon is only in general and in an indefinite way. When we come to know this in a special and determined way, we come to know something which we really already know. Precisely this "taking cognizance" is the genuine essence of learning, the μάθησις. The μαθήματα are the things insofar as we take cognizance of them as what we already know them to be in advance, the body as the bodily, the plant-like of the plant, the animal-like of the animal, the thingness of the thing, and so on. This genuine learning is therefore an extremely peculiar taking, a taking where he who takes only takes what he actually already has. Teaching corresponds to *this* learning. Teaching is a giving, an offering; but what is offered in teaching is not the learnable, for the student is merely instructed to take for himself what he already has. If the student only takes over something which is offered he does not learn. He comes to learn only when he experiences what he takes as something he himself already has. True learning only occurs where the taking of what one already has is a self-giving and is experienced as such. Teaching, therefore, does not mean anything else than to let the others learn, i.e., to bring one another to learning. Learning is more difficult than teaching; for only he who can truly learn—and only as long as he can do it—can truly teach. The genuine teacher differs from the pupil only in that he can learn better and that he more genuinely wants to learn. In all teaching, the teacher learns the most.

The most difficult learning is to come to know all the way what we already know. Such learning, with which we are here solely concerned, demands sticking rather closely to what appears to be nearest at hand; for instance, to the question of what a thing is. We steadfastly ask, considering its usefulness, *the same* obviously useless question of what a thing is, what tools are, what man is, what a work of art is, what the state and what the world are.

There was, in ancient times, a famous Greek scholar who traveled everywhere lecturing. Such people were called Sophists. Once this famous Sophist, returning to Athens from a lecture tour in Asia Minor, met Socrates on the street. It was Socrates' habit to hang around on the street and to talk with people, with a cobbler, for instance, over what a shoe is. Socrates had no other topic than what the things are. "Are you still standing there," condescendingly asked the much traveled Sophist of Socrates, "and still saying the same thing about the same thing?" "Yes," answered Socrates, "that I am. But you who are so extremely smart, you *never* say the same thing about the same thing."

The μαθήματα, the mathematical, is that "about" things which we really already know. Therefore we do not first get it out of things, but, in a certain way, we bring it already with us. From this we can now understand why, for instance, number is something mathematical. We see three chairs and say that there are three. What "three" is the three chairs do not tell us, nor three apples, three cats nor any other three things. Moreover, we can count three things only if we already know "three." In thus grasping the number three as such, we only expressly recognize something which, in some way, we already have. This recognition is genuine learning. The number is something in the proper sense learnable, a μάθημα, i.e., something mathematical. Things do not help us to grasp "three" as such, i.e., threeness. "Three"—what exactly is it? It is the number in the natural series of numbers that stands in third place. In "third"? It is only the third number because it is the three. And "place"—where do places come from? "Three" is not the third number, but the first number. "One" isn't really the first number. For instance, we have before us one loaf of bread and one knife, this one and, in addition, another one. When we take both together we say, "both of these," the one and the other, but we do not say, "these two," or 1 + 1. Only when we add a cup to the bread and the knife do we say "all." Now we take them as a sum, i.e., as a whole and so and so many. Only when we perceive it from the third is the former one the first, the former other the second, so that one and two arise, and "and" becomes "plus," and there arises the possibility of places and of a series. What we now take cognizance of is not created from any of the things. We take what we ourselves somehow already have. What must be understood as mathematical is what we can learn in this way.

We take cognizance of all this and learn it without regard for the things. Numbers are the most familiar form of the mathematical because, in our usual dealing with things, when we calculate or count, numbers are the closest to that which we recognize in things without creating it from them. For this reason numbers are the most familiar form of the mathematical. In this way, this most familiar mathematical becomes mathematics. But the essence of the mathematical does not lie in number as purely delimiting the pure "how much," but vice versa. Because number has such a nature, therefore, it belongs to the learnable in the sense of μάθησις.

Our expression "the mathematical" always has two meanings. It means, first, what can be learned in the manner we have indicated, and only in that way, and, second, the manner of learning and the process itself. The mathematical is that evident aspect of things within which we are always already moving and according to which we experience them as things at all, and as such things. The mathematical is this fundamental position we take toward things by which we take up things as already given to us, and as they should be given. Therefore, the mathematical is the fundamental presupposition of the knowledge of things.

Therefore, Plato put over the entrance to his Academy the words: Ἀγεωμέτρητος μηδεὶς εἰσίτω! "Let no one who has not grasped the mathematical enter here!"[16] These words do not mean that one must be educated in only one subject—"geometry"—but that he must grasp that the fundamental condition for the proper possibility of knowing is

---

[16] Elias Philosophus, sixth century A.D. Neoplatonist, in *Aristotelis Categorias Commentaria* (*Commentaria in Aristotelem Graeca*), A. Busse, ed. (Berlin, 1900), 118.18. *Trans.*

the knowledge of the fundamental presuppositions of all knowledge and the position we take based on such knowledge. A knowledge which does not build its foundation knowledgeably, and thereby takes its limits, is not knowledge but mere opinion. The mathematical, in the original sense of learning what one already knows, is the fundamental presupposition of "academic" work. This saying over the Academy thus contains nothing more than a hard condition and a clear circumscription of work. Both have had the consequence that we today, after two thousand years, are still not through with this academic work and never will be so as long as we take ourselves seriously.

This short reflection on the essence of the mathematical was brought about by our maintaining that the basic character of modern science is the mathematical. After what has been said, this cannot mean that this science employs mathematics. We posed our question so that, *in consequence* of this basic character of science, mathematics in the narrower sense first had to come into play.

Therefore, we must now show in what sense the foundation of modern thought and knowledge is essentially mathematical. With this intention we shall try to set forth an essential step of modern science in its main outline. This will make clear what the mathematical consists of and how it thus unfolds its essence, but also becomes established in a certain direction.

c. The Mathematical Character of Modern Natural Science; Newton's First Law of Motion

Modern thought does not appear all at once. Its beginnings stir during the later Scholasticism of the fifteenth century; the sixteenth century brings sudden advances as well as setbacks; but it is only during the seventeenth century that the decisive clarifications and foundations are accomplished. This entire happening finds its first systematic and creative culmination in the English mathematician and physicist, Newton, in his major work, *Philosophiae Naturalis Principia Mathematica*, 1686–87. In the title, "philosophy" indicates general science (compare *"Philosophia experimentalis"*); *"principia"* indicates first principles, the beginning ones, i.e., the *very first* principles. But these starting principles by no means deal with an introduction for beginners.

This work was not only a culmination of preceding efforts, but at the same time the foundation for the succeeding natural science. It has both promoted and limited the development of natural science. When we talk about classical physics today, we mean the form of knowledge, questioning, and evidence as Newton established it. When Kant speaks of "science," he means Newton's physics. Five years after the publication of the *Critique of Pure Reason*, exactly one hundred years after Newton's *Principia*, Kant published an essay entitled *The Metaphysical Principles of Natural Science* (1786). On the basis of the position reached in the *Critique of Pure Reason* it is a conscious supplement and counterpart to Newton's work. At the conclusion of the preface to his piece Kant expressly refers to Newton's work. The last decade of Kant's creativity was devoted to this sphere of inquiry.

As we glance at Newton's work (we cannot do more here), we thereby also preview Kant's concept of science, and we look at fundamental conceptions still valid in physics today, although no longer exclusively so.

This work is preceded by a short section entitled *"Definitiones."* These are definitions of *quantitas materiae*, *quantitas motus*, force, and, above all, *vis centripeta*. Then there follows an additional *scholium* which contains the series of famous conceptions of absolute and relative time, absolute and relative space, and finally of absolute and relative motion. Then follows a section with the title *"Axiomata, sive leges motus"* ("Principles or Laws of Motion"). This contains the proper content of the work. It is divided into three volumes. The first two deal with the motion of bodies, *de motu corporum*, the third with the system of the world, *de mundi systemate*.

Here we shall merely take a look at the first principle, i.e., that Law of Motion which Newton sets at the apex of his work. It reads: "Corpus omne preservare in statu suo quiescendi vel movendi uniformiter in directum, nisi quatenus a viribus impressis cogitur statum illum mutare." "Every body continues in its state of rest, or uniform motion in a straight line, unless it is compelled to change that state by force impressed upon it."[17] This is called the principle of inertia (*lex inertiae*).

The second edition of this work was published in 1713, while Newton was still alive. It included an extended preface by Cotes, then professor at Cambridge. In it Cotes says about this basic principle: "Natura lex est ab omnibus recepta philosophis." ("It is a law of nature universally received by all philosophers.")

Students of physics do not puzzle over this law today and have not for a long time. If we mention it at all and know anything about it, that and to what extent it is a fundamental principle, we consider it self-evident. And yet, one hundred years before Newton, at the apex of his physics, put this law in this form, it was still unknown. It was not even Newton himself who discovered it, but Galileo; the latter, however, applied it only in his last works and did not even express it as such. Only the Genoese Professor Baliani articulated this discovered law in general terms. Descartes then took it into his *Principia Philosophiae* and tried to ground it metaphysically. With Leibniz it plays the role of a metaphysical law (C. I. Gerhardt, *Die philosophischen Schriften von G. W. Leibniz* [Berlin, 1875-1890], IV, 518).

This law, however, was not at all self-evident even in the

---

[17] Isaac Newton, *Mathematical Principles of Natural Philosophy and His System of the World*, Andrew Motte, trans., 1729; revised translation, Florian Cajori (Berkeley: University of California Press, 1946), p. 13. *Trans.*

seventeenth century. During the preceding fifteen hundred years it was not only unknown, but Nature and Being in general were experienced in such a way that it would have been senseless. In its discovery and its establishment as the fundamental law lay a revolution that belongs to the greatest in human thought, and which first provides the ground for the turning from the Ptolemaic to the Copernican conception of the universe. To be sure, the law of inertia and its definition already had their predecessors in ancient times. Certain fundamental principles of Democritus (460–370 B.C.) tend in this direction. It has also been shown that Galileo and his age (partly directly and partly indirectly) knew of the thought of Democritus. But, as is always the case, that which can already be found in the older philosophers is seen only when one has newly thought it out for himself. Kant spoke very clearly about this fundamental fact in the history of thought when, after the publication of his main work, some contemporaries reproached him for saying only what Leibniz had "already" said. In order to oppose Kant in this way Professor Eberhardt of Halle, a disciple of the Wolff-Leibniz school, founded a special journal, the *Philosophische Magazin*. The criticism of Kant was so superficial and, at the same time, so arrogant that it found considerable response among ordinary people. When this activity went too far, Kant decided to take up the "disgusting" work of a polemic with the title: *On a Discovery, According to Which All New Critique of Pure Reason Is Made Dispensable by an Older One*. The essay begins as follows:

"Herr Eberhardt has made the discovery that Leibnizian philosophy also contains a critique of reason just as the recent one, which, in addition, introduces a dogmatism based upon an exact analysis of the possibility of knowledge, which contains all the truth of the latter, but even beyond that contains a well-grounded enlargement of the sphere of the understanding. How it could happen that people had not long ago seen these things in that great man's philosophy and its daughter, the Wolffian philosophy, is not explained by him. But how many discoveries, taken as new, are now seen by some clever interpreters very clearly in ancient ones after it had been indicated to them what to look for!"[18]

This also was the case during the age of Galileo. After the new inquiries were made, people could then again read Democritus. After people understood Democritus with the help of Galileo they could reproach the latter for not really reporting anything new. All great insights and discoveries are not only usually thought by several people at the same time, they must also be re-thought in that unique effort to truly say the same thing about the same thing.

d. The Difference Between the Greek Experience of Nature and That of Modern Times

d_1. The experience of nature in Aristotle and Newton

How does the aforementioned fundamental law relate to the earlier conception of nature? The idea of the universe (world) which reigned in the West up to the seventeenth century was determined by Platonic and Aristotelian philosophy. Scientific conceptional thought was especially guided by those fundamental representations, concepts and principles which Aristotle had set forth in his lectures on physics and the heavens (*De Caelo*), and which were taken over by the medieval Scholastics.

We must, therefore, briefly go into the fundamental conceptions of Aristotle in order to evaluate the significance of the revolution articulated in Newton's First Law. But we must first liberate ourselves from a prejudice which was partly nourished by modern science's sharp criticism

---

[18] "*Uber eine Entdeckung, nach der alle neue Kritik der reinen Vernunft durch eine ältere entbehrlich gemacht werden soll,*" Kant, *Gesammelte Schriften* (Berlin and Leipzig: Preussische Akademie der Wissenschaften, 1923), VIII, 187. *Trans.*

of Aristotle: that his propositions were merely concepts he thought up, which lacked any support in the things themselves. This might be true of later medieval Scholasticism, which often, in a purely dialectical way, was concerned with a foundationless analysis of concepts. It is certainly not true of Aristotle himself. Moreover, Aristotle fought in his time precisely to make thought, inquiry, and assertion always a λέγειν ὁμολογούμενα τοῖς φαινομένοις. (*De Caelo* 7, 306 a, 6.) ("To say that which corresponds to what shows itself on what is.")[19]

In the same place, Aristotle expressly says: τέλος δὲ τῆς μὲν ποιητικῆς 'επστήμης τὸ ἔργον, τῆς δὲ φυσικῆς τὸ φαινόμενον ἀεὶ κυρίως κατα τὴν αἴσθησιν. (*Ibid.*, 7, 306 a, 16–17.) ("And that issue, which in the case of productive knowledge is the product, in the knowledge of nature is the unimpeachable evidence of the senses as to each fact.")[20]

We have heard (p. 70 f.) that the Greeks characterize the things as φυσικά and ποιούμενα, such as occurs from out of itself, or such as is produced (*was her-gestellt, gemacht wird*). Corresponding to this there are two different kinds of knowledge ('επιστήμη), knowledge of what occurs from out of itself and knowledge of what is produced. Corresponding to this the τέλος of knowledge, i.e., that whereby this knowledge comes to an end, where it stops, what it really depends on, is different. Therefore, the above principle states, "That at which productive knowledge comes to a halt, wherein, from the beginning it halts or takes its footing, is the *work* to be produced. That, however, in which the knowledge of 'nature' takes its foothold is πὰ φαινόμενον, what shows itself on that which occurs out of itself. This is always predominant, the standard, especially for perception, i.e., for the mere 'taking-in-and-up' " (in contradistinction to making and concerning oneself busily

19 Translation of Heidegger's rendition. *Trans.*
20 Unless otherwise stated, all following references to the works of Aristotle are to *The Works of Aristotle*, W. D. Ross, ed. and trans., 11 vol. (Oxford: Clarendon Press, 1931). *Trans.*

with creating on the things) (*im Unterschied zum Machen und Sich-zu-schaffen-machen an den Dingen*). What Aristotle here expresses as a basic principle of scientific method differs in no way from the principles of modern science. Newton writes (*Principia Liber III, Regulae IV*): "In philosophia experimentale propositiones ex phaenomenis per inductionem collectae non obstantibus contrariis hypothesibus pro veris aut accurate aut quamproxime haberi debent, donec alia occurrerint phaenomena, per quae aut accuratiores reddedantur aut exceptionibus abnoxiae." ("In experimental philosophy we are to look upon propositions inferred by general induction from phenomena as accurate or very nearly true, notwithstanding contrary hypotheses that may be imagined, till such times as other phenomena occur, by which they may either be made more accurate, or liable to exceptions.")

But despite this similar basic attitude toward procedure, the basic position of Aristotle is essentially different from that of Newton. For *what* is actually apprehended as appearing and *how* it is interpreted are not the same.

d₂. The doctrine of motion in Aristotle

Nevertheless there is beforehand the common experience that what is, in the general sense of Nature—earth, sky, and stars—is in motion or at rest. Rest means only a special case of motion. It is everywhere a question of the motion of bodies. But how motion and bodies are to be conceived and what relation they have to each other is not established and not self-evident. From the general and indefinite experience that things change, come into existence and pass away, thus are in motion, it is a long way to an insight into the essence of motion and into the manner of its belonging to things. The ancient Greek conception of the earth is of a disc around which floats Okeanos. The sky overarches it and turns around it. Later Plato, Aristotle, and Eudoxus—though each differently—present the earth as a ball but still as a center of everything.

We restrict ourselves to the presentation of the Aristotelian conception which later became widely dominant, and this only sufficiently to show the contrast which expresses itself in the first axiom of Newton.

First, we ask, in general, what, according to Aristotle, is the essence of a thing in nature? The answer is: τὰ φυσικὰ σώματα are καθ' αὑτὰ κινητὰ κατὰ τόπον. ("Those bodies which belong to 'nature' and constitute it are, in themselves, movable with respect to location.") Motion, in general, is μεταβολή, the alteration of something into something else. Motion in this wide sense is, for instance, turning pale and blushing. But it is also an alteration when a body is transferred from one place to another. This being transported is expressed in Greek as φορά. Κίνησις κατὰ τόπον means in Greek what constitutes the proper motion of Newtonian bodies. In this motion there lies a definite relation to the place. The motion of bodies, however, is καθ' αὑτά, according to them, themselves. That is to say, how a body moves, i.e., how it relates to the place and to what it relates—all this has its basis in the body itself. Basis (*Grund*) is ἀρχή and has a double meaning: that from which something emerges, and that which governs over what emerges in this way. The body is ἀρχὴ κινήσεως. What an ἀρχὴ κινήσεως in this manner is, is φύσις, the primordial mode of emergence (*Hervorgehens*), which however remains limited only to pure movement in space. Herein there appears an essential transformation of the concept of physics. The body moves according to its nature. A moving body, which is itself an ἀρχὴ κινήσεως, is a natural body. The purely earthy body moves downward, the purely fiery body—as every blazing flame demonstrates —moves upward. Why? Because the earthy has its place below, the fiery, above. Each body has *its* place *according to its kind*, and it strives toward that place. Around the

earth is water, around this, the air, and around this, fire
—the four elements. When a body moves in its place, this
motion accords with nature, κατὰ φύσιν. A rock falls down
to the earth. However, if a rock is thrown upward by a
sling, this motion is essentially against the nature of the
rock, παρὰ φύσιν. All motions against nature are βίᾳ, violence.

The kind of motion and the place of the body are determined according to its nature. The earth is in the center
for all characterization and evaluation of motion. The rock
which falls moves toward this center, ἐπὶ τὸ μέσον. The fire
which rises, ἀπὸ τοῦ μέσου, moves away from the center. In
both cases the motion is κίνησις εὐθεῖα, in a straight line. But
the stars and the entire heavens move around the center,
περὶ τὸ μέσον. This motion is κύκλῳ. Circular motion and motion in a straight line are the simple movements, ἁπλαί. Of
these two, circular motion is first, that is, the highest, and
thus, of the highest order. For πρότερον τὸ τέλειον τοῦ ἀτελοῦς,
the complete precedes the incomplete. Their place belongs
to the motion of bodies. In circular motion the body has its
place in the motion itself, wherefore this motion is perpetual, and really existent. In rectilinear motion the place
lies only in a direction and away from another place, so
that motion comes to an end there. Besides these two
forms of simple motion, there are mixtures of both, μικτή.
The purest motion, in the sense of change of place, is circular motion; it contains, as it were, its place in itself. A body
which so moves itself, moves itself completely. This is true
of all celestial bodies. Compared to this, earthy motion is
always in a straight line, or mixed, or forced, but always
incomplete.

There is an essential difference between the motion of
celestial bodies and earthly bodies. The domains of these
motions are different. How a body moves depends upon its
species and the place to which it belongs. The *where* determines the *how* of its being, for being is called *presence*
(*Anwesenheit*). The moon does not fall earthward, be-

cause it moves in a circle, that is, it moves completely, permanently in the simplest motion. This circular motion is in itself completely independent of anything outside itself—for instance, from the earth as center. But, in contrast, to anticipate, in modern thought circular motion is understood only so that a perpetual attracting force (*Zug*) from the center is necessary for its formation and preservation. With Aristotle, however, this "force," δύναμις, the capacity for its motion, lies in the *nature* of the body itself. The kind of motion of the body and its relation to its place depend upon the nature of the body. The velocity of natural motion increases the nearer the body comes to its place, that is, increase and decrease of velocity and the ceasing of motion depend upon the nature of the body. A motion contrary to nature, i.e., a forced motion, has its cause in the force that affects it. However, according to its motion, the body, driven forcibly, must withdraw from this power, and since the body itself does not bring with it any basis *for* this forced motion, its motion must necessarily become slower and finally stop: πάντα γὰρ τοῦ βιαζομένου πορρωτέρω γιγνόμενα βραδύτερον φέρεται (Περὶ οὐρανοῦ A_8, 277 b, 6. τάχιστα φθειρόμενα τὰ παρὰ φύσιν, *ibid.*, A_2, 269 b, 9). This corresponds distinctly to the common conception: a motion imparted to a body continues for a certain time and then ceases, passing over into a state of rest. Therefore, we must look for the causes for the continuation or endurance of the motion. According to Aristotle, the basis for natural motion lies in the nature of the body itself, in its essence, in its most proper being (*seinem eigensten Sein*). A later Scholastic proposition is in accord with this: *Operari (agere) sequitur esse*. "The kind of motion follows from the kind of being."

d_3. Newton's doctrine of motion

How does Aristotle's descriptive observation of nature and concept of motion relate to the modern one, which got an essential foundation in the first axiom of Newton? We shall try to present in order a few main distinctions. For this purpose we give the axiom an abridged form: Every body left to itself moves uniformly in a straight line. ("Corpus omne, quod a viribus impressis non cogitur, uniformiter in directum movetur.") We shall discuss what is new in eight points:

1. Newton's axiom begins with "*corpus omne*," "every body." That means that the distinction between earthly and celestial bodies has become obsolete. The universe is no longer divided into two well-separated realms, the one beneath the stars, the other the realm of the stars themselves. All natural bodies are essentially of the same kind. The upper realm is not a superior one.

2. In accord with this, the priority of circular motion over motion in a straight line also disappears. And, even insofar as now, in reverse, motion in a straight line becomes decisive, still this does not lead to a division of bodies and of different domains according to their kind of motion.

3. Accordingly, the distinguishing of certain places also disappears. Each body can fundamentally be in any place. The concept of place itself is changed: place no longer is where the body belongs according to its nature, but only a position in relation to other positions. (Compare points 5 and 7). φορά and change of place in the modern sense are not the same.

With respect to the causation and determination of motion, one does not ask for the cause of the continuity of motion and, therefore, for its perpetual occurrence, but the reverse: being in motion (*Bewegtheit*) is presupposed, and one asks for the causes of a change from motion presupposed as uniform, and in a straight line. The circularity of the moon's motion does not cause its uniform perpetual motion around the earth. Precisely the reverse. It is this motion for whose cause we must search. According to the law of inertia, the body of the moon should move from every point of its circular orbit in a straight line, i.e., in the form of a tangent. Since the moon does not do so, the question based upon the presupposition of the law of inertia and out of it arises: Why does the moon decline from the line of a tangent? Why does it move, as the Greeks put it, in a circle? The circular movement is now not cause but, on the contrary, precisely what requires a reason. (We know that Newton arrived at a new answer when he proposed that the force according to which bodies fall to the ground is also the one according to which the celestial bodies remain in their orbits: gravity. Newton compared the centripetal declination of the moon from the tangent of its orbit during a fraction of time with this linear distance which a falling body achieves at the surface of earth in an equal time. At this point we see immediately the elimination of the distinction already mentioned between earthly and celestial motions and thus between bodies.)

4. Motions themselves are not determined according to different natures, capacities, and forces, the elements of the body, but, in reverse, the essence of force is determined by the fundamental law of motion: Every body, left to itself, moves uniformly in a straight line. According to this, a force is that whose impact results in a declination from rectilinear, uniform motion. "Vis impressa est actio in corpus exercita, ad mutandum eius statum vel quiescendi vel movendi uniformiter in directum" (*Principia*, Def. IV).[21] This new determination of force leads at the same time to a new determination of mass.

5. Corresponding to the change of the concept of place, motion is only seen as a change of position and relative position, as distances between places. Therefore, the determination of motion develops into one regarding distances, stretches of the measurable, of the so and so large.

---

[21] "An impressed force is an action exerted upon a body, in order to change its state, either of rest, or of uniform motion in a right line." *Trans.*

Motion is determined as the amount of motion, and, similarly, mass as weight.

6. Therefore, the difference between natural and against nature, i.e., forced, is also eliminated; the βία, violence, is as force only a measure of the change of motion and is no longer special in kind. The impact, for instance, is only a particular form of the *vis impressa*, along with pressure and centripetality.

7. Therefore, the concept of nature in general changes. Nature is no longer the *inner* principle out of which the motion of the body follows; rather, nature is the mode of the variety of the changing relative positions of bodies, the manner in which they are present in space and time, which themselves are domains of possible positional orders and determinations of order and have no special traits anywhere.

8. Thereby the manner of questioning nature also changes and, in a certain respect, becomes opposite.

We cannot set forth here the full implications of the revolution of inquiry into nature. It should have become clear only that, and how, the application of the first law of motion implies all the essential changes. All these changes are linked together and uniformly based on the new basic position expressed in the first law and which we call mathematical.

e. The Essence of the Mathematical Project (*Entwurf*)[22] (Galileo's Experiment with Free Fall)

For us, for the moment, the question concerns the application of the First Law, more precisely, the question in what sense the mathematical becomes decisive in it.

---

[22] Perhaps the best insight as to what Heidegger means by "project" is Kant's use of the word in the *Critique of Pure Reason*. "When Galileo experimented with balls whose weight he himself had already predetermined, when Torricelli caused the

How about this law? It speaks of a body, *corpus quod a viribus impressis non cogitur,* a body which is left to itself. Where do we find it? There is no such body. There is also no experiment which could ever bring such a body to direct perception. But modern science, in contrast to the mere dialectical poetic conception of medieval Scholasticism and science, is supposed to be based upon experience. Instead, it has such a law at its apex. This law speaks of a thing that does not exist. It demands a fundamental representation of things which contradict the ordinary.

The mathematical is based on such a claim, i.e., the application of a determination of the thing, which is not experientially created out of the thing and yet lies at the base of every determination of the things, making them possible and making room for them. Such a fundamental conception of things is neither arbitrary nor self-evident. Therefore, it required a long controversy to bring it into

---

air to carry a weight which he had calculated beforehand to be equal to that of a definite column of water, or, at a later time, when Stahl converted metal into lime and this again into metal by withdrawing something and then adding it, a light broke in on all investigators of nature. They learned that reason only gains insight into what it produces itself according to its own projects *(was sie selbst nach ihrem Entwurfe hervorbringt);* that it must go before with principles of judgment according to constant laws, and constrain nature to reply to its questions, not content to merely follow her leading-strings" (B XIII).

Literally *Entwurf* means "a throwing forth"; from *werfen* (to throw) and *ent-* (indicating separation or severing in the sense of "out," "away," "from," "forth"). In present day use it is a sketch, and the word "sketch" is sometimes used in this translation, as well as "project" and "projection." Originally a textile term referring to the building of a frame, in the seventeenth century it *(entwerfen)* took the sense of a preliminary or preparatory sketch. As Heidegger uses it in *SZ,* 145, it is a sketching which is a throwing forth of *Dasein* in which it "throws before itself the possibility as possibility and as such allows it to be." It is through understanding as project that the structure of the being of entities, including *Dasein,* becomes accessible. Project is constructive in that it *allows* the possibilities of entities *to be;* in the case of *Dasein* to achieve its openness to its own being (*See KM,* pp. 209–10). *Trans.*

power. It required a change in the mode of approach to things along with the achievement of a new manner of thought. We can accurately follow the history of this battle. Let us cite *one* example from it. In the Aristotelian view, bodies move according to their nature, the heavy ones downward, the light ones upward. When both fall, heavy ones fall faster than light ones, since the latter have the urge to move upward. It becomes a decisive insight of Galileo that all bodies fall equally fast, and that the differences in the time of fall only derive from the resistance of the air, not from the different inner natures of the bodies or from their own corresponding relation to their particular place. Galileo did his experiment at the leaning tower in the town of Pisa, where he was professor of mathematics, in order to prove his statement. In it bodies of different weights did not arrive at precisely the same time after having fallen from the tower, but the difference in time was slight. In spite of these differences and therefore really against the evidence of experience, Galileo upheld his proposition. The witnesses to this experiment, however, became really perplexed by the experiment and Galileo's upholding his view. They persisted the more obstinately in their former view. By reason of this experiment the opposition toward Galileo increased to such an extent that he had to give up his professorship and leave Pisa.

Both Galileo and his opponents saw the same "fact." But they interpreted the same fact differently and made the same happening visible to themselves in different ways. Indeed, what appeared for them as the essential fact and truth was something different. Both thought something along with the same appearance but they thought something different, not only about the single case, but fundamentally, regarding the essence of a body and the nature of its motion. What Galileo thought in advance about motion was the determination that the motion of every body is uniform and rectilinear, when every obstacle is excluded, but that it also changes uniformly when an equal force affects it. In his *Discorsi*, which appeared in 1638, Galileo said: "Mobile super planum horizontale projectum mente concipio omni secluso impedimento, jam constat ex his, quae fusius alibi dicta sunt, illius motum aequabilem et perpetuum super ipso plano futurum esse, si planum in infinitum extendatur." ("I think of a body thrown on a horizontal plane and every obstacle excluded. This results in what has been given a detailed account in another place, that the motion of the body over this plane would be uniform and perpetual if this place were extended infinitely.")

In this proposition, which may be considered the antecedent of the First Law of Newton, what we have been looking for is clearly expressed. Galileo says: "Mobile mente concipio omni secluso impedimento." ("I think in my mind of something moveable that is entirely left to itself.") This "to think in the mind" (*Sich-im-Geiste-denken*) is that giving-oneself-a-cognition (*Sich-selbst-eine-Kenntnis geben*) about a determination of things. It is a procedure of going ahead in advance, which Plato once characterized regarding μάθησις in the following way: ἀναλαβὼν αὐτὸς ἐξ αὑτοῦ τὴν ἐπιστήμην (*Meno* 85d), "bringing up and taking up— above and beyond the other—taking the knowledge itself from out of himself.")

There is a prior grasping together in this *mente concipere* of what should be uniformly determinative of each body as such, i.e., for being bodily. All bodies are alike. No motion is special. Every place is like every other, each moment like any other. Every force becomes determinable only by the change of motion which it causes—this change in motion being understood as a change of place. All determinations of bodies have one basic blueprint (*Grundriss*), according to which the natural process is nothing but the space-time determination of the motion of points of mass. This fundamental design of nature at the same time circumscribes its realm as everywhere uniform.

Now if we summarize at a glance all that has been said,

we can grasp the essence of the mathematical more sharply. Up to now we said only its general characteristic, that it is a taking cognizance of something, what it takes being something it gives to itself from itself, thereby giving to itself what it already has. We now summarize the fuller essential determination of the mathematical in a few separate points:

1. The mathematical is, as *mente concipere*, a project (*Entwurf*) of thingness (*Dingheit*) which, as it were, skips over the things. The project first opens a domain (*Spielraum*) where things—i.e., facts—show themselves.

2. In this projection there is posited that which things are taken as, what and how they are to be evaluated (*würdigt*) beforehand. Such evaluation (*Würdigen*) and taking-for (*Dafürhalten*) is called in Greek ἀξιόω. The anticipating determinations and assertions in the project are ἀξιώματα. Newton therefore entitles the section in which he presents the fundamental determinations about things as moved: *Axiomata, sive leges motus*. The project is axiomatic. Insofar as every science and cognition is expressed in propositions, the cognition which is taken and posited in the mathematical project is of such a kind as to set things upon their foundation in advance. The axioms are *fundamental* propositions.

3. As axiomatic, the mathematical project is the anticipation (*Vorausgriff*) of the essence of things, of bodies; thus the basic blueprint (*Grundriss*) of the structure of every thing and its relation to every other thing is sketched in advance.

4. This basic plan (*Grundriss*) at the same time provides the measure for laying out of the realm, which, in the future, will encompass all things of that sort. Now nature is no longer an inner capacity of a body, determining its form of motion and place. Nature is now the realm of the uniform space-time context of motion, which is outlined in the axiomatic project and in which alone bodies can be bodies as a part of it and anchored in it.

5. This realm of nature, axiomatically determined in outline by this project, now also requires for the bodies and corpuscles within it a mode of access (*Zugangsart*) appropriate to the axiomatically predetermined objects. The mode of questioning and the cognitive determination of nature are now no longer ruled by traditional opinions and concepts. Bodies have no concealed qualities, powers, and capacities. Natural bodies are now only what they *show* themselves as, within this projected realm. Things now show themselves only in the relations of places and time points and in the measures of mass and working forces. How they show themselves is prefigured in the project. Therefore, the project also determines the mode of taking in and studying of what shows itself, experience, the *experiri*. However, because inquiry is now predetermined by the outline of the project, a line of questioning can be instituted in such a way that it poses conditions in advance to which nature must answer in one way or another. Upon the basis of the mathematical, the *experientia* becomes the modern experiment. Modern science is experimental because of the mathematical project. The experimenting urge to the facts is a necessary consequence of the preceding mathematical skipping (*Uberspringen*) of all facts. But where this skipping ceases or becomes weak, mere facts as such are collected, and positivism arises.

6. Because the project establishes a uniformity of all bodies according to relations of space, time, and motion, it also makes possible and requires a universal uniform measure as an essential determinant of things, i.e., numerical measurement. The mathematical project of Newtonian bodies leads to the development of a certain "mathematics" in the narrow sense. The new form of modern science did not arise because mathematics became an essential determinant. Rather, that mathematics, and a particular kind of mathematics, could come into play and had come into play is a consequence of the mathematical

project. The founding of analytical geometry by Descartes, the founding of the infinitesimal calculus by Newton, the simultaneous founding of the differential calculus by Leibniz—all these novelties, this mathematical in a narrower sense, first became possible and, above all, necessary, on the grounds of the basically mathematical character of the thinking.

We would certainly fall into great error if we were to think that with this characterization of the reversal from ancient to modern natural science and with this sharpened essential outline of the mathematical we had already gained a picture of the actual science itself.

What we have been able to cite is only the fundamental outline along which there unfolds the entire richness of posing questions and experiments, establishing of laws and disclosing of new districts of what is. Within this fundamental mathematical position the questions about the nature of space and time, motion and force, body and matter remain open. These questions now receive a new sharpness; for instance, the question whether motion is sufficiently formulated by the designation "change of location." Regarding the concept of force, the question arises whether it is sufficient to represent force only as a cause that is effective only from the outside. Concerning the basic law of motion, the law of inertia, the question arises whether this law is not to be subordinated under a more general one, i.e., the law of the conservation of energy which is now determined in accordance with its *expenditure* and *consumption*, as *work*—a name for new basic representations which now enter into the study of nature and betray a notable accord with economics, with the "calculation" of success. All this develops within and according to the fundamental mathematical position. What remains questionable in all this is a closer determination of the relation of the mathematical in the sense of mathematics to the intuitive direct perceptual experience (*zur anschaulichen Erfahrung*) of the given things and to these things themselves. Up to this hour such questions have been open. Their questionability is concealed by the results and the progress of scientific work. One of these burning questions concerns the justification and limits of mathematical formalism in contrast to the demand for an immediate return to intuitively[23] given nature (*anschaulich gegebene Natur*).

If we have grasped some of what has been said up till now, then it is understandable that the question cannot be decided by way of an either/or, either formalism or immediate intuitive determination of things; for the nature and direction of the mathematical project participate in deciding their possible relation to the intuitively experienced and vice versa. Behind this question concerning the relation of mathematical formalism to the intuition of nature stands the fundamental question of the justification and limits of the mathematical in general, within a fundamental position we take toward what is, as a whole. But, in this regard the delineation of the mathematical has gained an importance for us.

f. The Metaphysical Meaning of the Mathematical

To reach our goal, the understanding of the mathematical as we have gained it up to now is not sufficient. To be sure, we shall now no longer conceive of it as a generalization of the procedure of a particular mathematical discipline, but rather the particular discipline as a particular form developing from the mathematical. But this mathematical must, in turn, be grasped from causes that lie even deeper. We have said that it is a fundamental trait of modern thought. Every sort of thought, however, is always only the execution and consequence of the historical mode

---

[23] *Anschauen*: "looking at." The usual English translation, "intuition," comes from the Latin *in* and *tueor* ("to see," "look," "gaze"). Intuition refers to immediate perception in contrast to conceptual inference. *Trans.*

of being (*Dasein*) at that time, of the fundamental position taken toward what is and toward the way in which what is, is manifest as such, i.e., to the truth.

What we have exhibited as the mathematical must now receive a clarification in this direction; for only in this way will what we are looking for become visible: precisely that formation of modern metaphysical thought in whose train something like the *Critique of Pure Reason* could and had to arise.

f₁. The principles: new freedom, self-binding and self-grounding

We inquire, therefore, about the metaphysical meaning of the mathematical in order to evaluate its importance for modern metaphysics. We divide the question into two subordinate ones: (1) What new fundamental position of *Dasein* shows itself in this rise of the dominance of the mathematical? (2) How does the mathematical, according to its own inner direction, drive toward an ascent to a metaphysical determination of *Dasein?*

The second question is the more important for us. We shall answer the first one only in the merest outline.

Up to the distinct emergence of the mathematical as a fundamental characteristic of thought, the authoritative truth was considered that of Church and faith. The means for the proper knowledge of what is were obtained by way of the interpretation of the sources of revelation, the writ and the tradition of the Church. Whatever more experience and knowledge had been won adjusted itself (as if by itself) to this frame. For basically there was no worldly knowledge. The so-called natural knowledge not based upon any revelation, therefore, did not have its own form of intelligibility or grounds for itself, let alone from out of itself. Thus, what is decisive for the history of science is not that all truth of natural knowledge was measured by the supernatural. Rather it is that this natural knowledge, disregarding this criterion, arrived at no independent foundation and character out of itself. For the taking over of the Aristotelian syllogism cannot be reckoned as such.

In the essence of the mathematical, as the project we delineated, lies a specific will to a new formation and self-grounding of the form of knowledge as such. The detachment from revelation as the first source for truth and the rejection of tradition as the authoritative means of knowledge—all these rejections are only negative consequences of the mathematical project. He who dared to project the mathematical project put himself as the projector of this project upon a base which is first projected only in the project. There is not only a liberation in the mathematical project, but also a new experience and formation of freedom itself, i.e., a binding with obligations which are self-imposed. In the mathematical project develops an obligation to principles demanded by the mathematical itself. According to this inner drive, a liberation to a new freedom, the mathematical strives out of itself to establish its own essence as the ground of itself and thus of all knowledge.

Therewith we come to the second question: How does the mathematical, according to its own inner drive, move toward an ascent to a metaphysical determination of *Dasein?* We can abridge this question as follows: In what way does modern metaphysics arise out of the spirit of the mathematical? It is already obvious from the form of the question that mathematics could not become the standard of philosophy, as if mathematical methods were only appropriately generalized and then transferred to philosophy.

Rather, modern natural science, modern mathematics, and modern metaphysics sprang from the same root of the mathematical in the wider sense. Because metaphysics, of these three, reaches farthest—to what is, in totality—and because at the same time it also reaches deepest toward the being of what is as such, therefore it is precisely metaphysics which must dig down to the bedrock of its mathematical base and ground.

As we pursue how modern philosophy grows up from this ground that it has laid in itself we grasp the historical possibility and necessity of a "critique of pure reason." Moreover, we shall come to understand why this work has the form it has and why we shall begin our interpretation of this work at *that* place at which we shall enter it.

f₂. Descartes: *Cogito Sum;* "I" as a special subject

Modern philosophy is usually considered to have begun with Descartes (1596–1650), who lived a generation after Galileo. Contrary to the attempts, which appear from time to time, to have modern philosophy begin with Meister Eckhart or in the time between Eckhart and Descartes, we must adhere to the usual beginning. The only question is how one understands Descartes' philosophy. It is no accident that the philosophical formation of the mathematical foundation of modern *Dasein* is primarily achieved in France, England, and Holland anymore than it is accidental that Leibniz received his decisive inspiration from there, especially during his sojourn in Paris from 1672–76. Only because he passed through that world and truly appraised its greatness in greater reflection was he in a position to lay the first foundation for its overcoming.

The following is the usual image of Descartes and his philosophy: During the Middle Ages philosophy stood—if it stood independently at all—under the exclusive domination of theology and gradually degenerated into a mere analysis of concepts and elucidations of traditional opinions and propositions. It petrified into an academic knowledge which no longer concerned man and was unable to illuminate reality as a whole. Then Descartes appeared and liberated philosophy from this disgraceful position. He began by doubting everything, but this doubt finally did run into something which could no longer be doubted, for, inasmuch as the skeptic doubts, he cannot doubt that he, the skeptic, is present and must be present in order to doubt at all. As I doubt I must admit that "I am." The "I," accordingly, is the indubitable. As the doubter, Descartes forced men into doubt in this way; he led them to think of themselves, of their "I." Thus the "I," human subjectivity, came to be declared the center of thought. From here originated the I-viewpoint of modern times and its subjectivism. Philosophy itself, however, was thus brought to the insight that doubting must stand at the beginning of philosophy: reflection upon knowledge itself and its possibility. A theory of knowledge had to be erected before a theory of the world. From then on epistemology is the foundation of philosophy, and that distinguishes modern from medieval philosophy. Since then, the attempts to renew Scholasticism also strive to demonstrate the epistemology in their system, or to add it where it is missing, in order to make it usable for modern times. Accordingly, Plato and Aristotle are reinterpreted as epistemologists.

This story of Descartes, who came and doubted and so became a subjectivist, thus grounding epistemology, does give the usual picture; but at best it is only a bad novel, and anything but a story in which the movement of being becomes visible.

The main work of Descartes carries the title *Meditationes de prima philosophia* (1641). *Prima philosophia*—this is the πρώτη φιλοσοφία of Aristotle, the question concerning the being of what is, in the form of the question concerning the thingness of things. *Meditationes de metaphysica*—nothing about theory of knowledge. The sentence or proposition constitutes the guide for the question about the being of what is (for the categories). (The essential historical-metaphysical basis for the priority of *certainty*, which first made the acceptance and metaphysical development of the mathematical possible—Christianity and the *certainty of salvation*, the security of the individual as such—will not be considered here.)

In the Middle Ages, the doctrine of Aristotle was taken over in a very special way. In later Scholasticism, through the Spanish philosophical schools, especially through the Jesuit, Suárez, the "medieval" Aristotle went through an extended interpretation. Descartes received his first and fundamental philosophical education from the Jesuits at La Flèche. The title of his main work expresses both his argument with this tradition and his will to take up anew the question about the being of what is, the thingness of the thing, "substance."

But all this happened in the midst of a period in which, for a century, mathematics had already been emerging more and more as the foundation of thought and was pressing toward clarity. It was a time which, in accordance with this free projection of the world, embarked on a new assault upon reality. There is nothing of scepticism here, nothing of the I-viewpoint and subjectivity—but just the contrary. Therefore, it is the passion of the new thought and inquiry to bring to clarification and display in its innermost essence the at first dark, unclear, and often misinterpreted fundamental position, which has progressed only by fits and starts. But this means that the mathematical wills to ground itself in the sense of its own inner requirements. It expressly intends to explicate itself as the standard of *all* thought and to establish the rules which thereby arise. Descartes substantially participates in this work of reflection upon the fundamental meaning of the mathematical. Because this reflection concerned the totality of what is and the knowledge of it, this had to become a reflection on metaphysics. This simultaneous advance in the direction of a foundation of mathematics and of a reflection on metaphysics above all characterizes his fundamental philosophical position. We can pursue this clearly in an unfinished early work which did not appear in print until fifty years after Descartes' death (1701). This work is called *Regulae ad directionem ingenii.*

(1) *Regulae:* basic and guiding propositions in which mathematics submits itself to its own essence; (2) *ad directionem ingenii:* laying the foundation of the mathematical in order that it, as a whole, becomes the measure of the inquiring mind. In the enunciation of something subject to rules as well as with regard to the inner free determination of the mind, the basic mathematical-metaphysical character is already expressed in the title. Here, by way of a reflection upon the essence of mathematics, Descartes grasps the idea of a *scientia universalis*, to which everything must be directed and ordered as the one authoritative science. Descartes expressly emphasizes that it is not a question of *mathematica vulgaris* but of *mathematica universalis*.

We cannot, here, present the inner construction and the main content of this unfinished work. In it the modern concept of science is coined. Only one who has really thought through this relentlessly sober volume long enough, down to its remotest and coldest corner, fulfills the prerequisite for getting an inkling of what is going on in modern science. In order to convey a notion of the intention and attitude of this work, we shall quote only three of the twenty-one rules, namely, the third, fourth, and fifth. Out of these the basic character of modern thought leaps before our eyes.

Regula III: "Circa objecta proposita, non quid alii senserint, vel quid ipsi suspicemur, sed quid clare et evidenter possimus intueri, vel certo deducere, quaerendum est; non aliter enim scientia acquiritur." ("Concerning the objects before us, we should pursue the questions, not what others have thought, nor what we ourselves conjecture, but what we can clearly and insightfully intuit, or deduce with steps of certainty, for in no other way is knowledge arrived at.")[24]

---

[24] Descartes, *Rules for the Direction of the Mind*, F. P. Lafleur, trans. (Liberal Arts Press, 1961), p. 8. *Trans.*

Regula IV: "Necessaria est methodus ad rerum veritatem investigandam." ("Method is necessary for discovering the truth of nature.")

This rule does not intend the platitude that a science
must also have its method, but it wants to say that the
procedure, i.e., how in general we are to pursue things
(μέθοδος), decides in advance what truth we shall seek out
in the things.

Method is not one piece of equipment of science among
others but the primary component out of which is first determined what can become object and how it becomes an
object.

Regula V: "Tota methodus consistit in ordine et disposi-
tione eorum ad quae mentis acies est convertenda, ut
aliquam veritatem inveniamus. Atquae hanc exacte ser-
vabimus, si propositiones involutas et obscuras ad simpli-
ciores gradatim reducamus, et deinde ex omnium simpli-
cissimarum intuitu ad aliarum omnium cognitionem per
eosdem gradus ascendere tentemus." ("Method consists
entirely in the order and arrangement of that upon which
the sharp vision of the mind must be directed in order to
discover some truth. But, we will follow such a method
only if we lead complex and obscure propositions back
step by step to the simpler ones and then try to ascend by
the same steps from the insight of the very simplest propositions to the knowledge of all the others.")

What remains decisive is how this reflection on the
mathematical affects the argument with traditional metaphysics (*prima philosophia*), and how, starting from
there, the further destiny and form of modern philosophy
is determined.

To the essence of the mathematical as a projection belongs the axiomatical, the beginning of basic principles
upon which everything further is based in insightful order.
If mathematics, in the sense of a *mathesis universalis*, is to
ground and form the whole of knowledge, then it requires
the formulation of special axioms.

(1) They must be absolutely first, intuitively evident in and of themselves, i.e., absolutely certain. This certainty participates in deciding their truth. (2) The highest axioms, as mathematical, must establish in advance, concerning the whole of what is, what is in being and what being means, from where and how the thingness of things is determined. According to tradition this happens along guidelines of the proposition. But up till now, the proposition had been taken only as what offered itself, as it were, of itself. The simple proposition about the simply present things contains and retains what the things are. Like the things, the proposition, too, is present-at-hand (*vorhanden*): it is the present (*vorhanden*) container of being.

However, there can be no pre-given things for a basically mathematical position. The proposition cannot be an arbitrary one. The proposition, and precisely it, must itself be based on its foundation. It must be a basic principle—*the* basic principle absolutely. One must therefore find such a principle of all positing, i.e., a proposition in which that about which it says something, the *subjectum* (ὑποκείμενον), is not just taken from somewhere else. That underlying subject must as such first emerge for itself in this original proposition and be established. Only in this way is the *subjectum* a *fundamentum absolutum*, purely posited from the proposition as such, a basis and, as such, a *fundamentum absolutum* at the same time *inconcussum*, and thus indubitable and absolutely certain. Because the mathematical now sets itself up as the principle of all knowledge, all knowledge up to now must necessarily be put into question, regardless of whether it is tenable or not.

Descartes does not doubt because he is a skeptic; rather, he must become a doubter because he posits the mathematical as the absolute ground and seeks for all knowledge a foundation that will be in accord with it. It is a question not only of finding a fundamental law for the realm of nature, but finding the very first and highest basic principle for the being of what is, in general. This absolutely mathematical principle cannot have anything in front of it and cannot allow what might be given to it beforehand. If anything is given at all, it is only the *proposition* in general *as such*, i.e., the positing, the position, in the sense of a thinking that asserts. The positing, the proposition, only has itself as that which can be posited. Only where thinking thinks itself, is it absolutely mathematical, i.e., a taking cognizance of that which we already have. Insofar as thinking and positing directs itself toward itself, it finds the following: whatever and in whatever sense anything may be asserted, this asserting and thinking is always an "*I* think." Thinking *is* always an "*I* think," *ego cogito*. Therein lies: I am, *sum*. *Cogito, sum*—this is the highest certainty lying immediately in the proposition as such. In "I posit" the "I" as the positer is co- and pre-posited as that which is already present, as what is. The being of what is is determined out of the "I am" as the certainty of the positing.

The formula which the proposition sometimes has, "*Cogito ergo sum*," suggests the misunderstanding that it is here a question of inference. That is not the case and cannot be so, because this conclusion would have to have as its major premise: *Id quod cogitat, est;* and the minor premise: *cogito;* conclusion: *ergo sum*. However, the major premise would only be a formal generalization of what lies in the proposition: "*cogito—sum*." Descartes himself emphasizes that no inference is present. The *sum* is not a consequence of the thinking, but vice versa; it is the ground of thinking, the *fundamentum*. In the essence of positing lies the proposition: I posit. That is a proposition which does not depend upon something given beforehand, but only gives to itself what lies within it. In it lies: "*I* posit": I am the one who posits and thinks. This proposition has the peculiarity of first positing that about which it makes an assertion, the *subjectum*. What it posits in this case is the "*I*." The I is the *subjectum* of the very first principle. The I is, therefore, a special something which under-lies (*Zugrundeliegendes*)—ὑποκείμενον, *subjectum*—the *subjectum* of the positing as such. Hence it came about that ever since then the "I" has especially been called the *subjectum*, "subject." The character of the ego as what is especially already present before one remains unnoticed. Instead the subjectivity of the subject is determined by the "I-ness" (*Ichheit*) of the "I think." That the "I" comes to be defined as that which is already present for represen-tation (the "objective" in today's sense) is not because of any I-viewpoint or any subjectivistic doubt, but because of the essential predominance and the definitely directed radicalization of the mathematical and the axiomatic.

This "I," which has been raised to be the special *sub-jectum* on the basis of the mathematical, is, in its meaning, nothing "subjective" at all, in the sense of an incidental quality of just this particular human being. This "subject" designated in the "I think," this I, is subjectivistic only when its essence is no longer understood, i.e., is not un-folded from its origin considered in terms of its mode of being (*seinsmässigen Herkunft*).

Until Descartes every thing present-at-hand for itself was a "subject"; but now the "I" becomes the special sub-ject, that with regard to which all the remaining things first determine themselves as such. Because—mathemati-cally—they first receive their thingness only through the founding relation to the highest principle and its "sub-ject" (I), they are essentially such as stand as something else in relation to the "subject," which lie over against it as *objectum*. The things themselves become "objects."

The word *objectum* now passes through a correspond-ing change of meaning. For up to then the word *objectum* denoted what was thrown up opposite one's mere imagin-ing: I imagine a golden mountain. This thus represented —an *objectum* in the language of the Middle Ages—is, ac-cording to the usage of language today, merely something "subjective"; for "a golden mountain" does not exist "objectively" in the meaning of the changed linguistic use. This reversal of the meanings of the words *subjectum* and *objectum* is no mere affair of usage; it is a radical change of *Dasein*, i.e., the illumination (*Lichtung*)[25] of the being of what is on the basis of the predominance of the *mathematical*. *It is a stretch of the way of actual history necessarily hidden from the naked eye*, a history which always concerns the openness of being—or nothing at all.

f₃. Reason as the highest ground: the principle of the I, the principle of contradiction

The I, as "I think," is the ground upon which, hereafter, all certainty and truth becomes based. But thought, assertion, logos, is, at the same time, the guideline for the determination of being, the categories. These are found by the guideline of the "I think," in viewing the "I." By virtue of this fundamental significance for the foundation of all knowledge, the "I" thus becomes the accentuated and essential definition of man. Up to that time and later, man had been apprehended as the *animal rationale*, as a rational living being. With this peculiar emphasis on the I, i.e., with the "I think," the determination of the rational and of reason now takes on a distinct priority. For thinking is the fundamental act of reason. With the *"cogito—sum,"* reason now becomes explicitly posited according to its own demand as the first ground of all knowledge and the guideline of the determination of the things.

Already in Aristotle, the assertion, the λόγος, was the guideline for the determination of the categories, i.e., the being of what is. However, the locus of this guideline—human reason, reason in general—was not characterized

---

25 "To say *Dasein* is 'illuminated' means that it is illumined in itself as being-in-the-world but not through any other entity, so that it *is* itself the illumination (*Lichtung*). What is present-at-hand hidden in the dark becomes accessible only for an entity illuminated in this way." (*SZ*, p. 133.) *Trans.*

as the subjectivity of the subject. But now reason has been expressly set forth as the "I think" in the highest principle as guideline and court of appeal for all determinations of being. The highest principle is the "I" principle: *cogito—sum*. It is the fundamental axiom of all knowledge; but it is not the only fundamental axiom, simply for this one reason, that in this I-principle itself there is included and posited with this yet another one, and therefore with every proposition. When we say *"cogito—sum,"* we express what lies in the *subjectum* (*ego*). If the assertion is to be an assertion, it must always posit what lies in the *subjectum*. What is posited and spoken in the predicate may not and cannot speak against the subject. The κατάφασις must always be such that it avoids the ἀντίφασις, i.e., saying in the sense of speaking against (*Dagegensprechen*), of contradiction. In the proposition as proposition, and accordingly in the highest principle as I-principle, there is co-posited equally basically as valid the principle of the avoidance of contradiction (briefly: the principle of contradiction).

Since the mathematical as the axiomatic project posits itself as the authoritative principle of knowledge, the positing is thereby established as the thinking, as the "*I* think," the I-principle. "I think" signifies that I avoid contradiction and follow the principle of contradiction.

The I-principle and the principle of contradiction spring from the nature of thinking itself, and in such a way that one looks only to the essence of the "I think" and what lies in it and in it alone. The "I think" is reason, is its fundamental act, what is drawn solely from the "I think," is gained solely out of reason itself. Reason so comprehended is purely itself, pure reason.

These principles, which in accord with the fundamental mathematical feature of thinking spring solely from reason, become the principles of knowledge proper, i.e., philosophy in the primary sense, metaphysics. The principles of mere reason are the axioms of pure reason. Pure reason, λόγος so understood, the proposition in this form, becomes the guideline and standard of metaphysics, i.e., the court of appeal for the determination of the being of what is, the thingness of things. The question about the thing is now anchored in pure reason, i.e., in the mathematical unfolding of its principles.

In the title, "pure reason," lies the λόγος of Aristotle, and in the "pure" a certain special formation of the mathematical.

6. The History of the Question About the Thing: Summary

The first chapter of the history of the question of the thing is characterized by the mutual relation of the thing and assertion (λόγος), the guideline along which the universal determinations of being (categories) are won. The second chapter conceives the assertion, the proposition, in a mathematical way, as principle; and accordingly sets forth the principles which lie in the essence of thinking, of the proposition, as such, i.e., the I-principle and the principle of contradiction. With Leibniz there is added the principle of sufficient reason (*Satz vom Grund*), which is also already co-posited in the essence of a proposition as a principle. These propositions originate purely out of mere reason, without the help of a relation to something previously given before one. They are a pure self-giving of that which thinking in its essence already has in itself.

It now remains to characterize the third chapter in the history of the question of the thing, i.e., to show how a *critique* of pure reason could and had to develop from this determination of things out of pure reason. For this purpose it is necessary that we acquire, although only roughly, an idea of how modern metaphysics developed according to the mathematical foundation from Descartes.

The philosophical fundamental axioms, i.e., the absolute axioms, are the I-principle, the principle of contradiction, and the principle of sufficient reason. The whole of metaphysics is to be based on them so that these axioms also dominate throughout the inner structure of metaphysics, i.e., the cognitive formation of its entire domain. Up to now this has hardly been mentioned. We have only said that metaphysics is the question concerning what is, as the whole and of the being of what is. But how do we mean this, what is as a whole? In the description of the turn from the earlier knowledge about nature to modern thought, we limited ourselves to a part of what is. Not only that, we also did not report how this limited district (nature) belongs into the whole of what is. However, since the ascendancy of Christianity in the West, not only throughout the medieval period but also through all of modern philosophy, nature and universe were considered as created. Modern metaphysics from Descartes to Kant, and also the metaphysics of German Idealism after Kant, are unthinkable without the Christian ideas that underlie them. Yet the relation to the dogma of the Church can be very loose, even broken. According to the predominance of the Christian concept of what is, a certain hierarchy and arrangement enters into what is, as a whole. What is most real and highest is the creative source of all that is, the one personal God as spirit and creator. All of what is that is not godlike is the created. But among all that is created, one is distinctive. This is man, and it is because his eternal salvation is in question. God as the creator, the world as the created, man and his eternal salvation; these are the three domains defined by Christian thought within what is, as a whole. Since metaphysics asks about what is, as a whole, what it is, why it is as it is, metaphysics proper, in a Christian sense, is concerned with God (theology), the world (cosmology), and man and his salvation (psychology). But, in accord with the fundamental mathematical character of modern thought, metaphysics, too, is formed out of the principles of pure reason, the *ratio*. Thus, the metaphysical doctrine of God becomes a theology, but a *theologia rationalis*, the doctrine of the world becomes a cosmology, but a *cosmologia rationalis*, and the doctrine of man, psychology, but a *psychologia rationalis*.

It is natural to arrange the whole state of modern metaphysics in the following way. For this form of metaphysics two concepts are essential: (1) the Christian conception of entities as *ens creatum* and (2) the basic mathematical character. The first instance concerns the content of metaphysics, the second its form. However, this characterization according to content and form is entirely too facile to be true. For this structure as determined by Christianity forms not only the content of what is treated in thought, but also determines the form, the how. Insofar as God as creator is the cause and the ground of all that is, the how, the way of asking, is oriented in advance toward this principle. Vice versa, the mathematical is not only a form clamped on over the Christian content, but it itself belongs to the content. Insofar as the I-principle, the "I think," becomes the leading principle, the "I" and, consequently, man, reach a unique position within this questioning about what is. It designates not only one domain among others, but just that one to which all metaphysical propositions are traced back and from which they stem. Metaphysical thought moves in the variously defined domain of subjectivity. Later Kant therefore says: All questions of metaphysics, i.e., those of the designated disciplines, can be traced back to the question: What is man? In the priority of this question there is concealed the priority of method coined in Descartes' *Regulae*.

If we use the distinction of form and content to characterize modern metaphysics, then we must say that the mathematical belongs just as much to the content of this metaphysics as the Christian belongs to its form.

According to the three fundamental directions of metaphysical questioning it deals each time with what is: God, world, man. The essence and the possibility of this what is must be determined in each case rationally, out of pure reason, i.e., from concepts gained in pure thought. But if what is and how it is must be decided in thinking and purely from thought, then before the definitions of what is as God, world, and man, there must obviously be a prior guiding concept of what is as such. Especially where this thinking conceives itself mathematically and grounds itself mathematically, the projection of what is as such must be expressly made the foundation of everything. Thus the inquiry into the special realms must be preceded by one which asks about what is in general, i.e., metaphysics as generally asking about what is, the *metaphysica generalis*. Viewed from it, theology, cosmology, and psychology become the *metaphysica specialis*, because they inquire into a particular realm of what is.

But because metaphysics is now mathematical, the general cannot remain what is only suspended above the particular, but the particular must be derived from the general as the axiomatic according to principles. This signifies that in the *mathematica generalis* what belongs to what is as such, what determines and circumscribes the thingness of a thing as such, must be determined in principle according to axioms, especially according to the first axiom, according to the schema of positing and thinking as such. What is a thing must be decided in advance from the highest principles of all principles and propositions, i.e., from pure reason, before one can reasonably deal with the divine, worldly, and human.

The universal, advance illumination of all things according to their thingness out of the pure reason of rational thought as such, the enlightening as this advance clarification of all things, is the *Enlightenment*, the spirit of the eighteenth century. In that century modern philosophy first received its proper form, into which Kant's thought grows and which also bears and determines his own most novel inquiry, the form of metaphysics, without which that of the nineteenth century would be unthinkable.

7. Rational Metaphysics (Wolff, Baumgarten)

Between Descartes and the Enlightenment stands
Leibniz. But he had an effect less through his own thinking
and work than through the form of the school of philosophy he determined.

During the eighteenth century scientific and philosophical thought in Germany was dominated by the doctrine
and school of Christian Wolff (1679–1754). He took his
philosophical equipment from a particular interpretation
of the philosophy of Leibniz. From there he strove for an
essential unification of the philosophical foundation
achieved by Descartes with traditional medieval Scholasticism and thus at the same time a reunification of Plato
and Aristotle. All of Western metaphysical knowledge was
to be gathered up in the rational clearness of the Enlightenment and the humanity of man to be based on itself
in pure reason. Christian Wolff treated philosophy in
widely distributed German and Latin textbooks. His textbook on metaphysics carries (in the German version) the
significant title, which, after what has been said, must now
be understandable, *Rational Thoughts of God, the World
and the Soul of Man, and Also of All Things in General*
(1719). Wolff first taught in Halle as professor of mathematics and soon transferred to philosophy. His thorough
and rigorous way of teaching presented a serious threat to
the shallow chatter of the theologians of the time; he was
thus driven out of Halle in 1723 through the efforts of his
theological opponents. He was threatened with hanging if
he remained. He taught at Marburg from 1723–40. However, Frederick the Great did not agree with the method of
refuting a philosophy by the threat of the gallows, and he
called Wolff back to Halle. There he became chancellor of
the University, privy councillor, vice-president of the
Petersburg Academy, and baron of the Holy Roman Em-
pire. Prominent among the many students of Wolff were

Gottsched (1700–76) and Alexander Baumgarten (1714–62); the latter also wrote a metaphysics (*Metaphysica*, 1739). Moreover, in accord with the general trend of the dominating form of pure reason, he attempted the experiment of submitting art to rational principles (and our relation to art, which, according to the prevailing interpretation, was taste). Taste and what is accessible in this capacity to judge (namely art) belong to the domain of the sensible, αἴσθησις. Just as thought is submitted to rational principles in logic, so also there is need for a rational doctrine of sensibility, a logic of the sensible, αἴσθησις. Baumgarten therefore called this rational theory of αἴσθησις the logic of sensibility or "aesthetics." And despite Kant's opposition to the use of this title, the philosophical doctrine of art has been called aesthetics ever since. This circumstance contains much more than the mere matter of a title, and can be understood only through modern metaphysics. It became decisive not only for the interpretation of art, but also for the position of art in human existence (*Dasein*) in the age of Goethe, Schiller, Schelling, and Hegel.

Through his teacher, the Wolffian disciple Martin Knutzen, Kant himself stands in the tradition of the Leibniz-Wolffian school. All his writings *before* the *Critique of Pure Reason* move within the sphere of inquiry and the mode of thought of the contemporary school-philosophy, even in parts where Kant already goes his own ways. Only incidentally, it might be mentioned, did Kant move beyond the school tradition and penetrate directly into the philosophy of Leibniz—insofar as this was then possible. In a similarly direct way he made the thinking through of English philosophy, especially Hume, fruitful for the formation of his own questioning. On the whole, however, the school-philosophy of Leibniz-Wolffian stamp remained so predominant that Kant, even after he gained the new position of this philosophy (after the publication of the *Critique of Pure Reason* and the works which followed it), kept up the tradition of using the textbooks of the school-philosophy in his lectures and of explaining them paragraph by paragraph. Kant never discussed his philosophy in his lectures, although, in later times, the new method of thought could not be completely excluded in the discussions of the textbooks or "readers," as they were then called. Kant used the previously mentioned textbook by Alexander Baumgarten in his lectures in metaphysics and appreciated this textbook "especially for the richness and precision of its teaching method." (*Nachricht von der Einrichtung seiner Vorlesungen im Winterhalbjahr 1765–66*, K. Vorländer, ed. [Meiner, *Der Philosophischen Bibliotek*, 1906], XLVIa, 155.) (Compare *Prolegomena*, 1-3.) In this short piece Kant indicates how he intends to adapt his former lectures on metaphysics, logic, ethics, and physical geography to a changed teaching method.

He introduces metaphysics, the "most difficult among all philosophical investigations," by preceding it with a metaphysical experiential science of man in order to lead to metaphysics step by step. This has the advantage in metaphysics "of putting into the greatest clarity" the abstract by presenting the concrete in advance. But this procedure has still another advantage. Kant says about it: "I cannot help thinking of another advantage, which should not be valued as slight, though it is based upon incidental causes only, an advantage which I want to draw from this method. Everyone knows how eagerly attended the first lectures are by the keen and unsettled youth, and how later the lecture room becomes somewhat roomier. Ontology, a science that is difficult to comprehend, scares him off from continuing; then what he could perhaps have understood cannot be of the slightest further use to him."

The textbook by Baumgarten presents us with the form of the customary metaphysics of the eighteenth century, which Kant had before him and which finally forced him to the work by which he lifted metaphysics from its hinges and put the question anew about metaphysics.

The *Metaphysica* of Baumgarten divides the entire material of metaphysics into exactly one thousand short paragraphs. According to Scholastic organization, the entire work is divided into four parts: (1) Ontology (*Metaphysica generalis*), §§4–350; (2) *Cosmologia*, §§351–500; (3) *Psychologia*, §§501–799; (4) *Theologia naturalis*, §§800–1000.

But the presentation of this external form does not tell us much about rational metaphysics, the metaphysics of pure reason, even when we remember what has been said about the fundamental characteristic of modern metaphysics and its foundation. On the other hand, we cannot go into the total content, which, although in itself is not so extensive, does, however, present a very involved structure because of its mathematical-rational form and formal proof.

And yet it is necessary that we provide ourselves with a more definite idea of this *Metaphysica,* in order to achieve with some understanding the transition from it to the *Critique of Pure Reason.* Let us characterize this metaphysics by discussing three questions: (1) How does metaphysics determine its own concept of itself? (2) How in this immediately pre-Kantian metaphysics is the essence of truth understood? (Metaphysics would represent the highest human realization of truth in knowledge.) (3) What is the inner structure of metaphysics?

By answering these three questions we once more carry out a unified consideration of the mathematical basis of modern metaphysics. We will see what this metaphysics of pure reason claims to be. Above all, we shall understand what form the question about the thing has taken in it.

1. How does metaphysics define its own concept? The first paragraph reads as follows: "Metaphysica est scientia prima cognitionis humanae principia continens." ("Metaphysics is the science which contains [embraces] the first principles of human knowledge.") This definition of metaphysics arouses the suspicion that metaphysics is

concerned with a doctrine of knowledge, thus with epistemology. But up to now metaphysics was considered as the
science of what is, as such, i.e., of the being of what is.
However, this metaphysics, just as the old one, is concerned with what is as well as with being; and yet the defining concept of metaphysics does not immediately say
anything about that. Not immediately. The definition,
however, says just as little that the object of metaphysics
is knowledge as such. We must understand this definition
of the concept of metaphysics in such a way that *cognitio
humana* does not mean the human faculty of knowledge,
but that which is knowable and known by the pure reason
of man. That is, what is. Its "fundamental principles" will
be exhibited, i.e., the fundamental determination of its
essence, being. But why does the definition of the concept
not simply say this, as Aristotle already defined it: Ἔστιν
ἐπιστήμη τις ἣ θεωρεῖ τὸ ὂν ἦ ὂν καὶ τὰ τούτῳ ὑπάρχοντα καθ'αὑτό.
("There is a science which investigates being as being and
the attributes which belong to this in virtue of its own
nature.") (*Metaphysics*, IV, from the beginning.)

Why are the knowable and knowledge now mentioned?
Because, since Descartes, the faculty of knowledge, pure
reason, has been established as that by whose guideline all
definitions of what is, the thing, are to be made in rigorous
proof and grounding. The mathematical is the *"mente
concipere"* of Galileo. In the development of metaphysics,
it is now a question of positing out of the essence of pure
rational knowledge a sketch of the being of what is, that
will be decisive for everything further knowable. This happens first in the fundamental discipline of metaphysics, in
ontologia. According to §4, it is the *scientia praedicatorum
entis generaliorum*. Kant (*Op. cit.*, pp. 115 f.) translates
this as follows: "The science of the general attributes of
all things." We see from this that the concept of the
"thing" is apprehended as very broad, as broadly as possible. "Thing" is anything that is. God, soul, and the world
are also things. We further recognize that the thingness of

things is determined on the basis of and by the guideline of the principles of pure reason. We have met three such principles, the I-principle, the principle of contradiction, and the principle of sufficient reason. With this we stand immediately before the answer to the second question.

2. In the pre-Kantian metaphysics of the eighteenth century, how is the nature of that truth understood, whose highest human realization in knowledge should be represented by metaphysics?

According to the traditional concept, truth (*veritas*) is the *adaequatio intellectus et rei*, the correspondence of thought and thing. Instead of *adaequatio* one also says *commensuratio* or *convenientia*, fitting or agreement. This essential definition of truth has a dual meaning which guided the question of the truth even in the Middle Ages. There is still cast over it the reflection and afterglow of an earlier, more primordial, although hardly understood, experience of the essence of truth at the beginning of the Greek existence (*Dasein*). Truth as *adaequatio* is, in one sense, a definition of *ratio*, the assertion, the proposition. A proposition is true insofar as it corresponds to things. The definition of truth as correspondence, however, not only concerns the proposition in relation to things, but also things, insofar as they are created, based on the project of a creative spirit, and as they correspond to it. Conceived in this way, truth is the commensurability of things with their essence, thought by God.

We are asking, in contrast, What is the essential definition of truth in modern metaphysics? In §92 of his *Metaphysik*, Baumgarten gives the following definition. "Veritas metaphysica potest definiri per convenientiam entis cum principiis catholicis." ("Metaphysical truth [that is, the truth of metaphysical knowledge] can be defined as an agreement of what is with the first most universal fundamental principles.") *Principia catholica* are the principles (axioms), specifically the "catholic ones" (according to the Greek καθόλου), i.e., principles directed upon the whole, which assert something about what is in totality and about the being of what is. All metaphysical propositions which establish being and its determinations must conform to these principles. These principles are ironclad principles of reason itself: the I-principle, the principle of contradiction, and the principle of sufficient reason. The truth about what things in their thingness are is determined according to the principles of pure reason, i.e., as we defined it above, in the essential sense: mathematical. The inner structure of the whole of metaphysics must be formed according to this conception of truth. Thus we arrive at the third question.

3. What is the inner structure of this metaphysics? We can already gather it from the external arrangement and sequence of the discipline. The foundation is ontology, and the apex of the building is theology. The first is concerned with what belongs to a thing as such, to anything that is in general (or *in communi*), to the *ens commune*. Theology is concerned with the highest being and that which is, in the most essential sense, the *summum ens*. With regard to content we also find this arrangement of metaphysics in the Middle Ages, in fact even in Aristotle. However, what is decisive is that, in the meantime, through the development and self-clarification of modern thought as the mathematical, the claim of pure reason has come to predominate. This means that the most general determinations of the being of what is are to be projected on the ground and with the guidance of the most universal principles of pure reason. At the same time, however, the entire knowledge of the world, soul, and God is to be derived from these most universal concepts in a purely rational analysis and sequence.

So the pure inner lawfulness of reason, from out of its fundamental principles and concepts, decides about the being of what is, about the thingness of things. In this pure rational knowledge, the truth about what is for all human reason receives its foundation and form as an indubitable and universally binding certainty.

Pure reason in this its self-formation, pure reason in this claim, pure reason as the authoritative court of appeal for the determination of the thingness of all things as such —it is this pure reason which Kant places into "critique."

II. The Question About the Thing in Kant's Main Work

1. What Does "Critique" Mean in Kant?

We will not pursue how Kant himself arrives at this "critique" and what the internal and external history of the origin of the work *Critique of Pure Reason* is. It is characteristic that we find out little even from letters of this silent period of his. However, even if we knew more, if we could exactly reckon what influenced Kant and so forth, in what sequence he worked out the individual parts of the work, this would neither explain the work itself (the creative is inexplicable), nor would this curiosity about Kant's workshop serve our understanding, supposing that we do not already know and comprehend what Kant wanted and achieved in his work. This is now our sole concern. More exactly, as preliminary, we want to understand the title.

We know now what "pure reason" means. It remains to inquire what "critique" signifies. It can here only be a matter of giving a preliminary explanation of what "critique" means. Usually we take this word at once and above all in a negative sense. Critique is for us faultfinding, a pointing to errors, emphasis on incompleteness and the corresponding rejection. In citing the title *"Critique of Pure Reason"* we must avoid this common and misleading meaning from the beginning. Moreover, that meaning does not correspond to the original meaning of the word. "Critique" comes from the Greek κρίνειν, which means "to sort" (*sondern*), "to sort out" and thus "to lift out that of special sort" (*das Besondere herausheben*). This contrast against others arises from an elevation of a new order. The sense of the term "critique" is so little negative that it means the most positive of the positive, the positing of what must be established in advance in all positing as what is determinative and decisive. Therefore, critique is a decision in this positing sense. Because critique is a separation and lifting out of the special, the uncommon and, at the same time, decisive, therefore, and only in consequence, is it also a rejection of the commonplace and unsuitable.

This meaning of the word "critique" appears in a unique way of its own during the second half of the eighteenth century in the discussions of art, of the form of the works of art and our relation towards them. Critique meant establishing the standard, the rules, legislation; and this at the same time means the elevation of the general over against the special. In this contemporary direction of meaning lies Kant's use of the term "critique," which he afterward also included in the titles of two other main works: *Critique of Practical Reason* and *Critique of Judgment*.

However, this word receives a fuller sense through Kant's work. It is this sense which must now be outlined. This will first make it possible to understand by implication the negative meaning, which the word also had in Kant. We shall try to make this clear by a retrospective glance at what has already been presented, without really having yet gone into Kant's work.

If critique has the designated positive meaning, the *Critique of Pure Reason* will not simply reject and find fault with pure reason. To "criticize" will rather aim to delimit what is decisive and peculiar to its proper essence. This laying of limits (*Grenzziehung*) is not primarily a demarcation against . . . but a delimiting in the sense of an exhibition of the inner construction of pure reason. The lifting out of the elements and the structure of pure reason is a lifting out of different possibilities of the uses of reason and their corresponding rules. As Kant once emphasized (*A* 768, *B* 796): the critique makes a complete review of the whole faculty of pure reason; it draws and sketches, in one of Kant's words, the "outline" (*Vorriss*) of pure reason (*B* xxiii, *N.K.S.*, p. 25).

Critique thus becomes the surveying which sets the boundaries for the entire domain of pure reason. This surveying does not take place, as Kant expressly and ever again enjoins, by referring to "facts" (*"Faktis"*), but it occurs from principles; not by determining qualities met somewhere, but by determining the whole essence of pure reason out of its own principles. Critique is a setting of boundaries, a surveying project of pure reason. Therefore, an essential moment belonging to critique is what Kant calls the architectonic.

Architectonic, the blueprint projected as the essential structure of pure reason, is as little a mere "ornament" (*Aufputz*) as the critique is a mere "censor" (*Zensur*). (For the use of the term "architectonic," *see* Leibniz, *De Primae Philosophiae Emendatione*, and Baumgarten, *Metaphysica*, §4, *ontologia* as *metaphysica architectonica*.)

In the execution of the "critique" of pure reason so understood, the "mathematical" in the fundamental sense first comes to its unfolding and, at the same time, to its being lifted up (*Aufhebung*), i.e., to its own limit. This also results from the "critique." Precisely, critique lies in the trend of modern thinking as such and in modern metaphysics in particular. But because of its basic character, Kant's "critique" leads to a new delimiting of pure reason and at the same time, therefore, of the mathematical.

2. The Relation of the "Critique" of Pure Reason to the "System of All Principles of the Pure Understanding"

It is no accident that Kant continually accompanies the critique of pure reason by a reflection on the essence of the mathematical and of mathematics, by a distinguishing between mathematical reason in the narrower sense over against metaphysical reason, i.e., the reasoning upon which a metaphysics, a projection of the being of what is, the thingness of things, must be based; for everything actually depends on this grounding of metaphysics. Let us recall Baumgarten's definition of metaphysics and of the definition of metaphysical truth. Critique of pure reason means to delimit the determination of the being of what is, the thingness of the things, from out of pure reason; it means to survey and project those principles of pure reason upon whose ground something like a thing in its thingness is determined.

We can already gather from this that in this "critique" the "mathematical" feature of modern metaphysics is retained, namely, to determine in advance out of principles the being of what is. The real effort aims at the formation and grounding of this "mathematical." The principles of pure reason must be grounded and demonstrated according to their own character. At the same time it lies in the essence of these principles that they exhibit a basic relation among themselves, belong together uniformly out of an inner unity. Kant calls such a unity according to principles a "system." The critique as a surveying of the inner structure and foundation of pure reason thus faces the fundamental task of exhibiting and grounding the *System of the Principles of Pure Reason.*

We know from our earlier discussion that, already for Aristotle, the proposition as simple assertion was the guideline for the determinations of being (the thingness) of things, i.e., the categories. The assertion "the house is high" is also called a judgment. Judging is an act of thought. Judging is a particular way in which reason takes place and acts. Pure reason as judging reason Kant calls understanding, the pure understanding. Propositions and assertions are acts of the understanding. The system of the principles of all propositions for which he sought is, therefore, the system of the principles of pure understanding.

We shall seek to understand Kant's *Critique of Pure*

Reason from its ground-providing center. Therefore, we begin our interpretation at the place entitled "System of All Principles of Pure Understanding" (*A* 148, *B* 187). The whole passage under discussion includes *A* 235 and *B* 294.

An aim of the interpretation will be to direct our inquiry and knowledge through this part in such a way that there results an understanding of the entire work. But even this understanding is only in the service of an insight into the question "What is a thing?"

In preparation, we can read some single sections from the work, where the real posing of the question does not immediately appear, but which are suited for shedding light on some of Kant's basic concepts. Attention is called to three such sections: (1) *A* 19, *B* 33–*A* 22, *B* 36.2; (2) *A* 50, *B* 74–*A* 62, *B* 86; (3) *A* 298, *B* 355–*A* 320, *B* 377.

In contrast, it is not recommended that one read the prefaces to *A* and *B* at this time, and especially not the corresponding Introductions, because they presuppose an insight into the whole work.

In our interpretation we shall not try to examine and paraphrase the structure of the work from the outside. Rather, we shall place ourselves within the structure itself in order to discover something of its framework and to gain the standpoint for viewing the whole.

For this we shall only follow a direction which Kant himself once stated in an incidental reflection. It concerns the evaluation of philosophic work: "One has to begin one's evaluation with the whole and to direct it to the idea of the work together with its ground. What remains belongs to the exposition in which much can be lacking and be improved." (Preussische Akademie edition, *op. cit.*, XVIII, No. 5025.)

Critique of pure reason is first a measuring and surveying of its essence and structure. The critique does not reject pure reason, but for the first time sets it within the boundaries of its nature and its inner unity.

"Critique" is the self-knowledge of reason placed before itself and upon itself. "Critique" is the accomplishment of the innermost rationality of reason. "Critique" fulfills the enlightenment (*Aufklärung*) of reason. Reason is knowledge from principles and therefore itself the faculty of principles (*Prinzipien*) and axioms (*Grundsätze*). A critique of the pure reason in the positive sense must, therefore, set forth the principles of pure reason in their inner unity and completeness, i.e., in their system.

3. Interpretation of the Second Main Section of the Transcendental Analytic: "System of All Principles of Pure Understanding"

The selection of just this section from the entire work may at first appear arbitrary. It can at least be justified in that this chapter provides us with special insight with regard to our leading question, the question of the thingness of the thing. Yet, at the moment, even this remains only an assertion. The question arises whether just this chapter has such a special meaning for Kant himself and for how he conceived his work, that is, whether we speak in Kant's sense when we call this section the center of the work. This question is to be answered affirmatively. For in the formation and unified proof of this system of all principles of pure understanding, Kant gains the ground upon which the truth of the knowledge of the things is based. In this way Kant lifts out and delimits (critique) a domain from which alone the status of the determination of the thing and the truth of all metaphysics up to now can be originally decided: whether the essence of truth is truly determined in it, whether in it a truly rigorously axiomatic, i.e., mathematical, knowledge, unequivocally follows its course and thereby reaches its goal; or whether this rational metaphysics, as Kant says, is only "a groping about," and indeed a groping about in "mere concepts" without a relation to the things themselves, thus remaining without justification and validity. The surveying of pure reason with regard to metaphysics must at the same time gauge (*ab-messen*), out of pure reason, how metaphysics (according to its definition as the science of the first causes of human knowledge) is possible. What is the status of human knowledge and its truth?

(The following interpretation makes up for what the writing *Kant and the Problem of the Metaphysics* (1929) lacked. Compare the preface to the second edition, 1950.

The title of that essay is not precise and therefore easily leads to the misunderstanding that *The Problem of Metaphysics* is concerned with a problematic whose overcoming was the task of metaphysics. Rather, *The Problem of Metaphysics* indicates that metaphysics as such is questionable.)

Kant offers a review of this second chapter, in which he treats the system of all principles. He does so at the beginning of the chapter entitled "The Ground of the Distinction of All Objects in General into Phenomena and Noumena" (*A* 235, *B* 294). In an intuitive simile he explains what mattered to him in establishing the "System of All Principles of Pure Understanding." "We have now not merely explored the territory of pure understanding, and carefully surveyed every part of it, but have also measured its extent, and assigned to everything its rightful place. This domain is an island, enclosed by nature itself within unalterable limits. It is the land of truth—enchanting name!—surrounded by a wide and stormy ocean, and the native home of illusion, where many a fog bank and many a swiftly melting iceberg give the deceptive appearance of farther shores, deluding the adventurous seafarer ever anew with empty hopes, and engaging him in enterprises which he can never abandon and yet is unable to carry to completion" (N.K.S., p. 257).

a. Kant's Concept of Experience

The measured and surveyed land, the solid ground of truth, is the domain of the established and establishable knowledge. Kant calls this "experience." Thus the question arises: What is the essence of experience? The "System of All Principles of Pure Understanding" is nothing other than a sketch of the essence and essential structure of experience. The essence of a fact (*Sache*), according to modern metaphysics, is what makes the fact as such in itself possible: the possibility, *possibilitas*, understood as that which renders possible. The question of the essence of experience is the question of its inner possibility. What belongs to the essence of experience? But at the same time this includes the question: What is the essence of what becomes truly accessible in experience? For when Kant uses the word "experience," he always understands it in an essentially twofold sense:

(1) Experiencing as happening to and an act of the subject I. (2) That as such which is experienced in such experience. Experience in the sense of the experienced and the experienceable, the object of experience, is nature, but nature understood in the sense of Newton's *Principia* as *systema mundi*. The grounding of the inner possibility of experience is, therefore, for Kant at the same time the answer to the question: How is nature in general possible? The answer is given in the "System of All Principles of the Pure Understanding." Kant, therefore, also says (*Prolegomena*, § 23) that these principles constitute "a physiological (*physiologisches*) system or system of nature." In §24 he also calls them the "physiological principles." "Physiology" is understood here in the original and archaic sense, and not in the sense of today. Physiology today is the doctrine of life processes, in distinction from morphology as the doctrine of living forms. In Kant's usage it meant λόγος of the φύσις, the fundamental assertions about nature, however, φύσις is now used in Newton's sense.

Only when we expressly and in a grounded way take possession of the solid ground of provable knowledge, of the land of experience and of the map of this land, do we take a position from which we can decide about the prerogative

and pretenses of traditional rational metaphy
about its possibility.

The setting up of the system of principles is tl
possession of the solid land of the possible truth (
edge. It is the decisive step of the whole task of the critique
of pure reason. This system of principles is the result of a
unique analysis of the essence of experience. Kant once
wrote in a letter to his pupil J. S. Beck, on January 20,
1792, ten years after the appearance of the *Critique of Pure
Reason:* "The analysis of experience in general and the
principles of possibility of the latter 'are' the most difficult
of the entire critique." (*Brief*, Cassirer X, 114; Akadamie
edition, XI, 313ff.) In the same letter, Kant gives these
instructions for lecturing on this most difficult part
of the *Critique of Pure Reason:* "In a word, since this
whole analysis has only the intention of setting forth the
fact that experience itself is possible only by means of
certain synthetic *a priori* principles, but since this can first
be made properly comprehensible only when these principles are actually presented, they are to be put to work as
quickly as possible." Here a twofold point must be
stressed:

1. The decisive thing for the proper insight into the
essence of experience, i.e., the truth of knowledge, is the
actual presentation of the system of principles.

2. The preparation for this presentation should be as
concise as possible.

Hence, we fulfill only a clear instruction of Kant's when
we single out the system of principles and set up the interpretation of this section in such a way that all preliminary requirements for it are summarized as concisely as
possible and are furnished in the development of the interpretation itself.

b. The Thing as a Natural Thing (*Naturding*)

The system of principles of pure understanding is, in
Kant's most exact sense, the inner supporting center of

the entire work. This system of principles is to unlock for us the question of how Kant determines the essence of the thing. What has been said in the preceding about the significance of the system of principles already gives us a preliminary interpretation (*Vordeutung*) of how Kant circumscribes the essence of the thing and in what way he holds it to be determinable at all.

"Thing"—this is the object of our experience. Since the inclusive concept of the possibly experienceable is nature, the thing must actually be conceived in truth as a *natural thing*. Kant does explicitly distinguish between the thing as an appearance (*Erscheinung*) and as thing-in-itself (*Ding an sich*). But the thing-in-itself, i.e., detached from and taken out of every relation of manifestation (*Bekundung*) for us, remains for us a mere *x*. In every thing as an appearance we unavoidably think also of this *x*. However, only the appearing natural thing is determinable in truth and knowable as a thing. We shall summarize in two propositions Kant's answer to the question about the essence of the thing which is accessible to us: (1) The thing is a natural thing. (2) The thing is the object of possible experience. Here every word is essential, and this in the definite meaning which it has acquired through Kant's philosophical work.

Let us now briefly recall the introductory considerations at the beginning of the whole lecture. There we placed the question about the thing into the circle of what first of all surrounds and encounters us every day. At that time the question arose how the objects of physics, i.e., the natural things, are related to the things immediately encountered. In view of Kant's essential definition of the essence of the thing as a natural thing, we can judge that from the beginning Kant does not pose the question of the thingness of the things that surround us. This question has no weight for him. His view immediately fixes itself on the thing as an object of mathematical-physical science.

That this viewpoint in the determination of the thingness of the thing became decisive for Kant has reasons which we now, after an acquaintance with the prehistory of the *Critique of Pure Reason,* can easily appraise. However, the definition of the thing as a natural thing also has consequences for which we cannot hold Kant in the least responsible. One could pay homage to the opinion that skipping over the things that surround us and the interpretation of their thingness is an omission for which we can easily make up and which can be fitted onto the definition of natural things, or perhaps could also be pre-arranged. But this is impossible because the definition of the thing and the way it is set up include fundamental presuppositions which extend over the whole of being and to the meaning of being in general. If we do not otherwise admit it, indirectly we can at least learn this from Kant's definition of the thing, namely, that a single thing for itself is not possible and, therefore, the definition of things cannot be carried out by considering single things. The thing as a natural thing is only definable from the essence of a nature in general. The thing, in the sense of what we encounter closest to us—before all theory and science—is adequately and first of all definable in a relational context which lies *before* and *above* all nature. This goes so far as to say that even technological things, though they are seemingly first produced on the basis of scientific natural knowledge, are in their thingness (*Dinghaftigkeit*) something other than natural things with the superimposition of a practical application.

But, all this only means again that asking the question of the thing is nothing less than the knowing man taking a decisive foothold in the midst of what is, taken as a whole. In thinking through the question of the thing sufficiently and in mastering, not mastering or neglecting it, there occur decisions whose temporal scope and span in our history are always to be considered only after centuries. This discussion of Kant's step should give us the proper proportions for such decisions.

c. The Threefold Division of the Chapter on the System of the Principles

The chapter (*"Hauptstück"*) of the *Critique of Pure Reason* which we shall try to expound begins at *A* 148, *B* 187 and is entitled "System of All Principles of Pure Understanding."

The whole chapter, which goes to *A* 235, *B* 294, is divided into three sections: I. "The Highest Principle of All Analytic Judgments" (*A* 150, *B* 189–*A* 153, *B* 193). II. "The Highest Principle of All Synthetic Judgments" (*A* 154, *B* 193–*A* 158, *B* 197). III. "Systematic Representation of All the Synthetic Principles of Pure Understanding" (*A* 158, *B* 197–*A* 235, *B* 287).

There follows a "General Note on the System of the Principles" (B 288–B 294).

With this threefold division of Kant's doctrine of the principles, we immediately think of the three principles of traditional metaphysics: contradiction, I-principle, and the principle of sufficient reason. It is to be supposed that Kant's threefold division has an inner relation with the threefold number of traditional principles. The exposition will show in what sense this is true. First, let us pay attention to the titles and first to those of the first two sections; we find the concept of *the highest principle*, and each time for a whole range of *judgments*. The general title of the whole chapter comprehends the principles as such of pure understanding. Now the discussion concerns principles of judgment. With what justification? Understanding is the faculty of thinking. But thinking is the uniting of representations (*Vorstellungen*) in one consciousness. "I think" means "I combine." Representationally, I relate something represented to another: "The room is warm"; "Wormwood is bitter"; "The sun shines." "The union of representations in one consciousness is judgment. Thinking, therefore, is the same as judging or relating representations to judgments." (*Prolegomena* § 22.)

Consequently, when instead of "pure understanding" as in the main title of the chapter, it now says "judgment" in the titles of the first two sections, this refers substantially to the same thing. Judgment is only the way in which the understanding as the faculty of thinking carries out the representing. Why in general "judgment" is used, and not pure understanding, will become clear in the content of the sections. (What "performs" these acts, the performance and what is performed, is the unity of representations, and it is that as itself a represented unity, e.g., the shining sun in the judgment: "The sun is shining.")

At the same time we obtain from the first two titles a distinction of judgments into *analytic* and *synthetic*. In his polemic against Eberhard, *On a Discovery, According to Which All New Critique of Pure Reason is Made Dispensable by an Older One* (1790), Kant once remarked that it is "indispensably necessary" in order to solve the chief problem of the critique of pure reason to "have a clear and distinct concept of what the critique *first* understands in general by synthetic judgments as distinct from the analytic." "The aforementioned distinction of judgments has never been properly comprehended" (*On a Discovery, op. cit.*, p. 228).

Accordingly, in the titles of the first and second sections of the chapter on the "System of All Principles of Pure Understanding," in the distinction between synthetic and analytic judgments and the highest principles belonging to them, something is pointed out which is decisive for the entire range of questions of the critique of pure reason. Therefore, it is not an accident that Kant, in the Introduction to this work, deals explicitly and in advance with "The Distinction between Analytic and Synthetic Judgments" (*A* 6 ff., *B* 10 ff.).

But just as important as the content of the first two titles is the title of the third section. This title does not concern principles of analytic nor of synthetic judgments, but synthetic principles of the pure understanding. And precisely the systematic "representation" (presentation) of these is the essential aim of the whole chapter.

It now seems appropriate to preface the interpretation of these three sections with a discussion of the difference between synthetic and analytic judgments. But in accordance with the overall plan of our interpretation we prefer to deal with this difference where the text immediately demands it. We pass over the introductory considerations to the chapter since these (A 148–B 187) are understandable only with reference to the preceding chapters of the work, into which we shall not enter. We begin immediately with the interpretation of the first section.

4. The Highest Principle of All Analytic Judgments. Knowledge and Object (A 150 ff., B 190 ff.)

In the title to Section I the principle of contradiction is meant as it was as one of three fundamental axioms of traditional metaphysics. But the fact that this principle is here called "the highest principle of all analytic judgments" already expresses Kant's special conception of this principle. With this he distinguishes himself both from the preceding metaphysics as well as from the German Idealism which follows, at least that of Hegel. Kant's general intent in his interpretation of the principle of contradiction is to contend against the leading role which this principle had assumed, especially in modern metaphysics. This role of the principle of contradiction as the highest axiom of all knowledge of being was already set forth by Aristotle even if in another sense (*Metaphysics*, IV, chap. 3–6).

At the end of the third chapter (1005 b 33) Aristotle says: φύσει γὰρ ἀρχὴ καὶ τῶν ἄλλων ἀξιωμάτων αὕτη πάντων. ("For this is naturally the starting point even for all the other axioms.")[26]

---

[26] Heidegger's translation: "Vom Sein her gesehen ist dieser Satz sogar auch der Grund (Prinzip) aller der anderen Axiome (Grundsätze)." *Trans.*

In 1755, in his qualifying lecture (*Habilitationsschrift*), Kant had already ventured a first, although as yet uncertain, thrust against the dominance in metaphysics of the principle of contradiction. This little writing bears the significant title *Principiorum primorum cognitionis metaphysicae nova dilucidatio (A New Illumination of the First Principles of Metaphysical Knowledge)*. This title could also head the *Critique of Pure Reason*, written nearly thirty years later.

a. Knowledge as Human Knowledge

It is true that the elucidation of the principle of contradiction in the *Critique of Pure Reason* moves on a different, expressly established plane and in a clear, fully thought out domain. This is immediately revealed in the first sentence with which the section begins: "The universal, though merely negative, condition of all our judgments in general, whatever be the content of our knowledge, and however it may relate to the object, is that they be not self-contradictory; for if self-contradictory, these judgments are in themselves, even without reference to the object, null and void." (*A* 150, *B* 189, N.K.S., p. 189.)

Here it is said in general that all our knowledge is under the condition that all its judgments be free of contradiction. Nevertheless, beyond this general content, we must note in this sentence of Kant's something different that is decisive for all that follows.

1. The sentence is about "our knowledge," which means *human* knowledge, not indefinitely any knowledge of any knowing being, not even about a knowledge simply and in general, of knowledge in an absolute sense. Rather it is we, mankind, our knowledge and only it is in question here and in the entire *Critique of Pure Reason*. Only in reference to a knowledge that is not absolute does it make sense at all to set up the principle of contradiction as a condition; for absolute unconditioned knowledge cannot be under conditions at all. What is a contradiction for finite

knowledge does not need to be one for absolute knowledge. Therefore, when in German Idealism Schelling and
especially Hegel at once posit the essence of knowledge as
absolute, then it is appropriate that for such knowing non-
contradiction is not a condition of knowledge, but rather
vice versa: contradiction becomes precisely the proper
element of knowledge.

2. It is said that our judgments and not our cognitions
(*Erkenntnisse*) must be without contradiction; this signifies that *judgments,* as acts of our understanding, constitute an essential, but only *one,* ingredient of our knowledge.

3. It is said of our knowledge that it always has some
content and is related in one way or another "to the object." Instead of *"Objekt,"* Kant often uses the word
"Gegenstand."

In order to understand, in their inner connection, these
three emphasized determinations of knowledge as human,
and to grasp from this Kant's ensuing expositions about
the principles, it is necessary to present as concisely as
possible Kant's basic interpretation of human knowledge
as it becomes clear for the first time in the *Critique of
Pure Reason.*

b. Intuition and Thought as the Two Essential
Components of Knowledge

In full consciousness of the scope of the definitions that
he has to offer, Kant places at the beginning of his work
the proposition which, according to his interpretation,
circumscribes the essence of human knowledge. "In whatever manner and by whatever means a mode of knowledge
may relate to objects, *intuition* is that through which it
is in immediate relation to them, and to which all thought
as a means is directed. But intuition takes place only insofar as the object is given to us. This again is only possible,
to man at least, insofar as the mind is affected in a certain
way." (*A* 19, *B* 33, N.K.S., p. 65.)

This essential definition of knowledge is the first and completely decisive blow against rational metaphysics. With it Kant moved into a new fundamental position of man in the midst of what is, or more precisely he lifted a position, which, at bottom, had always existed, into explicit metaphysical knowledge and laid a basis for it. That his concern is with *human* knowledge is further especially emphasized in the addition to the second edition: "to man at least." Human knowledge is representational relating of itself to objects. But this representing is not mere thinking in concepts and judgments, but—and this is emphasized by italics and by the construction of the whole sentence—"intuition" (*die Anschauung*). The really sustaining and immediate relation to the object is intuition. It is true that intuition alone as little constitutes the essence of our knowledge as does mere thought; but thought belongs to intuition and in such a way that it stands in the service of intuition. Human knowledge is conceptual, judgment-forming intuition. Human knowledge is thus a uniquely constructed unity of intuition and thought. Again and again throughout the whole work Kant emphasizes this essential definition of human knowledge. As an example, we can quote passage *B* 406, which first appears in the second edition where otherwise precisely a sharper emphasis on the role of thought in knowing makes itself felt. "I do not know an object merely in that I think" (this is spoken against rational metaphysics), "but only in so far as I determine a given intuition with respect to the unity of consciousness in which all thought consists." (*N.K.S.*, p. 368.) Passages *A* 719, *B* 747 express the same: "All our knowledge relates, finally, to possible intuitions, for it is through them alone that an object is given." (*N.K.S.*, p. 581.) In the order of the essential structure of knowledge this "finally" amounts to "first," in the first place.

Human cognition is in itself twofold. That is evident from the doubleness (*Zwiefalt*) of its structural elements. They are here called *intuition* and *thought*. But just as essential as this doubleness in contrast with singleness is how this doubleness is structured. Insofar as only the unity of intuition and thought results in a human knowledge, obviously these two permanent parts must bear some relation (*Verwandtschaft*) and have something in common (*Gemeinsamkeit*) in order to be unitable. This is that both intuition and thought are "representations" (*Vorstellungen*). Re-present (*Vor-stellen*) means to put something before oneself and to have it before one, as the subject to have something present toward oneself and back onto oneself (*etwas auf sich als das Subject zu, auf sich zurück, präsent haben: re-praesentare*). But how are intuition and thought distinguished as modes of representing within the common character of representing? We can now only provisionally clarify this: "This blackboard" —with that we address something that stands before us and is presented to us (*uns vorgestellt ist*). What is thereby represented is thus this certain flat extension with this coloring and in this light and of this hardness and material, etc.

What we have just enumerated is *immediately given* to us. We see and touch all this without more ado. We see and feel always precisely this extension, this hue, this lighting. The immediately represented is always "this," just that particular one which is just so and so. A representing that is immediate and therefore presents always just this particular one is intuiting. This essence of intuition becomes clearer in contrast with the other mode of representing, i.e., thought. Thought is not immediate, but mediate representing. What thought intends representationally is not the single "this," but just the universal. If I say "blackboard," the intuitively given is grasped and conceived as a blackboard. "Blackboard"—with that I represent something that is valid also for others, corresponding other givens in other classrooms. The representation of what is valid for many, and just as such a multivalid one, is the representation of something general. This universal one, which is common to all that belongs to it, is a concept (*Begriff*). Thought is the representation of something in general, i.e., in concepts. However, concepts are not immediately found in advance (*vor-gefunden*). A certain way and means is necessary to form them. Therefore, thinking is mediate representing.

c. The Twofold Determination of the Object in Kant

What has been said also makes clear that not only is knowing (*Erkennen*) twofold, but that the knowable (*Erkennbare*), the possible object (*Gegenstand*) of knowledge, must also be determined in a twofold way in order to be an object at all. We can clarify the facts of this case by examining the word *Gegenstand*. What we are supposed to be able to know must encounter us from somewhere, come to meet us. Thus the *"gegen"* (against)[27] in *Gegenstand*. But not just anything at all that happens to strike us (any passing visual or auditory sensation, any sensation of pressure or warmth) is already an *object* (Gegen*stand*). What encounters us must be determined as standing, something which has a stand and is, therefore, constant (*beständig*).[28] Nevertheless, this only gives us a preliminary indication of the fact that the object must obviously also be determined in a twofold way. But it has not yet been said exactly *what* an object of human knowledge truly is in the sense of Kant's concept of knowledge. An object in the strict sense of Kant is neither what is only sensed (*Empfundene*) nor what is perceived (*Wahrgenommene*). For example, if I point to the sun and address it as the sun, this thus named and intended is not the object (in the sense of "object of knowledge") in the

---

[27]*Gegen:* "Against," also means "toward," "in the direction of," "opposite to," "in the presence of," etc. Literally, *Gegenstand* means "standing against." *Trans*.

[28] "Das Begegnende muss bestimmt sein als stehend, als etwas, das Stand hat und so beständig ist." *Trans*.

strict Kantian sense, any more than the rock to which I point or the blackboard. Even if we go further and make some assertions about the rock and the blackboard, we do not penetrate into the objective in the strict Kantian sense. Likewise, if with reference to the given we repeatedly ascertain something, we still have not reached the comprehension of the object. We can, for instance, on the basis of repeated observations, say: When the sun shines on the rock it becomes warm. Here, indeed, are the given, the sun, sunshine, rock, warmth, and these are determined in a certain judgment-like way, i.e., sunshine and warmth of the rock are brought into relation. But the question is: In what relation? We say more clearly: Every time the sun shines, the rock becomes warm; every time I have a perception of the sun there follows in me after this perception of mine, the perception of the warm stone. This being together of the representations of sun and rock in the assertion "every time when . . . then," is simply a uniting of various perceptions, i.e., a perceptual judgment. Here my perceptions (as also those of every other perceiving "I") are always added to one another. This only determines how what is presently given to me appears to me.

If I say by contrast, "Because the sun shines, the rock will therefore become warm," then I express a cognition. The sun is now represented as the cause and the becoming warm of the rock as the effect. We could also express this knowledge in the sentence "The sun warms the rock." Sun and rock are now joined not simply on the basis of the subjectively ascertainable succession of the perceptions, but they are grasped in the universal concepts of cause and effect in themselves as they stand in themselves and to one another. Now an object (Gegen-stand) is grasped. The relation is no longer "every time when . . . then"; this refers to the succession of perceptions. The relation is now that of "If . . . then," ("because . . . therefore"). It refers to the fact (Sache) itself, whether I presently perceive it or not. This relation is now posited as necessary. What this judgment says is valid at all times and for everyone; it is not subjective but is true of the object (*Objekt*), of the object (*Gegenstand*) as such.

What encounters us in sensation and perception and is intuitively given—the sun and sunshine, rock and warmth —this "against" (*gegen*) only comes to the position of a state of affairs standing in itself when the given has already been represented universally and thought in such concepts as cause and effect, i.e., under the principle of causality in general. The permanent elements (*Bestandstücke*) of knowing, intuition, and concept, must be unified in a determinate way. The intuitively given must be brought under the universality of definite concepts. The concept must get over the intuition and must determine in a conceptual manner what is given in the intuition. With regard to the example, i.e., fundamentally, we must note the following:

The perceptual judgment (*Wahrnehmungsurteil*), "every time when . . . then," does not gradually change over after a sufficient number of observations, into the experiential judgment (*Erfahrungsurteil*), "if . . . then." This is just as impossible as it is out of the question for a *when* ever to change into an *if* and a *then* to change into a *therefore*, and vice versa.

The experiential judgment demands in itself a new step, another way of representing the given, that is, in the concept. This essentially different representation of the given, its apprehension as nature, first makes possible for observations to be taken as possible instances of experiential judgments, so that now, in the light of the experiential judgment the conditions of observation may be varied and the corresponding consequences of these varied conditions may be investigated. What we call hypothesis in science is the first step toward an essentially different, conceptual representing as over against mere perceptions. Experience does not arise "empirically" out of perception but becomes possible only through metaphysics: through a new conceptual representing peculiarly in advance of the given in the concepts of *cause-effect*. By this means a ground for the given is established: principles. An object in the strict sense of Kant is thus first of all the represented, wherein the given is determined in a necessary and universal way. Such a representation is human knowledge proper. Kant calls it experience (*Erfahrung*). Now, summarizing Kant's basic interpretation of knowledge, we say:

1. Knowledge for Kant is human knowledge.

2. Human knowledge is essentially experience.

3. Experience realizes itself in the form of mathematical-physical science.

4. Kant sees this science and with it the essence of real human knowledge in the historical form of Newtonian physics, which today one still calls "classical."

d. Sensibility and Understanding. Receptivity and Spontaneity

What we have said about human knowledge up to now should, to begin with, make the duality in its essential structure recognizable without presenting this structure in its innermost framework. Together with the duality of knowledge arose an initial understanding of the duality of the object. The mere intuitive "against" (*gegen*) is not yet an object (*Gegenstand*); but what is only conceptually thought in general, as something constant, is not yet an object either.

This also makes it clear what the words "content of knowledge" and "relation to the object" mean in the first sentence of this section. The "content" is always determined *by* what (and *as* what) is intuitively given: light, warmth, pressure (touch), color, sound. The "relation to the *object*" (*Objekt*), i.e., to the object (*Gegenstand*) as such, consists in the fact that something intuitively given has been brought to stand in the generality and unity of a concept (cause-effect). But we must carefully note that it is always something intuitive that is brought to stand. Conceptual pre-senting here takes on an essentially sharpened sense.

Therefore, when Kant stresses repeatedly: Through the intuition the object is given, through the concept the object is thought, the misunderstanding easily suggests itself that the given is already the object, or that the object is an object only through the concept. Both are equally wrong. Rather, it is true that the object stands only when the intuition is thought conceptually, and the object only confronts us if the concept designates something intuitively given. Consequently, Kant uses the term "object" in a narrow and proper sense, and in a wider and improper sense.

The object proper is only what is represented in experience as experienced. The improper object is every thing to which a representation as such refers—be it intuition or thought. Object in the wider sense is both what we have merely thought as such and what is only given in perception and sensation. Although in every case Kant is sure of what he means by "object," there is in this fluent usage an indication that Kant has broached and decided the question of human knowledge and its truth only in a certain respect. Kant has disregarded what is manifest (*das Offenbare*). He does not inquire into and determine in its own essence that which encounters us prior to an objectification (*Vergegenständlichung*) into an object of experience. Insofar as he apparently must return to this domain, as in the distinction of mere perception from experience, the procedure of comparing is always from experience to perception. This means that perception is seen from experience, and in relation to it, as a "not yet." However, it is just as important, above all, to show what experience is no longer, as scientific knowledge, in comparison to perception, in the sense of pre-scientific knowledge. For Kant, in view of rational metaphysics and its claims, this alone was decisive:

(1) To assert, in general, the intuitive (sensory) character of human knowledge as a fundamental component of its essence. (2) On the basis of this altered definition, to also determine anew the essence of the second component, thought and concepts.

Now we can characterize still more clearly the twofold character of human knowledge, and in different respects. Up to now we called the two different elements intuition and concept. The former was the immediately represented particular and the latter the mediately represented universal. The always different representations actually take place in correspondingly different behavior and performance of the human being. In intuition what is represented is pre-sented as object, i.e., the representing is a having before oneself what encounters. Insofar as it is to be taken as something, encountering it becomes what is taken up and in (*auf- und hingenommen*). The character of behavior in the intuition is that of taking-in (*Hinnehmen*), a reception, *recipere-receptio*, receptivity. In contrast, behavior in the conceptual representation is such that the representing from itself compares what is variously given, and in comparing refers them to one and the same and seizes this as such. In comparing spruce-beach-oak-birch we bring out, seize, and determine what these have in common as one and the same thing: "tree." The representing of this universal as such must unfold itself from out of itself and bring what is to be represented before itself. Because of this "from itself" character, thinking—as representing in concepts—is spontaneous, spontaneity.

Human intuition is never able to create what is to be viewed, the object itself, through the achievement of its intuiting as such. At most such is possible in a kind of imagination or fantasy. But in this the object itself is provided and viewed not as one that is (*Seiender*), but as imagined. Human looking (*Schauen*) is intuiting or looking at (*An-schauen*),[29] i.e., a view directed toward something already given.

Because human intuition depends upon something viewable given to it, the given must indicate itself. It must be able to announce itself. This happens through the sense organs. By means of these organs, our senses, such as sight, hearing, etc., are "stirred" (*gerührt*), as Kant says. Something is done to them; they are approached. That which so attracts us and how the attraction is initiated is sensation as affection. By contrast, in thought, in the concept, what is represented is such that we ourselves fashion and prepare it in its form. "In its form"—this means the *how* in which what is thought (*das Gedachte*), what is conceptually represented, is something represented, namely, in the *how* of the universal. On the contrary, the *what*, e.g., the "tree-like," must be given in its content. The execution and preparation of the concept is called function.

Human intuition is necessarily sensuous, i.e., such that the immediately represented must be given to it. Since human intuition depends upon such giving (*Gebung*), i.e, is sensuous, therefore it requires the sense organs. Thus, we have eyes and ears because our intuiting is a seeing and a hearing, etc. It is not because we have eyes that we see, nor do we hear because we have ears. *Sensibility* (*Sinnlichkeit*) is the capacity for human intuition. The capacity of thought, however, wherein the object as object (*der Gegenstand als Gegenstand*) is brought to stand, is *understanding*. We can now clearly arrange in order the different definitions of the twofoldness of human knowledge and also lay down the various respects in which, at any given time, these distinctions determine human knowledge:

Intuition—Concept (thought): the represented as such in the object.

[29] *See* note 23. *Trans.*

Receptivity—Spontaneity: modes of behaving in the representing.

Affection—Function: the character of event and result of the represented.

Sensibility—Understanding: representing as the capacities of the human mind, as sources of knowledge.

Depending on the context, Kant uses these different forms of the two essential elements.

e. The Apparent Superiority of Thought; Pure Understanding Related to Pure Intuition

With the interpretation of the *Critique of Pure Reason* and the explanation of Kant's philosophy in general, one cannot escape from the fact that, according to his doctrine, knowledge is composed of intuition and thought. But from this general statement it is still a long way to a real understanding of the role of these elements and the character of their unity, and above all to the correct evaluation of this essential definition of human knowledge.

In the *Critique of Pure Reason*, where Kant takes up the "most difficult task" of analyzing experience in its essential structure, the discussion of thought and the acts of understanding, those of the second component, not only occupy a disproportionately greater space, but the whole direction of the inquiry of this analysis of the essence of experience is aimed at the characterization of thought whose proper action we already have met as judgment. The doctrine of intuition, αἴσθησις, is the aesthetics. (Compare *A* 21, *B* 35, note.) The doctrine of thought, of judgment, λόγος, is logic. The doctrine of intuition includes *A* 19–*A* 49, i.e., thirty pages; *B* 33–*B* 73, i.e., forty pages. The doctrine of thought, *A* 50, *B* 74–*A* 704, *B* 732, takes up more than 650 pages.

The priority in the treatment of logic, its disproportionately greater extent within the whole work, is obvious. Also we can repeatedly ascertain in particular sections that the question of judgment and concept, thus the question of thought, stands in the foreground. We can also easily recognize this fact in the section upon which we based our interpretation and which we designated as the very center of the work. The headings say clearly enough that it is a question of judgments. The discussion is expressly about λόγος (reason) in the title of the whole work. On the basis of this obvious priority of logic, people have almost universally concluded that Kant sees the true essence of knowledge in thought, in judging. This opinion was supported by the traditional and ancient doctrine according to which judgment and assertion are the place of truth and falsity. Truth is the basic characteristic of knowledge. Therefore, the question about knowledge is nothing more than the question about judgment, and the interpretation of Kant must therefore begin at this decisive point.

How far this prejudice has prevented penetrating into the center of the work cannot and need not be further reported here. But it is important for the correct appropriation of this work to keep these facts continuously in mind. Generally, the neo-Kantian interpretation of the *Critique of Pure Reason* leads to a depreciation of intuition as the basic component of human knowledge. The Marburg school's interpretation of Kant even went so far as to eliminate altogether from the *Critique of Pure Reason* intuition as a foreign body. The downgrading of intuition had the consequence that the question of the unity of both components, intuition and thinking—or, more exactly, the question of the ground of the possibility of their unification—took a wrong turn, if it was ever seriously asked at all. All these misinterpretations of the *Critique of Pure Reason* as they still circulate in differing variations today have caused the importance of this work for its essential inherent and single question, concerning the possibility of a metaphysics, to be neither properly evaluated nor, above all, to be made creatively fruitful.

But how can it be explained that in spite of the fundamental and authoritative significance of intuition in human knowledge Kant himself places the main problem of the analysis of knowledge into the discussion of thought? The reason is as simple as it is obvious. Precisely because Kant—contrary to rational metaphysics, which put the essence of knowledge into pure reason and into mere conceptual thought—posits intuition as the supporting fundamental moment of human knowledge, thought must now be deprived of its former presumed superiority and exclusive validity. But the *Critique* could not be content with the negative task of disputing the presumption of conceptual thought. It had first and foremost to define and ground anew the essence of thought.

The extended discussion of thought and concept in the *Critique of Pure Reason* indicates no downgrading of intuition. On the contrary, this discussion of concept and judgment is the clearest proof that from now on intuition will remain the authority without which thought is nothing.

The extensive treatment of the one component of knowledge, of thought, is stressed even more in the second edition. In fact, it often looks as if the question of the essence of knowledge were exclusively a question of the judgment and its conditions. However, the priority of the question of judgment does not have its ground in the fact that the essence of knowledge really is judgment, but in the fact that the essence of judgment must be defined anew, because it is now conceived as a representation related in advance to intuition, i.e., to the object.

The priority of logic, the detailed treatment of thought, is therefore necessary, because thought in its essence does not have priority over intuition, but, rather, is based upon intuition and is always related to it. The priority of logic in the *Critique of Pure Reason* has its ground solely in the non-priority of the object of logic, i.e., in placing thought into the service of intuition. If correct thought is always based on intuition, then the proper logic belonging to this thought necessarily and precisely deals with this essential relation to intuition, consequently with intuition itself. The modest extent of the aesthetic—as the initial separate doctrine of intuition—is only an outward appearance. Since the aesthetic is now decisive, i.e., everywhere plays an authoritative part, therefore it makes so much work for logic. For this reason logic must turn out so extensive.

It is important to note this, not only for the overall comprehension of the *Critique of Pure Reason* as such, but, above all, for the interpretation of our chapter. For the titles of our first two sections, as well as the first sentence of Section I, read as though the question about human knowledge and its principles simply slips off into a question about judgments, about mere thought. However, we shall see that exactly the contrary is the case. With a certain exaggeration we can even say that the question of the principles of the *pure understanding* is the question of *the necessary role of intuition, which necessarily is the basis for the pure understanding. This intuition must itself be a pure one.*

"Pure" means "mere" (*bloss*), "unencumbered" (*ledig*), "being free from something else"; in this case, "free from sensation." Looked at negatively, pure intuition is free of sensation, although it is an intuition that belongs to the sphere of sensibility. "Pure" therefore means what is based only upon itself and existing first. This pure intuition, presented in an immediate representation, free of sensation, this single and only one, is *time*. Pure understanding means, in the first place, mere understanding detached from intuition. But because understanding as such relates to intuition, the determination "pure understanding" can only mean understanding based on intuition and, indeed, on pure intuition. The same is true concerning the title "pure reason." It is equivocal. Pre-critically it means mere reason. Critically, i.e., limited to its essence, it means reason which is essentially grounded in pure intuition and sensibility. The critique of pure reason is at once the delimitation of this reason which is founded upon pure intuition and, at the same time, the rejection of pure reason as "mere" reason.

f. Logic and Judgment in Kant

The insight into these relationships, i.e., the acquisition of the essential concept of a "pure understanding," is, however, the pre-condition for the understanding of the third section, which is supposed to present the systematic structure of pure understanding.

The clarification of the essence of human knowledge we have just carried out enables us to read the first sentence of our section with a different eye than at the beginning. "The universal, though merely negative, condition of all our judgments in general, whatever be the content of our knowledge, and however it may relate to the object, is that they be not self-contradictory; for if self-contradictory, these judgments are in themselves, even without reference to the object, null and void." (*A* 150, *B* 189, *N.K.S.*, p. 189.) We realize that our knowledge is here immediately examined in a certain respect, namely, in terms of the second essential component of knowing, the act of thought, the judgment. More precisely it is said here that freedom from contradiction is the "condition, though merely negative, of all our judgments in general." This is said of "all our judgments in general," and not yet of "analytic judgments," which are set forth as the theme in the title. Furthermore, he speaks of "a merely negative condition," and not about a highest principle (*Grund*). It is true that the text speaks of contradiction and of judgments in general, but not yet of the principle of contradiction as the highest principle of all analytic judgments. Kant here considers judgment as before its differentiation into analytic and synthetic judgments.

In what respect is judgment viewed here? What is a judgment? How does Kant define the essence of the judgment? The question sounds simple enough, and yet the inquiry immediately becomes complicated. For we know that judging is the function of thought. Thought has experienced a new characterization through Kant's essential definition of human knowledge: It enters essentially into the service of intuition. Therefore, the same must also be valid for the act of thought of the judgment. Now one could say that through stressing the subservience of thought and judgment only a particular purpose (*Abzweckung*) of thought has been introduced. Thought itself and its determination have not been thereby essentially touched. On the contrary, the essence of thought (judgment) must already be defined, in order for thought to enter into this subservient position.

The essence of thought, i.e., the judgment, has, since ancient times, been determined by logic. Although Kant did determine a new conception of knowledge along the lines we discussed, he could only add to the current definition of the essence of thought (judging) the further one that thought stands in the service of intuition. He could take over unchanged the logic of the existing doctrine of thought in order to supplement the addition that logic, if it deals with human knowledge, must always stress that thought must be related to intuition.

In fact, this is how Kant's position looks with respect to traditional logic and thereby also toward its essential definition of judgment. What is still more important, Kant himself frequently viewed and presented the situation in this way. Only slowly and with great difficulty did he come to recognize that his discovery of the peculiar subservience of thought might be more than just an additional definition of it; that, on the contrary, with it the essential definition of thought and thus of logic changes basically. There is a saying of Kant about logic which is often quoted, though understood in an opposite and, therefore, false sense. This saying testifies to his sure presentiment of this revolution which he had initiated. It is no accident that it occurs only in the second edition: "That *logic* has already, from the earliest times, proceeded upon this sure path is evidenced by the fact that since Aristotle it has not required to retrace a single step, unless, indeed, we care to count as improvements the removal of certain needless subtleties or the clearer exposition of its recognised teaching, features which concern the elegance rather than the certainty of the science. It is remarkable also that to the present day this logic has not been able to advance a single step, and is thus to all appearance a closed and completed body of doctrine." (*B* viii, *N.K.S.*, p. 17.) Roughly speaking, this means that from now on this appearance proves itself to be void. Logic is to be newly founded and transformed.

In certain places Kant has clearly arrived at this insight, but he has not developed it. That would have meant nothing less than to construct metaphysics upon the ground which had been cleared by the *Critique of Pure Reason*. Such, however, was not Kant's intention, since to him "critique" (in the specified sense) had to be first and alone essential. It also did not lie within Kant's capacity, because such a task exceeds even the capacity of a great thinker. It demands nothing less than to jump over one's own shadow. No one can do this. However, the greatest effort in attempting this impossibility—that is the decisive ground-movement of the action of thought. We experience something of this fundamental movement in quite different ways in Plato, Leibniz, and, above all, in Kant and later in Schelling and Nietzsche. Hegel alone apparently succeeded in jumping over this shadow, but only in such a way that he eliminated the shadow, i.e., the finiteness of man, and jumped into the sun itself. Hegel skipped over (*überspringen*) the shadow, but he did not, because of that, surpass the shadow (*über den Schatten*). Nevertheless, every philosopher *must* want to do this. This "must" is his vocation. The longer the shadow, the wider the jump. This has nothing to do with a psychology of the creative personality. It concerns only the form of motion belonging to the work itself as it works itself out in him.

Kant's attitude toward such an apparently dry question, "What is the essence of the judgment?" reveals something of this fundamental movement. The relation of the first to the second edition of the *Critique of Pure Reason* shows how difficult it was for Kant to establish in its whole range an adequate essential definition of judgment from out of his new conception of knowledge. In terms of content all decisive insights had been achieved in the first edition. Yet only in the second edition does Kant succeed in bringing forward, at the decisive spot, that essential delineation of judgment which accords with his own fundamental position.

Kant stresses again and again the fundamental importance of the newly proposed distinction of judgments into analytic and synthetic. This means nothing other than that the essence of judgment as such has been newly defined. The distinction is only a necessary consequence of this essential definition, and, retrospectively, at the same time, a method for designating the newly conceived essence of the judgment.

We must take all that has been said into account, in order not to take too lightly the question: "According to Kant, of what does the essence of judgment consist?" and so that we are not surprised if we cannot find our way uniformly through his definitions without further ado. For Kant has nowhere developed a systematic description of his essential definition of judgment on the basis of the insights at which he himself arrived. Certainly this is not developed in his lecture on logic which has been handed down to us, where, if anywhere, one would expect to find it. In general, this lecture must be consulted cautiously because (1) lecture notebooks and notes are, at any rate, a questionable matter, especially in the sections which discuss difficult things; and (2) in his lectures, Kant purposely adhered to the traditional doctrines and took their scholarly traditional order and presentation as his guide. Thus he was not guided, in these notes, by the inner system of the subject matter itself as it presented itself in his thought. Kant chose as the textbook in his logic lectures the *Auszug aus der Vernunftlehre*, a schoolbook whose author, Meier (1718–1777), was a student of Baumgarten, the aforementioned student of Wolff.

With this reading of the treatment of the question of the judgment by Kant, we are compelled, in the most exact conformity with Kant, to give a systematically freer, but short, presentation of his essential definition of judgment. According to what has been said, this will automatically lead to a clarification of the decisive distinction between analytic and synthetic judgments.

The question "Of what does judgment consist?" can be posed in two respects: first, in the direction of the traditional definition of thought, and second, in the direction of Kant's new delineation. This latter does not simply exclude the traditional characteristics of judgment, but includes them into the essential structure of judgment. This indicates that this essential structure is not as simple as the pre-Kantian logic thought it was, and as one views it again today—in spite of Kant. The intrinsic basis for the difficulty in seeing the whole essence of judgment does not lie in the incompleteness of Kant's system, but in the essential structure of judgment itself.

At this point we should remember that we have already schematically indicated the organized structure of the judgment when we showed (*supra*, pp. 35–38) how far since Aristotle and Plato λόγος, i.e., the assertion, has been the guide for the definition of the thing. We did this with the aid of the fourfold meaning of "assertion." What we only touched on there now finds its essential elaboration in a short systematic presentation of Kant's essential definition of judgment.

5. Kant's Essential Definition of the Judgment

a. The Traditional Doctrine of Judgment

We begin with the traditional doctrine of judgment. The differences and changes that appear in its history must be left aside. We recall only Aristotle's general definition of the assertion (judgment), λόγος: λέγειν τι κατά τινος, "to say something about something": *praedicere.* Therefore, to assert is to relate a predicate to a subject—"The board is black." Kant expresses this universal characteristic of judgment in such a way that, at the beginning of the important section "The Distinction between Analytic and Synthetic Judgments" (Introduction, *A* 6, *B* 10, *N.K.S.*, p. 48), he remarks that in judgments "the relation of a subject to the predicate is thought." The judgment is a relation in which and through which the predicate is attributed to or denied of the subject. Accordingly, we have either attributive, affirmative, or denying, negative judgments. "This board is not red." It is important to keep in view that without exception, since Aristotle, and also in Kant, the simple affirmative (and true) assertion has been posited as the standard fundamental form of all judging.

Corresponding to the tradition, Kant says of the judgment that in it "the relation of a subject to the predicate is thought." In general, this statement proves true. However, the question remains whether this exhausts the essence of judgment, and whether the heart of the matter is understood. As to Kant, the question arises whether he would admit that the cited characteristic of judgment he himself applied had hit upon its essence. Kant would not admit that. On the other hand, it is not clear what should be added to the essential definition of judgment. In the end it is also unnecessary to add further determinations. On the contrary, we must note the opposite, that the given definition omits essential moments of the judgment, so that it is only a question of seeing how in precisely the given definition there lie indications of the essential moments.

In order that we may take Kant's new step with and after him, it is advisable, first, to cite briefly the view of judgment that prevailed in his time, and to which he paid attention. For this purpose we choose the definition of judgment given by Wolff in his large "Logic." In §39 we read: "Actus iste mentis, quo aliquid a re quadam diversum eidem tribuimus, vel ab ea removemus, iudicium appellature." ("That action of mind by which we attribute to a certain thing something which is different from it—*tribuer* [κατάφασις]—or hold away from it—*removere* [ἀπόφασις]—is called judgment [*iudicium*].") Accordingly, §40 asserts: "Dum igitur mens iudicat, notiones duas vel coniungit, vel separat." ("When [as] the mind judges, it either connects or separates two concepts.") In accordance §201 notes: "In enunciatione seu propositione notiones vel coniunguntur, vel separantur." ("In a proposition, or sentence, concepts are either bound or separated.")

A student of a student of this master of conceptual analysis, Professor Meier defines it as follows in his *Auszug aus der Vernunftlehre*, §292: "A judgment (*iudicium*) is a representation of a logical relation of several concepts." It is particularly "logical" that in this definition *Logos* is defined as a representation of a logical relation. However, aside from this, the textbook used by Kant only reproduces the definition of Wolff in a trite way. Thus, judgment is "the representation of a relation between several concepts."

b. The Insufficiency of the Traditional Doctrine; Logistics

We first contrast this definition of judgment from the Scholastic philosophy with Kant's definition that most sharply expresses the greatest difference. It is found in the second edition of the *Critique of Pure Reason* in connection with a section that Kant thoroughly reworked for the second edition, eliminating obscurities without changing anything of the fundamental position. It is the section on the "Transcendental Deduction of the Pure Concepts of Understanding." The essential definition of the judgment is found in §19 (*B* 140, *N.K.S.*, p. 158). The paragraph begins with the words: "I have never been able to accept the interpretation which logicians give of judgment in general. It is, they declare, the representation of a relation between two concepts." "Interpretation" (*Erklärung*) means to make something clear, not to derive something causally. What Kant here rejects as inadequate is just the definition of Meier, i.e., of Baumgarten and Wolff. What is meant is the definition of judgment as an assertion, familiar in logic since Aristotle, λέγειν τι κατά τινος. However, Kant does not say that this definition is false. He merely states that it is unsatisfactory. He himself makes use of this definition of judgment, and still uses it several times in the period after publishing his *Critique of Pure Reason*, even after the second edition. In investigations carried on around the year 1790, Kant says: "The understanding shows its capacity only in judgments, which are nothing other than the unity of consciousness in the relation of concepts in general. (*"Fortschritte der Metaphysik,"* K. Vorländer, ed., p. 97.) Where a relation is represented, a unity is always represented which supports the relation and becomes conscious through the relation so that what we are conscious of in judgment has the character of a unity. The same was already expressed by Aristotle (*De Anima*, 6, 430a, 27 f.): There is in judgment σύνθεσίς τις ἤδη νοημάτων ὥσπερ ἐν ὄντων, "a putting together of objects of thought in a certain unity." This characterization of judgment is valid for judgment in general. We shall use some examples which we must employ later: "This board is black"; "All bodies are extended"; "Some bodies are heavy." Without exception, a relation is represented here.

Representations are connected. We find the linguistic expression of this connection in the "is" or the "are." Therefore, this "little relation word" (Kant) or "bond" is called *copula*. The understanding, therefore, is the faculty of connecting representations, i.e., of representing this subject-predicate relationship. The characterization of the assertion as the connection of representations is correct but unsatisfying. This correct, but inadequate, definition of assertion became the basis for a view and treatment of logic which today and for a number of decades has been much talked about and is called symbolic logic (*"Logistic"*). With the help of mathematical methods people attempt to calculate the system of the connectives between assertions. For this reason, we also call this logic "mathematical logic." It proposes to itself a possible and justified task. However, what symbolic logic achieves is anything but logic, i.e., a reflection upon λόγος. Mathematical logic is not even logic of mathematics in the sense of defining mathematical thought and mathematical truth, nor could it do so at all. Symbolic logic is itself only a mathematics applied to propositions and propositional forms. All mathematical logic and symbolic logic necessarily place themselves outside of every sphere of logic, because, for their very own purpose, they must apply λόγος, the assertion, as a mere combination of representations, i.e., basically inadequately. The presumptuousness of logistic in posing as the scientific logic of all sciences collapses as soon as one realizes how limited and thoughtless its premises are. It is also characteristic for logistic to consider everything that reaches beyond its own definition of assertion as a connection of representations, as a matter of "finer distinctions" which don't concern it. But here it is not a question of fine or gross distinctions, but only this: Whether or not the essence of the judgment has been hit upon.

When Kant says that the cited "interpretation" of judgment in Scholastic logic is unsatisfying, this dissatisfaction is not simply a personal one in regard to his own particular wishes. On the contrary, this interpretation does not satisfy those demands which come from the essence of the situation itself.

c. The Relation of the Judgment to Object and Intuition. Apperception

What is Kant's new definition of judgment? Kant said (*B* 141, cited above) "that a judgment is nothing but the manner in which given modes of knowledge are brought to the objective unity of apperception." We cannot yet fully and immediately grasp this definition and its determining elements (*Bestimmungsstücke*). Meanwhile, something strikes the eye. The discussion is no longer of representations and concepts, but of "given cognitions," i.e., of the given in knowledge, consequently, of intuitions. He speaks of "objective unity." Here judging as an action of understanding is not only related to intuition and object, but its essence is defined from this relation and even *as* this relation. Through the essential definition of judgment, as it is anchored in intuition and object-relation, this relationship is, at the very beginning, outlined and expressly set into the unified structure of knowledge. From here a new concept of understanding arises. Understanding is now no longer merely the faculty of connecting representations, but: "*Understanding* is, to use general terms, *the faculty of knowledge*. This knowledge consists in the determinate relation of given representations to an object. . . ." (§ 17, *B* 137, *N.K.S.*, p. 156.)

We can clarify this new situation with a diagram. This diagram will later serve us as a reference point when we develop the essential distinction between analytic and synthetic judgments from this new interpretation of judgment.

The definition of judgment quoted earlier concerns simply a relation of concepts, subject and predicate. That the representing of such a relation demands an *actus mentis* is self-evident, since some mode of action belongs to every act of the understanding. In contrast with this the new definition speaks of the objective unity of knowledge, i.e., the unity of the intuitions, which is represented as a

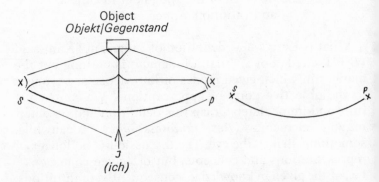

unity belonging to the object and determining it. This relation of representations, as a whole, is related to objects. Therewith, for Kant, there is also posited the relation to the "subject" in the sense of the I that thinks and judges. In the essential definition of judgment, this I relation is called apperception. *Percipere* is the simple apprehension and grasping of the objective. In apperception the relation to the I is grasped and perceived in a certain way, along with the object. The standing-over-against (*Entgegenstehen*) of the object as such is not possible unless what encounters, in its standing-over-against, is present for that which represents, which thereby at the same time has itself present along with the object, although not as an object, but only insofar as what encounters in its againstness (*Entgegen*) at all demands a directed relation to that which is aware of that which encounters.

According to the way in which we have now contrasted the two definitions of judgment, i.e., the traditional one and Kant's, it looks as though Kant only added something to the definition of judgment which had been omitted up till then. But it is not a question of a "mere extension," but of a more primordial grasp of the whole. Therefore, we must begin with Kant's essential definition in order to be able to evaluate the position of the traditional definition. If we take this latter for itself, then we can clearly see that we select one component and that this, so taken, represents only an artificial construction which has been uprooted from the supporting basis of the relations to the object, and to the knowing I.

From this it is easy to judge why the traditional definitions of judgment never could satisfy Kant, i.e., put him at peace with the matter itself. In regard to the question of the possibility of metaphysics, the question concerning the essence of human knowledge had to become decisive for him.

To understand Kant's new definition of judgment more clearly is nothing else than to clarify the aforementioned distinction between analytic and synthetic judgments. We ask in what respect these judgments are distinguished. What does this key respect imply for the new definition of the nature of judgment?

The various twisted, slanted, and fruitless attempts to come to terms with Kant's distinction all suffer in advance from being based on the traditional definition of judgment, but not on that attained by Kant.

The distinction brings into view nothing else than the changed conception of the *Logos* and all that belongs to it, i.e., the "logical." Up to then the essence of the logical was seen in the connection and relation of concepts. Kant's new definition of the logical, contrasted with the traditional one, is something absolutely strange and almost nonsensical, insofar as it asserts that the logical precisely does not just consist in this mere relation of concepts. Obviously with full knowledge of the scope of his new definition of the logical, Kant put it into the title of that important §19: "The Logical Form of All Judgments Consists in the Objective Unity of the Apperception of the Concepts

Which They Contain." To read this as a methodical guide means that all discussion of the essence of the judgment must arise from the entire structure of judgment as it is established, in advance, from the relations to the object and to the knowing human.

d. Kant's Distinction Between Analytic and Synthetic Judgments

What is the purpose of the distinction between analytic and synthetic judgments? In what respect does its clarification give us a more fulfilled insight into the nature of judgment? Hitherto we know only that this distinction directs the division between the first two sections of our chapter. We cannot get much from the names. Pursuing them we can easily fall into error, mostly because the designated distinction can also be met in the traditional definition of judgment and had already been applied even at the time of its first formation by Aristotle. Analytic means analysis, dissolving, taking apart, διαίρεσις; synthesis, on the other hand, means putting together.

If we observe once again the view of judgment as the relation between subject and predicate, then it immediately follows that this relation, i.e., the attributing of the predicate to the subject, is a synthesis, e.g., of "board" and "black." On the other hand, these two relational elements must be separated in order to be combinable. There is an analysis in every synthesis, and vice versa. Therefore, every judgment as a relation of representations is not only incidentally but necessarily analytic and synthetic at the same time. Therefore, because every judgment as such is both analytic and synthetic, the distinction into analytic and synthetic judgments is nonsensical. This reflection is correct. However, Kant does not base his distinction upon the nature of judgment as traditionally intended. What analytic and synthetic mean to Kant is not derived from the traditional, but from the new, essential delineation

(*Wesensumgrenzung*). In order really to see the difference and its main point, we call upon the aid of the diagram and of examples of analytic and synthetic judgments.

"All bodies are extended" is, according to Kant, an analytic judgment. "Some bodies are heavy" (*Prolegomena* §2a) is, according to Kant, a synthetic judgment. With regard to these examples, one could base the difference between analytic and synthetic judgments by saying that the analytic judgment speaks of "all" bodies, while the synthetic, on the contrary, speaks about "some." This difference between the two judgments is certainly not accidental. However, it does not suffice in order to grasp the required difference, particularly not when we understand it only in the sense of traditional logic and assert that the first judgment is universal and the second particular. "All bodies" here means "body in general." According to Kant, this "in general" is represented in the concept. "All bodies" means the body taken according to its concept, with regard to what we mean at all by "body." Taking body according to its concept, according to what we represent by it, we can and even must say that body is extended, whether it be a purely geometrical body or a material and physical one. The predicate "extended" lies in the concept itself; a mere dissecting of the concept finds this element. In the judgment "The body is extended," the represented unity of the relation of subject and predicate, the belonging together of both, has the basis of its fundamental determination in the concept of the body. If I judge about bodies in any way at all, I must already have a certain cognition of the object in the sense of its concept. If nothing more is asserted about the object than what lies in the concept, i.e., if the truth of the judgment is based only upon a dissection of the concept of the subject as such, then this judgment is an analytic one. The truth of the judgment rests on the analyzed concept as such.

The following diagram clarifies the above:

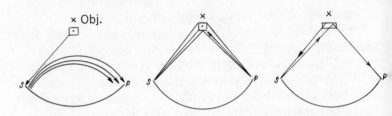

According to the new definition, there belongs to the judgment the relation to the object (x), i.e., the subject is meant in its relation to the object. However, this relation can now be represented in various ways. First, so that the object is represented only insofar as it is cited in general, in the concept.

In the concept we already have a knowledge of the object, and by skipping the object (X), without detouring through X, purely by remaining in the subjective concept "bodily," we can draw the predicate out of it. Such an analyzing judgment only presents more clearly and purely what we already represent in the subjective concept. Therefore, according to Kant, the analytic judgment is only a clarifying one. It does not increase the content of our knowledge. Let us take another example. The judgment "The board is extended" is an analytic judgment. In the concept of the board as corporeal lies being extended. This judgment is self-evident, i.e., the putting-into-relation of subject and predicate already has its ground in the concept we have of a board. In contrast, if we say, "The board is black," then our assertion is not self-evident. The board could just as well be gray, white, or red. The being red does not already lie in the concept of a board, as being extended does. How the board is colored, that it is black, can be decided only from the object itself. Therefore, to reach the grounds of the determination in which this relation of subject and predicate is based, our representation has to take another way than in the analytic judgment, namely, the way via the object and its particular givenness.

Viewed from the analytic judgment this means that we cannot stay within the subject's concept and appeal only to what belongs to a board as such. We have to step out of the subject and pass beyond the concept and go by way of the object itself. This, however, means that in addition to the concept of the object, the object itself must be represented. This additional representation (*Mit-dazu-vorstellen*) of the object is a synthesis. Such a judgment, where the predicate is annexed to the subject via passage through the X and recourse to it, is a *synthetic* judgment. "For that something outside the given concept must be added as a substratum, which makes it possible to go beyond my predicate, is clearly indicated by the expression synthesis." (*Über eine Entdeckung . . . , op. cit.,* p. 245.)

In the sense of the traditional definition of judgment, a predicate is added to the subject also in the analytic judgment. With respect to the subject-predicate relationship the analytic judgment, too, is synthetic. Conversely, the synthetic is also analytic. But this respect is not decisive for Kant. We now see more clearly what this general judging relationship amounts to, when it is selected in isolation and alone alleged to be the judging relationship. Then it is only the neutralized relation of subject and predicate which is present in general in the analytic and synthetic judgment, but in essentially different ways. This leveled and faded form is stamped as the essence of judgment. It remains ominous that it is always right. Now our diagram becomes misleading insofar as it could give the impression that the subject-predicate relationship was first and foremost the main support, and the rest were just accessories.

The decisive respect in which analytic and synthetic judgments are distinguished is the reference of the subject-predicate relationship *as such to the object*. If this object is only represented in its concept, and if this is posited as what is given beforehand, then the object is in a certain sense a standard, but only as the given concept. This concept can yield the determinations only insofar as it is *dissected*, and only what is dissected and thus thrown into relief is attributed to the object. The grounding of the judgment takes place within the realm of the dissection of the concept. The object is a standard in the analytic judgment, too—but solely within its concept. (Compare: ". . . of that which as concept is contained and is thought in the knowledge of the object. . . ." [*A* 151, *B* 190, *N.K.S.*, p. 190])

But, if the object is an immediate standard for the subject-predicate relationship, if the asserting is proven by taking its way via the object itself, if the object itself participates as the foundation and grounds, then the judgment is synthetic.

The distinction classifies judgments according to the possible difference of the basis for the determination of the truth in the subject-predicate relationship. If the basis for the determination is contained in the concept as such, then the judgment is analytic. If this basis is contained in the object itself, then the judgment is synthetic. From out of the object itself this judgment adds something to the erstwhile knowledge of the object; it *extends (erweiternd)*. The analytic judgment, however, is only *clarifying (erläuternd)*.

It must have become clear that the above distinction between judgments presupposes the new concept of judgment, i.e., the relation to the objective unity of the object itself; and that, at the same time, it serves to convey a definite insight into the full essential structure of the judgment. Nevertheless, we still do not see clearly what the distinction into analytic and synthetic judgments has to do with the task of the critique of pure reason. We have defined this positively as the essential delimiting of pure reason, i.e., what it has the power to do; negatively put, as rejection of the presumptuousness of metaphysics based upon mere concepts.

e. *A Priori—A Posteriori*

To what extent is the designated distinction one of fundamental importance for the execution of the critique? We can answer this question just as soon as we have characterized analytic and synthetic judgments in one more respect, which up to now has been intentionally postponed.

In the clarification of the nature of the mathematical and in the description of the development of mathematical thought in modern natural science and modern modes of thought in general, we ran into a striking fact. For example, Newton's first principle of motion and Galileo's law of falling bodies both have the peculiarity that they leap ahead of what verification and experience, in a literal sense, offer. In such principles, something has been anticipated in respect to things. Such anticipations rank ahead of and precede all further determinations of things. In Latin terms such anticipations are *a priori* rather than anything else. This does not mean that in the order of the historical development of our knowledge these anticipations as such become familiar to us first. Rather, the anticipating principles are first in rank when it is a question of grounding and constructing our knowledge in itself. Thus a natural scientist can for a long time have various kinds of information and knowledge of nature without knowing the highest law of motion as such; yet what is posited in this law is always already the ground for all particular assertions made in the domain of statements concerning processes of motion and their regularity.

The priority *(Priorität)* of the *a priori* concerns the essence of things. What enables the thing to be what it is *pre-cedes* the thing as regards the facts and nature, although we only grasp that which precedes after taking account of some of the most obvious qualities of the thing. (On *prioritas naturae,* compare Leibniz' "Letter to Volder of January 21, 1704," in *Leibniz,* Gerhardt, ed., II, 263.) In the order of explicit apprehension, what objectively *precedes is later.* The πρότερον φύσει is ὕστερον πρὸς ἡμᾶς. Because what objectively precedes is later in the order of coming to know, this easily again and again leads to the error that it is also objectively something later and thus an unimportant and basically indifferent fact. This widespread as well as convenient opinion corresponds to a peculiar blindness for the essence of things and for the decisive importance of the cognition of essence. The predominance of such a blindness to essence is always an obstacle for a change in knowledge and the sciences. On the other hand, the decisive changes in human knowledge and scientific attitude are based upon the fact that what objectively precedes (*das sachlich Vorgängige*) can be grasped in the right way also for inquiry as the preceding (*das Vorherige*) and constantly as an advance projection.

The *a priori* is the title for the essence of things. According to how the thingness of the thing is grasped and the being of what is is understood, so also is the *a priori* and its *prioritas* interpreted. We know that for modern philosophy the I-principle is the first principle in the order of precedence of truth and principles, i.e., that which is thought in the pure thought of the I as the prime subject. Thus it happens that, conversely, everything thought in the pure thought of the subject holds good *a priori.* That is *a priori* which lies ready in the subject, in the mind. The *a priori* is what belongs to the subjectivity of the subject. Everything else, on the contrary, which first becomes accessible only by going out of the subject and entering into the object, into perceptions, is—as seen from the subject—later, i.e., *a posteriori.*

We cannot enter here into the history of this distinction —*a priori*, preceding in rank, and *a posteriori*, correspondingly later. Kant in his way takes it over from modern thought and with its help characterizes the distinction of judgments into analytic and synthetic. An analytic judgment, which has the fundamental determination of the truth of its subject-predicate relationship solely in the concept, remains from the outset in the sphere of conceptual analysis, i.e., the sphere of mere thought. It is *a priori*. All analytic judgments according to their essence are *a priori*. Synthetic judgments are *a posteriori*. Here we must first move out of the concept to the object, from which we "afterward" derive the determinations.

f. How Are Synthetic Judgments *A Priori* Possible?

Let us now look at traditional metaphysics from the vantage point of Kant's clarification of the essence of judgment. A critique of this traditional metaphysics must circumscribe the essence of thought and judgment achieved and claimed in it. What kind of judgment does traditional modern metaphysics demand, in the light of Kant's theory of judgment? As we know, rational metaphysics is a knowledge out of mere concepts, therefore *a priori*. But this metaphysics does not desire to be a logic, analyzing only concepts; but it claims to know the supersensible domains of God, the world and the human soul, hence objects themselves. Rational metaphysics wants to enlarge our knowledge about such things. The judgments of this metaphysics are synthetic in their claim yet at the same time *a priori*, because they are derived from mere concepts and mere thought. The question concerning the possibility of the rational metaphysics can thus be expressed in the formula: How are the judgments claimed in it possible, i.e., how are synthetic judgments which are also *a priori* possible? We say "also," since how synthetic judgments are possible *a posteriori* is understood without difficulty. An enlargement of our knowledge (synthesis) results whenever we move beyond the concept and allow the givens of perception and sensation, the *a posteriori*, the later (as seen by thought, i.e., by that which precedes [*Vorherigen*]), to have their say.

How analytic judgments *a priori* are possible, on the other hand, is also clear. They simply reproduce by clarification what already lies in the concept. On the contrary, it remains incomprehensible, at first, how synthetic judgments *a priori* are to be possible. According to what has been said, at least, the mere conception of such a judgment is contradictory in itself. Since synthetic judgments are *a posteriori*, we could replace the word synthetic by *a posteriori* to see the nonsense of this question. It runs: How are *a posteriori* judgments possible *a priori?* Or, since all analytic judgments are *a priori*, we can replace the word *a priori* by analytic and reduce the question to the form: How are synthetic judgments analytically possible? That is as if we would say: How is fire possible as water? The answer is self-evident. It is: "Impossible."

The question concerning the possibility of synthetic judgments *a priori* looks like a demand to make out something binding and determinative about the object, without going into and back to the object.

Yet, the decisive discovery of Kant consists precisely in allowing us to see that and how synthetic judgments *a priori* are possible. To be sure, the question concerning the "how" of the possibility had for Kant a double meaning: (1) in which sense and (2) under what conditions.

Synthetic judgments *a priori* are indeed, as will be shown, possible only under exactly determined conditions, which conditions rational metaphysics is not able to fulfill. Therefore, synthetic judgments *a priori* are not achievable in it. The most special intention of rational metaphysics collapses in itself. Note: It does not collapse because it does not reach the set goal in consequence of outer obstacles and limits, but because the conditions of that knowledge which metaphysics claims in its very character are not fulfillable on the basis of this character.

The rejection of rational metaphysics on the basis of its inner impossibility does presuppose a positive demonstrating of those conditions which make possible synthetic judgments *a priori*. Out of the mode of these conditions is also determined how, i.e., in what sense alone, synthetic judgments *a priori* are possible, namely, in a sense about which philosophy and human thought in general knew nothing until Kant.

By ascertaining these conditions—that is to say, the circumscription of the nature of such judgments—Kant not only recognizes in what respect they are possible, but also in what respect they are necessary. Namely, they are necessary to make possible human knowledge as experience. According to the tradition of modern thought, which, despite everything, Kant held to, knowledge is founded in principles. Those principles which necessarily underlie our human knowledge as conditions of its possibility must have the character of synthetic judgments *a priori*. In the third section of our chapter there occurs nothing more than the systematic presentation and grounding of these synthetic and yet, at the same time, *a priori* judgments.

g. The Principle of the Avoidance of Contradiction as the Negative Condition of the Truth of Judgment

From the above we now understand more easily why two sections precede this third one. The first is concerned with analytic, the second with synthetic judgments. Upon the background of these first two sections, what is peculiar and new in the third section and the meaning of the center of the whole work first becomes visible. On the basis of the achieved clarification of the distinction between analytic and synthetic judgments, we also understand why the discussion concerns the highest principles of these judgments, what this means.

Analytic and synthetic judgments are distinguished

with regard to their different kinds of relations to the object, i.e., according to the respective kinds of bases for determining the truth of the subject-predicate relationship. The highest principle is the positing of the first and proper ground in which the truth of the respective kind of judgment is based. Thus we can say, by turning the whole thing around:

The first two sections of our chapter enable the original insight into the essence of analytic as well as synthetic judgments insofar as they respectively deal with what constitutes the essential distinction between the two kinds of judgments. As soon as the discussion is of analytic and synthetic judgments in Kant's sense, then judgments and the essence of the judgment in general are understood in and out of their relation *to the object* and, therefore, in accord with the new concept of judgment achieved in the *Critique of Pure Reason*.

When, therefore, our chapter is concerned throughout with judgments, this no longer means that thought is examined for the sake of itself, but that the relation of thought to the object and thus to intuition is in question.

This short systematic reflection on Kant's theory of judgment was intended to enable us to understand the following discussion of the first section, i.e., to gain an advance view of the inner connections of what Kant says in the following.

A judgment is either analytic or synthetic, i.e., the basic ground of its truth is either in the given subjective concept or in the object itself. We can consider a judgment as simply a subject-predicate relationship. By this we only comprehend a residue of the structure of judgments. Even for this residue to be what it is, to provide a subject-predicate relationship at all, it still stands under the condition that subject and predicate are unitable, i.e., that they are attributable to each other and do not contradict each other. But, this condition does not yield the complete basis for the truth of the judgment, because judgment is yet not fully comprehended.

The mere unitability of subject and predicate only says that an assertion as λέγειν τι κατά τινος, i.e., a saying (*Spruch*) in general, is possible at all, insofar as no contradiction hinders it. However, this unitability as a condition for assertion does not yet reach into the sphere of the essence of judgment. In this case the judgment is as yet considered without any regard for the giving of grounds and object relation. The mere unitability of subject and predicate tells so little about the truth of the judgment that, in spite of being free from contradiction, a subject-predicate relationship can be false or even groundless. "But even if our judgment contains no contradiction it may connect concepts in a manner not borne out by the object, or else in a manner for which no ground is given, either *a priori* or *a posteriori,* sufficient to justify such judgment, and so may still, in spite of being free from all inner contradiction, be either false or groundless." (*A* 150, *B* 190, *N.K.S.,* pp. 189 f.)

Only now does Kant give us the formula of the famous "principle of contradiction": "No predicate contradictory of a thing can belong to it" (*A* 151, *B* 190, *N.K.S.,* p. 190). In his lecture on metaphysics ([Erfurt: Pölitz, 1821], p. 15) the formula runs: "Nulli subjecto competit praedicatum ipsi oppositum." ("To no subject does a predicate belong that contradicts it.") These two formulations do not differ essentially. The one from the *Critique of Pure Reason* expressly names the thing to which the subjective concept is related; the lecture names the subjective concept itself.

In the last paragraph of our first section Kant explains why he formulates the principle of contradiction in this way that deviates from the traditional wording. "Although this famous principle is thus without content and merely formal, it has sometimes been carelessly formulated in a manner which involves the quite unnecessary admixture of a synthetic element. The formula runs: It is impossible that something should *at one and the same time both be and not be.*" (*A* 152, *B* 191, *N.K.S.,* p. 190.) In

Aristotle the principle of contradiction runs: τὸ γὰρ αὐτὸ ἅμα ὑπάρχειν τε καὶ μὴ ὑπάρχειν ἀδύνατον τῷ αὐτῷ καὶ κατὰ τὸ αὐτό (*Metaphysics*, IV, 3, 1005b, 19). ("It is impossible for the same to occur as well as not to occur at the same time in the same and with respect to the same.")[30] ("Unmöglich kann dasselbe zugleich vorkommen sowohl als nicht vorkommen am selben in Hinsicht auf das selbe.") Wolff writes in his *Ontologie*, §28: "Fieri non potest, ut idem simul sit et non sit." ("It cannot happen that the same at the same time is and is not.") The terms for the determination of time (ἅμα, *simul*, *zugleich*) are conspicuous in these formulations. Kant's own wording omits "at the same time." Why is it omitted? "At the same time" is a determination of time and therefore characterizes the object as temporal, i.e., as an object of experience. However, insofar as the principle of contradiction is understood only as the negative condition of the subject-predicate relationship in general, the judgment is meant in its separation from the object and its temporal determination. But even when one attributes a positive meaning to the principle of contradiction, as is soon done, "at the same time," as a determination of time, does not according to Kant belong to its formula.

h. The Principle of the Avoidance of Contradiction as the Negative Formulation of the Principle of Identity

In what sense can a positive application of the principle of contradiction be made so that it does not only represent a negative condition of the possibility of a subject-predi-

---

[30] W. D. Ross translates this passage: "It is, that the same attribute cannot at the same time belong and not belong to the same subject and in the same respect." (Aristotle, *op. cit.*, VIII.) Hugh Tredennick's translation runs: "It is impossible for the same attribute at once to belong and not to belong to the same thing and in the same relation." (*The Metaphysics* [Cambridge: Harvard University Press, 1947], p. 161.) Heidegger seems to translate this passage more cautiously than these. *Trans.*

cate relationship at all, i.e., for all possible judgments, but also a highest principle for a certain kind of judgment? Traditional rational metaphysics was of the opinion that the principle of contradiction was the principle of all judgments in general. Using Kant's terms, all judgments would include analytic as well as synthetic. This distinction of judgments enables Kant to draw more exactly than was done up to that time the range of the axiomatic validity of the principle of contradiction, i.e., to delimit it negatively and positively. A principle, in contrast to a mere negative condition, is a proposition in which there is posited the ground for possible truth, i.e., something sufficient for supporting the truth of the judgment. This ground is always presented as something that supports and is sufficient in supporting; it is *ratio sufficiens*. If the judgment is taken only as a subject-predicate relationship, then it is not at all considered with regard to the grounds that determine its truth. However, it is in this regard that the distinction of analytic and synthetic judgments becomes determinative. The analytic judgment takes the object simply according to its given concept and desires only to retain this concept in the selfsameness of its contents, in order to clarify it. The selfsameness of the concept is the only and sufficient standard for the attributing and denying of the predicate. The principle which establishes the ground of the truth of the analytic judgment must, consequently, establish the selfsameness of the concept as the ground for the subject-predicate relationship. Understood as a rule, the principle must posit the necessity of adhering to the concept in its selfsameness, identity. The highest principle of analytic judgments is the principle of identity.

But did we not say that the highest principle examined in this first section is the principle of contradiction? Were we not justified in saying this since Kant nowhere speaks about the principle of identity in the first section? But it must puzzle us that there is the talk about a twofold role of the principle of contradiction. The talk about the positive use of the principle of contradiction not only speaks of the application of this principle as a basis for determination, but that this application is possible only if the negative content of the principle is turned into its positive one at the same time. Presented in a formula, it is: We have advanced from $A \neq$ non A, to $A = A$.

Positively used, the principle of contradiction is the principle of identity. Kant indeed does not mention the principle of identity in our section, but in the Introduction he labels the analytic judgments as those "in which the connection of the predicate with the subject is thought through identity" (A 7, B 10, $N.K.S.$, p. 48); here "identity" is presented as the ground of the analytic judgment. Similarly, in a polemical pamphlet, *Über eine Entdeckung . . .* (*op. cit.*, VIII, 245), analytic judgments are designated as those "which rest entirely either on the principle of identity or contradiction." In the following second section (A 154–55, B 194, $N.K.S.$, pp. 191 f.) identity and contradiction are mentioned together. The relation of these two principles has not been decided even today. Nor it is possible to decide it formally, because this decision remains dependent on the conception of being and truth as such. In Scholastic rational metaphysics the principle of contradiction had priority. For this reason Kant intentionally terminates the discussion on the principle of contradiction in our section. For Leibniz, on the contrary, the principle of identity becomes the first principle, especially since for him all judgments are identities (*Identitäten*). Kant himself points out, against Wolff, in his habilitation treatise (Part I: *De Principio Contradictionis, Propositio* I) as follows: Veritatum omnium non datur principium *unicum*, absolute primum, catholicon.[31] *Proposito* III shows the *praeferentia* of the *principium identitatis . . . prae principio contradictionis.*

---

[31] "The principle alone is not given as the absolutely first and universal of all truths." *Trans.*

In analytic judgments, the object is thought only according to its concept and not as an object of experience, i.e., as a temporally determined object. Therefore, the principle of these judgments in its formula does not need to contain any temporal determination.

i. Kant's Transcendental Reflection; General and Transcendental Logic

The principle of contradiction and the principle of identity belong solely to logic, and, therefore, concern only the judgment considered logically. When Kant speaks thus, he certainly looks beyond the difference in the use of the principle of contradiction that he introduced, and views as only logical all thought which in its establishment does not take the way over the object itself. Logic, in the sense of "general logic," disregards all relations to the object (*A* 55, *B* 79, *N.K.S.*, p. 95). It knows nothing of anything like synthetic judgments. All judgments of metaphysics, however, are synthetic. Therefore—and this is now all that matters—the principle of contradiction is not a principle of metaphysics.

Therefore—and this is the further decisive consequence which mediates between sections one and two—metaphysical knowledge and every objective synthetic cognition demand another foundation altogether. Other principles must be established.

Considering the importance of this step, we shall try to conceive more clearly the limitation of the principle of contradiction as the principle of analytic judgments, especially with regard to the guiding question about the thingness of the thing. The traditional definition of the thingness of the thing, i.e., of the being of what is (*Sein des Seienden*), has the assertion (the judgment) as its guideline. Being is determined from out of thought and the laws of conceivability or inconceivability. However, the first section of our chapter, which we have just discussed, asserts nothing else than that mere thought can-not be the final court of appeal for the determination of the thingness of the thing, or, as Kant would say, for the objectivity of the object. Logic cannot be the basic science of metaphysics. However, in determining the object, which according to Kant is the object of human knowl-edge, it is necessary that thought participates, namely, as thought referred to intuition, i.e., as synthetic judgment. Hence logic, as the doctrine of thought, also has a say in metaphysics. According to the transformed definition of the essence of thought and judgment, the essence of logic, insofar as it is related to it, must also be changed. It must be a logic which considers thought inclusive of its relation to the object. Kant calls this kind of logic "transcendental logic."

The transcendental is what concerns transcendence. Viewed transcendentally, thought is considered in its passing over to the object. Transcendental reflection is not directed upon objects themselves nor upon thought as the mere representation of the subject-predicate relation-ship, but upon the passing over (*Überstieg*) and the re-lation to the object *as this relation*. (Transcendence: 1. Over to [the other side]—as such [*Hinüber zu—als solches*] 2. Passing up, passing beyond [*Über-weg*].) (For Kant's definition of "transcendental," compare *Critique of Pure Reason*, *A* 12, *B* 25.[32] In a note (Academie edition, *op. cit.*, xv, No. 373), it reads as follows: "A determination of a thing with regard to its essence as a thing is trans-cendental.")

According to this line of thought, Kant calls his philoso-phy transcendental philosophy. The system of principles is its foundation. In order to be clearer here and in what follows we bring into relief several views of the inquiry.

---

[32] Kant's *Critique of Pure Reason, A* 12, *B* 25, *N.K.S.*, p. 59: "I entitle *transcendental* all knowledge which is occupied not so much with objects as with the mode of our knowledge of objects insofar as this mode of knowledge is to be possible *a priori*. A sys-tem of such concepts might be entitled transcendental philos-ophy." *Trans.*

We customarily express our cognitions, and even our questions and modes of considering, in sentences. The physicist and the lawyer, the historian and the physician, the theologian and the meteorologist, the biologist and the philosopher all speak similarly in sentences and assertions. Yet the domains and objects to which the assertions refer remain distinct. Hence, the content of what is said differs in each case.

Thus it comes about that no other difference is generally noticed than a difference in content when, for example, we speak in a biological line of questioning of the division of cells, growth, and propagation, or when we talk about biology itself—its direction of inquiry and assertion. People think that to talk biologically about the objects of biology differs from a discussion about biology itself only with respect to content. He who can do the first, and precisely he, must surely also be able to do the second. However, this is an illusion, for one cannot deal biologically with biology. Biology is not something like algae, mosses, frogs and salamanders, cells, and organs. Biology is a science. We cannot put the biology itself under the microscope as we do the objects of biology.

The moment we talk "about" a science and reflect upon it, all the means and methods of this science in which we are well versed fail us. The inquiry about a science demands a point of view whose accomplishment and direction are even less self-evident than is the mastery of this science. If it is a matter of an elucidation about a science, then the opinion easily gains a footing that such reflections are "universal," in distinction to the "particular" questions of the science. However, it is here not simply a matter of quantitative differences, of the more or less "universal." A qualitative difference appears, in the essence, in point of view, in concept-formation and in demonstration. In fact, this difference already lies in each science itself. It belongs to it insofar as it is a free historical action of man. Therefore, continual self-reflection belongs to every science.

Let us recall the example: "The sun warms the rock." If we follow this assertion and its own essential line of assertion, then we are plainly directed to the objects sun, rock, and warmth. Our representation is incorporated into what the object itself offers. We do not pay attention to the assertion as such. To be sure, by a specific turn in the point of view of our representing, we can turn away from sun and rock and consider the assertion as such. That happened, for instance, when we characterized the judgment as a subject-predicate relationship. This subject-predicate relationship itself has nothing in the least to do with the sun and the rock. We take the assertion, the λόγος, "The sun warms the rock," now purely "logically." Not only do we thereby disregard the fact that the assertion refers to natural objects. We do not regard its objective relation at all. Besides this first representational direction (directly to the object) and besides this second (to the objectless assertory relation in itself) there is now a third. In the characterization of the judgment "The sun warms the rock," we said that the sun is understood as the cause and the warmth of the rock as the effect. If, in this respect, we hold on to the sun and the warm rock, we are indeed directed toward sun and rock, and yet not directly. We do not only mean the sun itself and the warm rock itself, but we now consider the object "sun" in regard to how this object is an object *for us*, in what respect it is meant, i.e., how our thought thinks it.

We do not now take a direct view of the object (sun, warmth, rock) but with regard to the mode of its objectivity (*Gegenständlichkeit*). This is the respect in which we refer to the object *a priori*, and in advance: as cause and effect.

We are now not only not directed to the object of the assertion, but also not to the form of the assertion as such, but rather to how the object is the object of the assertion, how the assertion represents the object in advance, how our knowledge passes over to the object, *transcendit*, and how, thereby, and in what objective determination the object encounters. Kant calls this way of considering transcendental. In a certain sense the object stays in our view and in a certain sense so does the assertion, because the *relation* between the assertion and the object is to be grasped.

This transcendental consideration, however, is not an external hooking up of psychological and logical modes of reflection, but something more primordial, from which these two sides have been separately lifted out. Whenever, within a science, we reflect in some way upon that science itself, we take the step into the line of vision and onto the plane of transcendental reflection. Mostly we are unaware of this. Therefore our deliberations in this respect are often accidental and confused. But, just as we cannot take one reasonable or fruitful step in any science without being familiar with its objects and procedures, so also we cannot take a step in reflecting on the science without the right experience and practice in the transcendental point of view.

When, in this lecture, we constantly ask about the thingness of the thing and endeavor to place ourselves into the realm of this question, it is nothing else than the exercises of this transcendental viewpoint and mode of questioning (*Fragestellung*). It is the exercise of that way of viewing, in which all reflection on the sciences necessarily moves. The securing of this realm, the acknowledged and knowing, taking possession of it, being able to walk and to stand in its dimensions, is the fundamental presupposition of every scientific *Dasein* which wants to comprehend its historical position and task.

j. Synthetic Judgments *A Priori* Necessarily Lie at the Basis of All Knowledge

When we approach the domain of the objects of a science, the objects of this domain are already determined such and so in advance. However, this does not occur accidentally nor from a lack of attention on our part as if this pre-determination of the object ever could be prevented. On the contrary, this pre-determination is necessary, so necessary that without it we could not stand before objects at all, as before something according to which our assertions are directed and *on which* they are measured and proven (*ausweisen*). How can a scientific judgment correspond with its object? How, for instance, can a judgment about art history really be an art-historical judgment if the object is not defined in advance as a work of art? How can a biological assertion about an animal be truly a biological judgment if the animal is not already pre-defined as a living creature?

We must always already have a knowledge of content, of what an object is according to its objective nature, i.e., for Kant a synthetic knowledge. And we must have it in advance, *a priori*. Objects could never confront us as objects at all without synthetic judgments *a priori;* by these objects we "then" guide ourselves in particular investigations, inquiries, and proofs, in which we constantly appeal to them.

Synthetic judgments *a priori* are already asserted in all scientific judgments. They are pre-judgments (*Vorurteile*) in a true and necessary sense. How scientific a science is depends not on the number of books written, nor the number of institutes and certainly not on the usefulness it offers at the moment. Rather, it depends on how explicit and defined is its work with which it strives to do something on its pre-judgments. There is no presuppositionless science, because the essence of science consists in such presupposing, in such pre-judgments about the object. Kant has not only affirmed all this, but has also shown it, and not simply shown but also grounded it. He has set this grounding as a completed work into our history in the form of the *Critique of Pure Reason*.

If we take the essence of truth in the traditional sense

as the correspondence of the assertion with the object—and Kant, too, takes it in this way—then truth understood in this way cannot be, unless the object (*Gegenstand*) has been brought to a standing-against (*Gegen-stehen*) in advance, by synthetic judgments *a priori*. Therefore, Kant calls synthetic judgments *a priori*, i.e., the system of principles of pure understanding, the "source of all truth" (*A* 237, B 296, *N.K.S.*, p. 258). The inner connection of what has been said with our question about the thingness of the thing is obvious.

For Kant, true (*wahrhaft*) things., i.e., things of which a truth for us can come to be, are objects of experience. However, the object only becomes accessible to us when we transcend the mere concept to that other which first has to be added to it and placed beside it. Such putting-along-side *(Beistellung)* occurs as a synthesis. In the Kantian sense, we encounter things first and only in the domain of synthetic judgments; and, accordingly, we first encounter the thingness of the thing only in the context of the question of how a thing as such and in advance is possible as a thing, i.e., at the same time how synthetic judgments *a priori* are possible.

6. On the Highest Principle of All Synthetic Judgments

If we put together all that has been said about the outer limits of analytic judgments, then the two first principles of the second section will become understandable:

> The explanation of the possibility of synthetic judgments is a problem with which general logic has nothing to do. It need not even so much as know the problem by name. But in transcendental logic it is the most important of all questions; and indeed, if in treating of the possibility of synthetic *a priori* judgments we also take account of the conditions and scope of their validity, it is the only question with which it is concerned. For upon completion of this enquiry, transcendental logic is in a position com-

pletely to fulfill its ultimate purpose, that of determining the scope and limits of pure understanding.

In the analytic judgment we keep to the given concept, and seek to extract something from it. If it is to be affirmative, I ascribe to it only what is already thought in it. If it is to be negative, I exclude from it only its opposite. But in synthetic judgments I have to advance beyond the given concept, viewing as in relation with the concept something altogether different from what was thought in it. This relation is consequently never a relation either of identity or of contradiction; and from the judgment, taken in and by itself, the truth or falsity of the relation can never be discovered. (*A* 154 f., *B* 193 f., *N.K.S.*, pp. 191 f.)

The "altogether different" is the object. The relation of this "altogether different" to the concept is the representational putting-along-side (*Beistellen*) of the object in a thinking intuition: synthesis. Only while we enter into this relation and maintain ourselves in it does an object encounter us. The inner possibility of the object, i.e., its essence, is thus co-determined out of the possibility of this relation to it. In what does this relation to the object consist, i.e., in what is it grounded? The ground on which it rests must be uncovered and properly posited as the ground. This occurs in the statement and establishment of the highest principle of all synthetic judgments.

The condition of the possibility of all truth is grounded in this posited ground. The source of all truth is the principles of pure understanding. They themselves and therefore this source of all truth go back to a still deeper source, which is brought to light in the highest principle of all synthetic judgments.

With the second section of our chapter, the whole work of the *Critique of Pure Reason* reaches its deepest basis, founded by it itself. The highest principle of all synthetic judgments (or, as we can also say, the basic determination of the essence of human knowledge, its truth and its object) is expressed in this formula at the end of the second section: ". . . The conditions of the *possibility of experience* in general are likewise conditions of the *possibility of the objects of experience*. . . ." (*A* 158, *B* 197, *N.K.S.*, p. 194.)

Whoever understands this principle understands Kant's *Critique of Pure Reason*. Whoever understands this does not only know one book among the writings of philosophy, but masters a fundamental posture of the history of man, which we can neither avoid, leap over, nor deny in any way. But we have to bring this by an appropriate transformation to fulfillment in the future.

The third section also takes precedence over the second, the latter being only an unfolding of the former. Therefore, a complete and definite understanding of this decisive second section is possible only if we already know the third one. Therefore, we shall skip the second section and only return to it after the exposition of the third, at the close of our presentation of the question of the thing in the *Critique of Pure Reason*.

All synthetic principles of the pure understanding are systematically presented in the third section. What makes an object into an object, what delimits the boundaries of the thingness of the thing, is described in its inner connection. Also in the exposition of the third section we immediately begin with the presentation of the particular principles. The preliminary consideration need be clarified only so far as to gain a more definite concept of the principle in general and of the point of view of the division of the principles.

For that purpose, the first sentence of the third section gives us the key: "That there should be principles at all is entirely due to the pure understanding. Not only is it the faculty of rules in respect of that which happens, but is itself the source of principles according to which everything that can be presented to us as an object must conform to rules. For without such rules appearances would never yield knowledge of an object corresponding to them." (*A* 158 f., *B* 197 f., *N.K.S.*, pp. 194 f.)

7. *Systematic Representation of All the Synthetic Principles of Pure Understanding*

a. The Principles Make Possible the Objectivity of the Object; The Possibility of Establishing the Principles

In our pursuit of the question about the thingness of the thing, we were led to Kant's doctrine of the principles of the pure understanding. In what way? For Kant the thing accessible to us is the object of experience. Experience for him means the humanly possible theoretical knowledge of what is. This knowledge is twofold. Therefore, Kant says: *"Understanding* and *sensibility,* with us, can determine objects *only when they are employed in conjunction."* (*A* 258, *B* 314, *N.K.S.*, p. 274.) An object is determined *as object* by the conjunction, i.e., by the unity of what is intuited in intuition and what is thought in thought. To the essence of object (*Gegenstand*) belongs the "against" (*Gegen*) and the "standing" (*Stand*). The essence of this "against," its inner possibility and ground, as well as the essence of this "standing," its inner possibility and ground, and, finally and above all, the primordial unity of both, the "againstness" as well as the "constancy," constitute the objectivity of the object.

That the determination of the essence of the object results from principles at all is not immediately obvious. Nevertheless, it becomes understandable when we attend to the traditional direction of the question of the thing in Western philosophy. According to this, the basic mathematical characteristic is the decisive: the recourse to axioms in every determination of what is. *Kant remains within this tradition.* However, the way he conceives and establishes these axioms brings about a revolution. The hegemony of the highest principle of all judgments hitherto, the principle of contradiction, is removed from its position of dominance. What principles replace it?

First of all, it must be noticeable that Kant does not speak of axioms. "Axioms" are for him a certain kind of principle *a priori*, namely, those which are immediately certain, i.e., which are verifiable without further ado from intuition of an object. However, such principles are not under discussion in this present context, which is already indicated since it is concerned with principles of the pure understanding. But, as principles they must also include the grounds for other principles and judgments. Thus they themselves cannot be based on earlier and more universal cognitions. (*A* 148 f., *B* 188, *N.K.S.*, pp. 188 f.) This does not exclude the fact that they have a foundation. Only the question remains wherein they have their foundation. Principles which ground the essence of an object cannot be grounded upon the object. The principles cannot be extracted by experience from the object, since they themselves first make possible the objectivity of the object. Nor can they be grounded in mere thought alone, because they are principles of *objects*. Consequently, the principles do not have the character of general formal logical propositions, such as "A is A," of which we say that they are self-evident. Recourse to common sense fails entirely here. In the realm of metaphysics it is "an expedient which always is a sign that the cause of reason is in desperate straits." (*A* 784, *B* 812, *N.K.S.*, p. 622.) What the nature of the basis of proof for these principles of the pure understanding is and how they distinguish themselves through the nature of the basis of their proof must be shown from the system of these principles itself.

b. Pure Understanding as the Source and Faculty of Rules; Unity, Categories

That the determination of the thing in Kant leads back to principles is an indication for us that Kant remains within the tradition. However, this historical characterization is still not an explanation of the content. When Kant defines the essence of thought anew, he must also demonstrate, on the basis of this new formulation of the nature of understanding, why and to what extent principles belong to this.

Kant was the first to be able not simply to accept and affirm the rule of principles, but to ground it from the nature of the understanding itself. The first proposition of the third section points to this connection. There he says expressly that the pure understanding is itself the source of the principles. We must show how far this proves to be true, especially with reference to all that we have heard up till now about the nature of the understanding. General logic, which defines the judgment as the relationship of the representations of subject and predicate, knows the understanding as the faculty of connecting representations. Thus, just as the logical conception of the judgment is correct but insufficient, so also this conception of the understanding remains correct but unsatisfactory. The understanding must be viewed as a representing that refers to the object, i.e., as a connecting of representations so constructed that the connecting refers to the object. The understanding must be formulated as that representing which grasps and constitutes this reference to an object as such.

The connection between subject and predicate is not merely a connecting in general, but a definitely determined connecting every time. Let us recall the objective judgment "The sun warms the rock." Here sun and rock are represented objectively in that the sun is conceived of as the cause, and the rock's becoming warm as the effect. The connection of subject and predicate occurs on the grounds of the general relation of cause and effect. Connection is always a putting-together (*Zusammensetzen*) with regard to a possible kind of unity which characterizes the "together" (*Zusammen*). In this characterization of the judgment, the primordial sense of λόγος as a gathering-together (*Sammlung*) still faintly shines through.

Each kind of subject-predicate connection in judgments presupposes and bears in itself the representation of a *unity* as the guiding regard, according to which and in whose sense the connecting occurs. The anticipating representing of such unities, which guides connection, belongs to the essence of the understanding. The representations of these unities as such and in general are "concepts," according to the definition given earlier. Concepts of such unities belonging to the understanding's action of connecting are, however, not derived from any objects given beforehand; they are not concepts which have been drawn out of perceptions of individual objects. The representations of these unities belong to the functions of the understanding, to the essence of connecting. They lie purely in the essence of the understanding itself and for this reason are called pure concepts of the understanding: categories.

General logic has worked out a variety of forms of judgment, modes of subject-predicate connection which can be arranged in a table of judgments (*Urteilstafel*). Kant took over from tradition and augmented this table of judgments, the exhibition and classification of the different modes of subject-predicate connection (*A* 70, *B* 95). The dimensions of classification are quantity, quality, relation, and modality. The table of judgments can, therefore, give an indication of just as many kinds of unities and concepts of unity, which guide the different connecting. According to the table of judgments, one can formulate a table of the concepts of unity of the pure understanding, of its root concepts (*Stammbegriffe*) (*A* 80, *B* 106, *N.K.S.*, p. 113). If anything at all is introduced as a condition for the unifying and unified positing of something manifold, this represented condition is used as the rule of the connecting. The understanding is fundamentally the capacity for rules, since the anticipating representing of unities, which regulates this connecting, belongs to the essence of the understanding as a connection of representations, and since these regulating unities belong to the essence of the understanding itself. Therefore, Kant says: "We may now characterize it [the understanding] as the *faculty of rules*"; and he adds: "This distinguishing mark is more fruitful, and approximates more closely to its essential nature." (*A* 126, *N.K.S.*, p. 147.) The same is said in our spot at the beginning of the third section: The understanding is the "*faculty of rules*." Here the metaphysical definition of the essence of the understanding shows itself.

But in the section in question, the definition of the essence of the understanding traces back still one step further into the essence. The pure understanding is "not only the faculty of rules," but even the source of rules. This means that the pure understanding is the ground of the necessity of rules at all. That which shows itself (*Sichzeigendes*) must have in advance the possibility of coming to a stand and constancy, so that what encounters, what shows itself, i.e., what appears, can come before us at all as standing before us (*Gegenstehendes*). However, what stands in itself (*Insichstehendes*) and does not fall apart (*Nichtauseinanderfahrendes*) is what is collected in itself (*Insichgesammeltes*), i.e., something brought into a unity, and is thus present and constant in this unity. This constancy is what uniformly in itself and out of itself exists as presented toward. (*Die Ständigkeit ist das einheitliche in sich von sich aus An-wesen.*) This presence to it is made possible *with* the participation of the pure understanding. Its activity is thought. Thought, however, is an "*I* think"; I represent something to myself in general in its unity and in its belonging together. The presence (*Präsenz*) of the object shows itself in the representing, in which it becomes present *to me* (*auf mich zu Präsentwerden*) through the thinking, i.e., connecting representing. But to whom this presence of the object is presented, whether to me as a contingent "I" with its moods, desires, and opinions, or to me as an "I" that puts behind itself everything "subjective," allowing the object itself to be what it is, this depends on the "I," namely, upon the comprehensiveness and the reach of the unity and the rules under which the connecting of the representations is brought, i.e., fundamentally upon the range and kind of freedom by virtue of which I myself am a self.

The pre-senting (*vor-stellend*) connecting is only possible for the understanding if it contains in itself modes of uniting, rules of the unity of the connecting and determining, if the pure understanding allows rules to emerge and is itself their origin and source. The pure understanding is the ground of the necessity of rules, i.e., the occurrence of principles, because this ground, the understanding itself, is necessary in fact, according to the essence of that to which the pure understanding belongs, according to the essence of human knowledge.

If we human beings are merely open to the pressure of all that in the midst of which we are suspended, we are not equal to this pressure. We master it only when we serve it out of a superiority, i.e., by letting the pressure stand over against us, bringing it to a stand, thus forming and maintaining a domain of possible constancy. The metaphysical necessity of the pure understanding is grounded in this need that the pressure must be free-standing. According to this metaphysical origin of the source of principles, that source is the pure understanding. These principles, in turn, are the "source of all truth," i.e., of the possibility for our experiences to be at all able to correspond to objects.

Such correspondence to . . . is only possible when the wherewith (*Womit*) of correspondence already comes before us in advance and stands before us. Only so does something objective address us in the appearances; only so do they become recognizable with respect to an object speaking in them and "corresponding" to them. The pure understanding provides the possibility of the correspondence to the object thanks to the objectivity of appearances, i.e., of the thingness of things for us.

c. The Mathematical and Dynamical Principles as Metaphysical Propositions

On the basis of this explanation, we can understand the decisive proposition which introduces the third section. (*A* 158, *B* 197 f., *N.K.S.*, p. 194 f.) The principles of pure reason lay the groundwork for the objectivity of objects. In them—namely in their connection—those modes of representation are achieved in virtue of which the "against" of the object and the "stand" of the object are opened up in their primordial unity. The principles always concern this twofold unity of the essence of the object (*Gegenstand*). Therefore, they must first lay the ground in the direction of the "against," the "againstness" (*Gegenheit*), and simultaneously in the direction of the "stand" (*Standes*), the constancy. Thereby, from the essence of the principles follows their division into two groups. Kant calls them the mathematical and dynamical principles. What is the objective reason for this distinction? How is it intended?

Kant defines the natural thing as the thing approachable by us, the body which *is* as an object of experience, i.e., of mathematical-physical knowledge. The body is something in motion or at rest in space, so that the motions, as changes of place, can be determined numerically in terms of their relations. This mathematical determination of the natural body is not an accidental one for Kant, not only a form of calculating that is merely added on to it. Rather, the mathematical, in the sense of what is movable in space, belongs first of all to the definition of the thingness of the thing. If the possibility of the thing is to be metaphysically grasped, there is need for such principles in which this mathematical character of the natural body is grounded. For this reason, one group of the principles of pure understanding is called "the mathematical principles." This designation does not mean that the principles themselves are mathematical belonging to mathematics, but that they concern the mathematical character of natural bodies, the metaphysical principles which lay the ground of this character.

The thing in the sense of a natural body is, however, not only what is movable in space, what simply occupies space, i.e., is extended, but what fills a space, keeping it occupied, extending, dividing, and maintaining itself in this occupying; it is resistance, i.e., force. Leibniz first set forth this character of a natural body, and Kant took over these defining determinations. That which is space-filling, which is spatially present, we know only through forces which are effective in space (*A* 265, *B* 321, *N.K.S.*, p. 279). Force is the character by which the thing is present in space. By being effective (*wirkt*) it is actual (*wirklich*). The actuality (*Wirklichkeit*), the presence, the *Dasein* of the things, is determined from the force (*dynamis*), i.e., dynamically. For that reason Kant calls those principles of pure understanding which determine the possibility of the thing with respect to its *Dasein* the dynamical principles. Here, also, is to be noted what has been said regarding the designation "mathematical." These are not principles of dynamics as a discipline in physics, but metaphysical principles which first render possible the physical principles of dynamics. Not by accident does Hegel give the title "Force and Understanding" to an important section in the *Phenomenology of the Spirit*, in which he delimits the nature of the object as a thing of nature.

We find this twofold direction of the determination of natural bodies, the mathematical and the dynamical, clearly prefigured by Leibniz. (Compare Gerhardt, *op. cit.*, IV, 394 f.) But only Kant succeeded in demonstrating and explaining its inner unity in the system of principles of the pure understanding.

The principles contain those determinations of things

as appearances, which belong to them in advance, *a priori*, with reference to the possible forms of the unity of the understanding-like conjunctions, i.e., the categories. The table of categories is divided into four parts. This division corresponds to that of the principles. The mathematical and dynamical principles are each divided into two groups, the whole system into four:

(1) Axioms of intuition. (2) Anticipations of perception. (3) Analogies of experience. (4) Postulates of empirical thought in general. We shall attempt in the following to understand the titles of the principles from the exposition itself. Kant remarks expressly, "These titles I have intentionally chosen in order to give prominence to differences in the evidence and in the application of the principles." (*A* 161, *B* 200, *N.K.S.*, p. 196.) Under discussion are the principles of quantity, quality, relation, and modality.

The understanding of the principles is gained only by going through their demonstrations; for these demonstrations are nothing other than the exhibition of the "principles," the grounds upon which they are based and from whence they create what they themselves are. For this reason everything depends on these demonstrations. The formulas of the principles do not say much, especially since they are not self-evident. Therefore, Kant has put a great deal of effort into these demonstrations. He reworked them for the second edition, especially the first three groups. Each is constructed according to a definite schema, which corresponds to the essential contents of these principles. The wordings of the particular principles and, above all, their titles are also different in the first and second editions. These differences give important indications of the direction which Kant's intention to clarify takes, and how the real meaning of these principles is to be understood.

Once again we take everything in view in order to have

available hereafter the essentials of the positing and proof of the principles of pure understanding. The principles are "Principles of the Exposition" of appearances. They are the grounds upon whose basis the exposing of an object in its appearing is possible. They are the conditions for the objectivity of the object.

From what has now been said about the principles of pure understanding in general, we can already more clearly discern in what sense they are synthetic judgments *a priori* and how their possibility must be proved. Synthetic judgments are such that they extend our knowledge of the object. This generally happens in that we derive the predicate by way of perception from the object, *a posteriori*. But we are concerned now with predicates as determinations of the object, which belong to it *a priori*. These determinations are those from which and upon the ground of which it is first determined in general what belongs to an object as object, those determinations which bring together the determinations of the objectivity of the object. They must obviously be *a priori*; for only insofar as we know in general about objectivity are we able to experience this or that possible object. But how is it possible to determine the object as such in advance—before experience, and for it? This possibility is shown in the proofs of the principles. The respective proofs, however, accomplish nothing more than raising to light the ground of these principles themselves, which finally must be ever one and the same and which we then encounter in the highest principles of all synthetic judgments. Accordingly, the authentic principles of the pure understanding are those in which is expressed each time the principle (*Prinzip*) of the propositions (*Sätze*) of the four groups. Thus, the real principles (*Grundsätze*) are not the axioms, anticipations, analogies, and postulates themselves. The real principles are the *principles* of the axioms, anticipations, analogies, and postulates.

d. The Axioms of Intuition

Let us now notice the difference of the wording of *A* and *B* (*A* 162, *B* 202, *N.K.S.*, p. 197) already mentioned.

(*A*) "Principle of the pure understanding: All appearances are, in their intuition, extensive magnitudes."

(*B*) "Their principle is: All intuitions are extensive magnitudes."

The wording in *B* is not always more precise than in *A*. They supplement one another, and are therefore of special value, because this large domain, discovered by Kant, was still not as thoroughly clarified by him as he envisioned in the task of a system of transcendental philosophy. But for us who come after him, just the inconsistencies, the back and forth, the new starts, the envisioned still in process are more essential and fruitful than a smooth system wherein all the joints are filled and painted over.

Before we go through the process of proof for the first principle we ask what the discussion is about, i.e., concerning the "elements" (*Bestandstücke*). We know that it deals with the determination of the essence of the object. The ob-ject (*Gegen-stand*) is determined by intuition and thought. The object is the thing insofar as it appears. The object is appearance. Appearance never means semblance (*Schein*) here, but the object itself in its being present and standing there (*Dastehen*). In the same place in which, at the beginning of the *Critique of Pure Reason*, Kant names the two elements of knowledge, intuition and thought, he also characterizes appearance. "That in the appearance which corresponds to sensation I term its *matter;* but that which so determines the manifold of appearance that it allows of being ordered in certain relations, I term the *form* of appearance." (*A* 20, *B* 34, *N.K.S.*, p. 65.) Form is the wherein (*Worinnen*) of the order of colors, sounds, etc.

d₁. *Quantum* and *Quantitas*

The first principle concerns appearances "with respect to their intuition," thus with the object in regard to its "against" (*gegen*), the encountering, the coming-before-us (*Vor-uns-kommen*). In this respect it is said that appearances as intuitions are extensive magnitudes.

What do "magnitude" and "extensive magnitude" mean? The German expression *"Grösse"* is equivocal in general and especially in relation to Kant. For this reason Kant likes to add distinguishing Latin expressions in parentheses, or he often uses only the Latin in order to tie down the distinction which he was first to posit clearly. We find at the end of one paragraph and at the beginning of the one following the two labels for magnitude (*Grösse*) (*A* 163 f., *B* 204, *N.K.S.*, p. 199): magnitude as *quantum* and magnitude as *quantitas*. Magnitude as *quantitas* (Cf. *Reflex.* 6338a, Akademie ed., *op. cit.*, XVIII, 659 ff.) answers the question "How big?" It is the measure, the how much of a unity taken many times. The magnitude of a room is so and so many meters long, wide, and high. However, this magnitude of the room is only possible because the room as spatial at all, is an up, down, back, front, and beside; it is a *quantum*. By this Kant understands what we can call sizable (*Grosshafte*) at all. On the other hand, magnitude as *quantitas* is the measure and measurement of the sizable. At any given time it is a determinate unity in which the parts precede and compose the whole. In contrast, in magnitude as *quantum*, in the sizable, the whole is before the parts. It is indefinite in regard to the aggregate (*Menge*) of parts and in itself continuous. *Quantitas* is always *quantum discretum*. It is possible only through a subsequent division and a corresponding combination (synthesis) within and upon the ground of the *quantum*. This latter, however, never becomes what it is only through a synthesis. Magnitude as *quantitas* is always something that can be compared, because determined by so and so many parts, while the spatial (*Raumhaftes*)—disregarding *quantitas*—is always in itself the same.

Magnitude as *quantitas* always has to do with the generation of magnitudes. If this happens in the progress from parts to parts to the whole through successive piecing together of the separated parts, then the magnitude (*quantitas*) is an extensive one. "The magnitude of the amount (aggregate) is extensive." (*Reflex.* 5887, cf. 5891.)

Magnitude as *quantitas* is always the unity of a repeated positing. The representation of such a unity contains at first only what the understanding in such a repeated positing "does for itself"; there "is nothing contained therein which calls for sensory perception." (*Reflex.* 6338a.) Quantity is a pure conception of the understanding. But this is not true of magnitude as *quantum;* it is not produced through a positing but is simply *given* for an intuiting.

d₂. Space and time as *Quanta,* as forms of pure intuition

What does it mean that appearances as intuitions are extensive magnitudes? It is evident from the comparative definitions of magnitude as *quantitas* and as *quantum* that *quantitas* always presupposes *quantum,* that magnitude as measurement, as so much, must always be a measurement of something sizable. Accordingly, appearances as intuitions (i.e., intuitions as such) must be *quanta,* sizable, if they are to be quantities at all. According to Kant, however, space and time are of such a nature (*quanta*). That space is a magnitude does not mean that it is something so and so big. Space is at first precisely never so and so big, but it is what first makes possible magnitude in the sense of *quantitas.* Space is not composed of spaces. It does not consist of parts, but each space is simply a limitation of the whole of space, and in such a way that even the bounds and border presuppose space and spatial extension, and remain in space, just as the part of space remains in space. Space is a magnitude (*quantum*) in which the finite, measurably-determined parts and combinations always come too late, where the finite of this sort simply has no right and achieves nothing for the definition of its essence. For this reason, space is called an "infinite magnitude" (*A* 25, *N.K.S.*, p. 69). This does not mean "endless" with respect to finite determinations as *quantitas*, but as *quantum*, which presupposes nothing end-like as its condition. Rather, on the contrary, it is itself the condition of every division and finite partitioning.

Space and time are equally *quanta continua*, basically sizable, in-finite magnitudes and, consequently, possible extensive magnitudes (quantities). The principle of the axioms of intuition reads: "All appearances are, in their intuition, extensive magnitudes." (*A* 162, *N.K.S.*, p. 197.) But how can intuitions be extensive magnitudes? For this they must be basically sizables (*quanta*). Kant rightly calls space and time such. But space and time still are not intuitions; they are space and time.

Earlier we defined intuition as the immediate representing of a particular. Something is given to us through this representing. Intuition is a giving representing, not a making one, or one which first forms something through combining. Intuition (*Anschauung*) in the sense of something looked at (*Angeschaut*)[33] is the represented, in the sense of a given. In the spot where Kant defines space as an in-finite magnitude, he says, however, "Space is represented as an infinite given magnitude" (*A* 25, *N.K.S.*, p. 69), and "Space is represented as an infinite *given* magnitude" (*B* 40, *N.K.S.*, p. 69). The representing which brings space as such before us is a giving representation,

---

[33] In interpreting both Kant and Heidegger it is helpful to recall that the Latin and English "intuition" is the usual translation of the ordinary German word "looking at" (*Anschauung*). *Trans.*

i.e., an intuition. Space itself is something one looks at and in this sense is intuition (*Anschauung*). Space is immediately given. Where is it given? Is space anywhere at all? Is it not rather the condition of the possibility of every "where" and "there" and "here"? One spatial characteristic is, for example, proximity (*Nebeneinander*). However, we do not acquire this "beside" (*neben*) by first comparing objects lying beside one another. In order to experience these objects as beside one another, we must already immediately represent the beside, and, similarly, the before, behind, and above, one another. These extensions do not depend upon appearances, upon what shows itself, since we can imagine all objects omitted from space, but not space itself. In all cases of things showing themselves in perception, space as a whole is represented in advance necessarily and as immediately given. But this one, general given, this represented, is not a concept, is not something represented in general such as "a tree in general." The general representation "tree" contains all individual trees *under* it as that of which it is assertable. Space, however, contains all particular spaces *in* itself. Particular spaces are simply respective limitations of the one originally single space as an only one. Space as *quantum* is immediately given as a single "this." To immediately represent a particular is called intuiting (*anschauen*). Space is something intuited, and it is something intuited and standing in view in advance of all appearing of objects in it. Space is not apprehended through sensation, it is something intuited in advance—*a priori*—i.e., purely. Space is pure intuition. As this purely intuited it is what determines in advance everything empirically given, sensibly intuited, as the "wherein" in which the "manifold can be ordered." Kant also calls it form, that which determines, in contrast to matter, which is the determinable. Seen in this way, space is the pure form of sensible intuition, specifically that of the external sense. In order that certain sensations might be referable to something outside of me (i.e., to something in another place in space other than the one in which I find myself), this extension of the outside and the out-to (*Hinaus-zu*) must already be given.

Space, according to Kant, is neither a thing that is itself present at hand (*an sich vorhandenes Ding*) (Newton), nor a manifold of relationships which result from the relations of things that are themselves present at hand (*an sich vorhandene Dinge*) (Leibniz). Space is the single whole of beside one another, behind and over one another, which is immediately represented in advance in our receiving what encounters. Space is only the form of all appearance of the outer senses; i.e., a way in which we take in what encounters us. It is thus a determination of our sensibility. "It is, therefore, solely from the human standpoint that we can speak of space, of extended things, etc. If we depart from the subjective condition under which alone we can have outer intuition . . . the representation of space stands for nothing whatsoever." (*A* 26, *B* 42, *N.K.S.*, p. 71.)

The corresponding holds good for time. With this general clarification of the nature of space we have been trying only to make understandable what it means when Kant defines space as a *pure intuition* and thereby wants to have achieved the metaphysical concept of space as such. For it seems strange at first how anything at all is delimited by being characterized as an intuition. Trees, desks, houses, and men are also intuited. But the essence of the house consists in no way in being an intuition. The house is intuited insofar as it encounters us. But being a house does not mean being intuited. Nor would Kant ever define the essence of the house in such a way. But what is right for the house should also be fair for space. This would certainly be true if space were a thing of the same sort as a house, a thing in space. But space is not in space.

Kant does not say simply: Space is intuition, but "pure intuition" and "form of external intuition." Also, intuiting is and remains a mode of pre-senting (*Vor-stellen*) something, a way of approach to something and a kind of givenness of something, but not this something itself.

Only if the way in which something is given constitutes this something in its "being" would a characterization of something as intuition become possible and even necessary. Space, taken as intuition, then means not only that space is given in such a way, but that being space consists in such a being given. Indeed, Kant *so* means it. The spatial being of space consists in the fact that it places space (*einräumt*) into what shows itself (*das sich Zeigenden*), the possibility of showing itself in its extension (*Ausbreitung*). Space places space (*räumt ein*) by giving position and place, and this placing into is its being. Kant expresses this placing by saying that space is what is purely intuited, what shows itself in advance, before all and for all; and as such it is the form of intuition. Being-intuited (*Angeschautsein*) is the space-placing spatial being of space. We do not know of any other being of space. Neither do we have any possibility of inquiring after such. Undeniably, there are difficulties in Kant's metaphysics of space—entirely disregarding the fact that a metaphysics that no longer contains any difficulties has already ceased to be one. Only the difficulties of the Kantian interpretation of space do not lie where most people like to find them, be it from the standpoint of psychology or from the standpoint of mathematical natural science (theory of relativity). The chief difficulty lies not in the formulation of the problem of space itself, but in attributing space as pure intuition to a human subject, whose being is insufficiently defined. (On how the problem of space is constructed out of a fundamental overcoming of the relationship to the subject, compare *SZ* §§ 19–24 and §70.)

It is now important for us to show only how space and time are at all conceivable as intuitions. Space gives itself only in this pure intuiting, wherein space as such is held-before (*vor-gehalten*) us in advance and is pre-sented as something capable of being viewed (*Anblickbares*), something "pre-formed" (*vor-gebildet*) as that sizable character of the beside one another and over or behind one another, a manifoldness which gives out of itself the possibility of its own delimitations and boundaries.

Space and time are pure intuitions. Intuition is dealt with in the "Aesthetic." Intuition, accordingly, is what belongs *a priori* to the objectivity of the object, what allows appearances to show themselves; pure intuition is *transcendental*. The transcendental aesthetic gives us only a preliminary view. Its real thematics reaches its goal only in the treatment of the first principle.

d₃. The proof of the first principle. All principles are based on the highest principle of all synthetic judgments

With what has been said the essentials have been prepared for our understanding of the proof of the first principle and the principle itself. The proof consists of three propositions which are clearly distinguished from each other. The first proposition begins with "All," the second with "Now is" and the third with "Thus." (*A* 162, *B* 203, *N.K.S.*, pp. 197 f.)[34] Unmistakably these three prop-

---

[34] Full text of proof from Kemp Smith's translation (pp. 197 f.): "(All) appearances, in their formal aspect, contain an intuition in space and time, which conditions them, one and all, *a priori*. They cannot be apprehended, that is, taken up into empirical consciousness, save through that synthesis of the manifold whereby the representations of a determinate space or time are generated, that is, through combination of the homogeneous manifold and consciousness of its synthetic unity. (Now) consciousness of the synthetic unity of the manifold [and] homogeneous in intuition in general, insofar as the representation of an object first becomes possible by means of it, is, however, the concept of magnitude *(quantum)*. (Thus) even the perception of an object, as appearance, is only possible through the same synthetic unity of the manifold of the given sensible intuition as that whereby the unity of the combination of the manifold [and] homogeneous is thought in the concept of a *magnitude*. In other words, appearances are all without exception *magnitudes*, indeed, *extensive magnitudes*. As intuitions in space or time, they must be represented through the same synthesis whereby space and time in general are determined." We have added (All), (Now), and parentheses around "Thus" to correspond to Heidegger's reference. *Trans.*

ositions are connected in the form of a syllogism: major premise, minor premise, and conclusion. Each of the following proofs is constructed in this way—the proofs for the anticipations and analogies—which, as is true of the proofs of the axioms, are found only in the second edition.

We carry out the three steps of the deduction by clarifying what is still unclear in each proposition.

The proof begins by indicating that all appearances show themselves in space and time. With regard to the manner of their appearing, in regard to their form, they contain an intuition of the kind mentioned. What does this mean in regard to the objective character of appearances? We say, "The moon is in the sky." According to its sensible and perceptual givenness it is something shining, colored, with variously distributed brightness and darkness. It is given outside us, there, in this definite form, of this magnitude, at this distance from other heavenly bodies. The space—the wherein of the givenness of the moon—is limited and bounded to this shape, of this magnitude, in these relationships and distances. Space is a determined space, and only this determination constitutes the space of the moon, the spatiality of the moon. Being determined to this shape, this extension, this distance from others, is grounded in a determining. The determining is an ordered putting in connection, a lifting out of particular extensional parts which are themselves homogeneous in their parts, for instance the parts of the circumference of the shape. Only as the manifoldness of an in itself indefinite space is divided into parts and is put together out of these parts in a particular sequence and with determined limits can the bright-colored show itself to us as moon-shape with this magnitude and distance, i.e., become received and taken up by us in the domain of what always already encounters us and stands-over-against-us (*Gegen-uns-stehenden*).

That which appears, according to its intuition and the form of its intuitedness, that is, with respect to space and its prior undifferentiated manifoldness, is a such and such determined one: a composed homogeneity. This compositeness, however, is so only on the ground of a unity of the shape represented therein in such and such a way, i.e., the magnitude. Unity governs in the synthesis and regulates the representation and consciousness of it. With this we have set in relief the essential content of the major premise. The minor premise begins with what was last said, i.e., with the consciousness of the synthetic unity of the manifold (*B* 203, *N.K.S.*, p. 198).

"Consciousness of the synthetic unity of the manifold [and] homogeneous in intuition in general, insofar as the representation of an object first becomes possible by means of it, is, however, the concept of a magnitude (*quanti*)." Here it is stated through what the unity of something manifold becomes possible at all. Let us begin with what is manifold and homogeneous itself. Homogeneity is the consequence of serializing and connecting of the many equal ones into one, a result of multiplicity without differences. The unity of such is always a "so and so much," i.e., quantity as such. Unity as such of a multiplicity as such is the governing notion of connecting (*Verbinden*), of an "I think," a pure concept of the understanding. But insofar as this concept of the understanding, "unity," as the rule of unification, refers to something sizable, to *quantum* as such, it is the concept of a *quanti*. This concept, quantity, brings what is homogeneous and manifold to a stand in a unified collectedness (*Gesammeltheit*). By this means the representation of an object, the "I think" and the over-against for the I, first become possible. Now, as suggested in the major premise, insofar as appearances appear in the form of space and time the first determination of the encountering as such is this composite, shaped unification with respect to *quantitas*.

Now the conclusion follows with necessity: It is thus the same unity and unification which permit the encountering of the appearances as shaped, so and so big, in the separations of space and time, and which bring the homogeneous to a stand in the composition of quantities of a multiplicity (*Menge*). Therefore, appearances are from the beginning extensive magnitudes with respect to their intuition and the way of their encountering standing-against (*Gegenstehen*). The *quantum*, space, is always determined as these appearing spatial formations only in the synthesis of quantity. The same unity of quantity permits what encounters to stand-over-against (*entgegenstehen*) collectedly. With this the principle has been proved. However, thereby it is also established why all principles which say something about the pure manifoldness of extension (e.g., the shortest distance between two points is a straight line) as mathematical principles are valid for the appearances themselves, why mathematics is applicable to the objects of experience. This is not self-evident and is possible only under certain conditions. These are presented in the proof of the principle. Therefore, Kant calls this principle the "transcendental principle of the mathematics of appearances" (*A* 165, *B* 206, *N.K.S.*, p. 200). Under the title "Axioms of Intuition" these axioms are not themselves laid down or discussed. The principle is proved in that the ground of the objective truth of the axioms is posited, i.e., their ground as necessary conditions of the objectivity of objects. The applicability of the axioms of the mathematics of extension and number, and, therewith of mathematics as such, is necessarily justified, because the conditions of mathematics itself, those of *quantitas* and *quantum*, are at the same time the conditions of appearance of that to which mathematics is applied.

With this we hit upon that ground which makes possible this ground and all others, to which every proof of every principle of the pure understanding is referred. This is the connection which we now for the first time bring more clearly into view:

The condition of experiencing appearances (here with

regard to shape and size)—namely, the unity of the synthesis as quantity—this condition of experiencing is at the same time the condition of the possibility of an object of experience. In this unity the encountering manifoldness of the "against" (*Gegen*) first comes to a "stand" (*Stand*) —and is object (*Gegenstand*). The particular *quantitas* of spaces and times makes possible the reception of the encountering, the apprehension, the first permitting of a standing-against of the object (*das erste Gegenstehenlassen des Gegenstandes*). Our question about the thingness of the thing, about the objectivity of the object, is answered by the principle and its proof as follows: because objectivity as such is the unity of the collection of something manifold into a representation of unity, and is a conception in advance, and because what is manifold encounters in space and time, what encounters must itself stand against us in the unity of quantity as extensive magnitude.

Appearances must be extensive magnitudes. Thereby is asserted about the being of objects themselves something which does not already lie in the conception of something in general about which we assert in a judgment. With the determination of being an extensive magnitude something is synthetically attributed to the object; but it is attributed *a priori*, not on the ground of perceptions of single objects, but in advance, out of the essence of experience as such.

What is the hinge upon which the whole proof revolves, i.e., what is the ground upon which the principle itself rests? What is, therefore, primordially expressed by the highest principle itself and thus brought into the light?

What is the ground of the possibility of this principle as a synthetic judgment *a priori?* In it the pure concept of the understanding, quantity, is transferred to the *quantum* space, and so to the objects which appear in space. How can a pure concept of the understanding become determinant at all for something like space? These totally heterogeneous pieces must conform in some respect if they are to be united at all as determinable and determining, and it must be in such a way that there *is* an object by virtue of this unity of intuition and thought.

Because these questions repeat themselves in each of the principles and their proofs, they are not to be answered right now. We first want to see that these questions constantly and unavoidably return in the treatment of the principles. However, we do not wish to postpone the answer until the close of the exposition of the principles, but shall expound it after the discussion of the following principle, in the transition from the mathematical to the dynamical principles.

e. The Anticipations of Perception

The ground and inner possibility of the object is posited in the principles. The mathematical principles grasp the object with respect to the "against" and its inner possibility. Hence, the second principle as well as the first speaks of appearances with respect to their appearing. "The principle which anticipates all perceptions, as such, is as follows: In all appearances sensation, and the *real* which corresponds to it in the object (*realitas phaenomenon*), has an *intensive magnitude*, that is, a degree." (*A* 166, *N.K.S.*, p. 201.) "Their principle is:[35] *In all appearances, the real that is an object of sensation has intensive magnitude, that is, a degree.*" (*B* 207, *N.K.S.*, p. 201.)

Here appearances are taken in another respect than in the first principle. In the first principle appearances are considered as intuitions with respect to the form of space and time in which the encountered encounters. The principle of the "anticipations of perception" does not attend to the form, but to that which is determined through

[35] *N.K.S.* leaves out "Their principle is:" *Trans.*

the determining form. It is the determinable as matter of the form. Matter does not mean here the material stuff present at hand. Matter and form are understood as "concepts of reflection," and indeed as the most general ones which result from reflecting back (*Rückbesinnung*) on the structure of experience. (*A* 266 ff., *B* 322 ff., *N.K.S.*, p. 280.)[36]

In the proof of the "anticipations" the discussion is of sensations, of the real, and also again of magnitude, specifically of intensive magnitude. It is now not a question of axioms of *intuition*, but of basic aspects of *perception*, i.e., the sort of representing "in which sensation is to be found" (*B* 207, *N.K.S.*, p. 201).

e₁. The several meanings of the word "sensation"; the theory of sensation and modern natural science

In human cognition the cognizable must encounter and must be given, because what is, is something other than ourselves, and because we have not ourselves made or created what is. One does not first have to show a shoe to a shoemaker for him to know what a shoe is. He knows this without the encountering shoe, and knows it better and more exactly without this, because he can produce one. By contrast, what he cannot make must be presented to him from somewhere else. Since we human beings have not created what is as such as a whole and could never create it, it must be shown to us if we are to know of it.

In this showing of what is in its openness, that doing (*Tun*) has a special task which shows things by creating them in a certain sense, the creation of a work of art. Work makes world. World within itself first reveals things. The

---

[36] Heidegger refers here to the fourth section of the "Appendix: The Amphiboly of Concepts of Reflection: *'Matter* and *Form.'"* These two concepts underlie all other reflection, so inseparably are they bound up with all employment of the understanding. *Trans.*

possibility and necessity of the work of art is only *one* proof that we come to know what is, only when it is specially given to us.

However, this usually happens through encountering things in the realm of everyday experience. For this to occur, they must approach us, affect us, obtrude and intrude upon us. Thus occur impressions, sensations. Their manifoldness (*Mannigfaltigkeit*) is divided into the different areas of our senses: sight, hearing, etc. In sensation and its pressure we find that "which constitutes the distinctive difference between empirical and *a priori* knowledge" (*A* 167, *B* 208 f., *N.K.S.*, p. 202). The empirical is the *a posteriori*, that which is second, viewed from us—considering us as first. It is always subsequent and playing along side of us. The word "sensation," like the word "representation," has at first two senses: in one sense it means what is sensed—red as perceived, the sound, the red-sensation, the sound-sensation. It also means the sensing as a state of ourselves. Yet this differentiation is not its point (*Bewenden*). What is designated as "sensation" is for this reason so equivocal, because it occupies a peculiar intermediate position between the things and the human beings, between object and subject. The interpretation and explanation of the essence and role of sensation changes according to how we interpret what is objective and according to the conception of the subjective. Here let us only cite an interpretation which prevailed very early in Western thought and is not completely overcome even yet. The more one passed over to seeing things according to their mere appearance, their shape, position, and extension (Democritus and Plato), the more obtrusive in contrast to spatial relation became that which fills intervals and places, i.e., the sensory given. Consequently, the givens of sensations—color, sound, pressure, and impact —became the first and foremost building blocks out of which a thing is put together.

As soon as things were broken up into a manifold of the sensory givennesses, the interpretation of their uniform essence could proceed only by saying: Things are really only collections of sensory data. In addition they also have value and an aesthetic value, and—insofar as we know them—a truth value. Things are collections of sensations with values attached. In this view sensations are represented as something in themselves. They are themselves made into things, without first saying what that thing might be, through whose splitting the fragments (the sensations) remain as allegedly original.

But the next step is to interpret the fragment-things, the sensations, as effects of a cause. Physics establishes that the cause of color is light waves, endless periodic undulations in the ether. Each color has its determined number of vibrations per second. For example, red has the wave length of 760 $\mu\mu$ and 400 billion vibrations per second. That *is* red. This is the objective red in contrast to the mere subjective impression of the red sensation. It would be even nicer if we could trace the red sensation back to a stimulation of electric currents in the nerve pathways. When we get that far we know what things are objectively.

Such an explanation of sensation appears to be very scientific, and yet it is not, insofar as the domain of the givenness of sensations and what is to be explained, i.e., color as given, has at the same time been abandoned. Besides, it goes unnoticed that there is still a difference, whether we mean by color the determinate color of a thing, this red on the thing, or the red sensation as given in the eye. This last-mentioned givenness is not given immediately. A very complicated and artful focus is necessary to grasp the color sensation as such in contrast to the color of the thing. If we observe—apart from any theory of knowledge—the givenness of the color of the thing, e.g., the green of a leaf, we do not find the slightest cause which might produce an effect on us. We are never aware of the green of the leaf as an effect on us, but as the green of the leaf.

Where, however, the thing and the body are represented as extended and resisting things, as in modern mathematical physics, the viewable manifold sinks to one of sensory givennesses. Today the given for experimental atomic physics is only a manifold of light spots and streaks on a photographic plate. Now fewer presuppositions are necessary for the interpretation of this given than for the interpretation of a poem. It is only the solidity and tangibility of the measuring apparatus which gives rise to the appearance that this interpretation stands on firmer ground than the allegedly subjective basis of the interpretations of poets in the arts.

Fortunately, there first still exists (apart from the light waves and nerve currents) the coloring and shine of things themselves, the green of the leaf and the yellow of the grain field, the black of the crow and the gray of the sky. The reference to all that is not only also here, but must be constantly presupposed as that which the physiological-physical inquiry breaks up and reinterprets.

The question arises as to what more truly is (*was ist seiender*), that crude chair with the tobacco pipe depicted in the painting by Van Gogh, or the waves which correspond to the colors used in the painting, or the states of sensation which we have "in us" while looking at the picture? The sensations play a role each time, but each time in a different sense. The color of the thing is, for instance, something different from the stimulus given in the eye, which we never grasp immediately as such. The color of the thing belongs to the thing. Neither does it give itself to us as a cause of a state in us. The thing's color itself, the yellow, for instance, is simply this yellow as belonging to the field of grain. The color and its bright hue are always determined by the original unity and kind of the colored thing itself. This is not first composed of sensations.

The reference serves only to make it clear to us that it is not immediately clear what is meant by sensation. The undelimited ambiguity of the word and the uncontrolled diversity of the fact intended only reflect the uncertainty and bafflement which prevent a conclusive definition of the relation between man and thing.

Furthermore, the opinion reigns that the comprehension of things as a mere manifold of sensory givens is the presupposition for the mathematical-physical definition of bodies. The theory of knowledge according to which knowledge essentially consists of sensations is held to be the reason for the rise of modern natural science. But the contrary is really the case. The mathematical starting point concerning the thing as something extended and movable in space and time leads to the consequence that the usual everyday given (*das umgänglich alltäglich Gegebene*) is apprehended as mere material (*als blosses Material*) and is fragmented into the manifoldness of the sensations. Only the mathematical starting point effected a favorable hearing for a corresponding theory of sensation. Kant also remains at the level of this starting point. Like the tradition before and after him, he skips that sphere of things in which we know ourselves immediately at home, i.e., things as the artist depicts them for us, such as Van Gogh's simple chair with the tobacco pipe which was just put down or forgotten there.

e_2. Kant's concept of reality; intensive magnitudes

Although Kant's critique remains from the beginning within the sphere of the experience of the object of mathematical-physical natural knowledge, his metaphysical interpretation of the givenness of sensations differs from all before and after him, i.e., it is superior to all of them. The interpretation of the objectivity of the object in regard to the sensory given in it is carried out by Kant in the positing and proof of the principle of the anticipations of perception. It is characteristic of the usual interpretations of Kant that they have either overlooked this section altogether or misunderstood it in every respect. The proof of this is the bafflement with which a fundamental concept is manhandled, which plays an essential role in the principle. We are referring to the concept of the *real* and of *reality*.

The clarification of this concept and of its application by Kant belongs to the first elementary course in the introduction to the *Critique of Pure Reason*. The expression "reality" is usually used today in the sense of actuality or existence. Thus one speaks of the question of the reality of the external world and one means by this the discussion whether something really and truly exists outside of our consciousness. To think *Realpolitisch* means reckoning with the actually existing situations and circumstances. Realism in art is the mode of representation in which one copies only what is actual and what one takes to be actual. We have to drop the currently familiar meaning of "reality" in the sense of actuality in order to understand what Kant means by the real in appearance. This meaning of "reality" current today, moreover, corresponds neither with the original meaning of the word nor the initial use of the term in medieval and modern philosophy up to Kant. Instead, the present use has presumably come about through a failure to understand and through a misunderstanding of Kant's usage.

Reality comes from *realitas*. *Realis* is what belongs to *res*. That means a something (*Sache*). That is real which belongs to something, what belongs to the what-content (*Wasgehalt*) of a thing, e.g., to what constitutes a house or tree, what belongs to the essence of something, to the *essentia*. Reality sometimes means the totality of this definition of its essence or it means particular defining elements. Thus, for example, extension is a reality of a natural body as well as weight, density, resistance. All such is real, belongs to the *res*, to the something "natural body," regardless of whether the body actually exists or not. For instance, materiality (*Stofflichkeit*) belongs to the reality of a table. For this the table does not need to be real in the present-day sense of "real." Actual being or existence is something which must first be added to the essence, and in this regard *existentia* itself was considered a reality. Only Kant first demonstrated that actuality, being present-at-hand, is not a real predicate of a thing; that is, a hundred possible dollars do not in the least differ from a hundred real dollars according to their *reality*. It is the same, one hundred dollars, the same what (*Was*), *res*, whether possible or actual.

We distinguish actuality from possibility and necessity. Kant unites all three categories under the title of modality. From the fact that "reality" is *not* found in this group, we can see that reality does not mean actuality. To which group does *reality* belong? What is its most general sense? It is *quality*—*quale*—a so and so, a that and that, a *what*. "Reality" as thinghood (*Sachheit*) answers the question of *what* a thing is and not whether it exists. (*A* 143, *B* 182, *N.K.S.*, p. 184.) The real, that which constitutes the *res*, is a determination of *res* as such. Pre-Kantian metaphysics explains the concept of reality in this way. In Kant's use of the metaphysical concept of reality, he follows the textbook of Baumgarten in which the tradition of medieval and modern metaphysics is discussed after the manner of the classroom.

The fundamental character of *realitas* according to Baumgarten is *determinatio*, determinateness. Extension and materiality are realities, i.e., determinations which belong to the *res*, "body." Viewed more exactly, *realitas* is a *determinatio positiva et vera*, a determinateness belonging to the true essence of something, and posited as such. The opposite concept is a what which does not determine a thing positively, but in regard to what is missing in it. Thus blindness is a privation (*Fehlen*) which is lacking in what is seeing. However, blindness, obviously, is not nothing. While it is not a positive determination, it is a negative one, i.e., a "negation." Negation is the concept opposite to reality.

Kant gives a new critical interpretation to *realitas*, as he does to all the fundamental concepts he takes from traditional metaphysics. Objects are the things as they appear. Appearances always bring something (a what) to a showing of itself. What thereby presses and attacks us and approaches us, this first what and thinglike (*Sachhafte*) is called "*the real*" in appearance. "*Aliquid sive obiectum qualificatum* is the occupation of space and time." (Akademie edition, *op. cit.*, XVIII n. 6338a, p. 663.) The real in appearances, the *realitas phaenomenon* (*A* 168, *B* 209) is that which, as the first what-content (*Wasgehalt*), must occupy the void of space and time, in order for anything to appear at all, so that appearance and the press of an against (*eines Gegen*) become possible.

The real in the appearance, in Kant's sense, is not what is actually in the appearance as contrasted with what is inactual in it and could be mere semblance and illusion (*Schein und Dunst*). The real is that which must be given at all, so that something can be decided with respect to its actuality or inactuality. The real is the pure and first necessary *what* as such. Without the real, the something, the object is not only inactual, it is nothing at all, i.e., without a *what*, according to which it can determine itself as this or that. In this *what*, the real, the object qualifies itself as encountering thus and so. The real is the first *quale* of the object.

Along with this critical concept of reality Kant also uses the term in the traditionally wider sense for each thinghood, which co-determines the essence of the thing, the thing as an object. Accordingly, we frequently meet with the expression "objective reality," precisely in a fundamental inquiry of the *Critique of Pure Reason*. This twist has induced and promoted the epistemological misunderstanding of the *Critique of Pure Reason*. The term "objective reality" was explained in our discussion of the first principle. Here it is a question as to whether and how the pure concepts of the understanding, which, although not taken empirically from the object, at the same time belong to the content of the object; for example, whether quantity actually has objective reality. This question is not whether quantity is actually present-at-hand, or whether something outside consciousness corresponds to it. Rather it is asked whether and why quantity belongs to the object as object. Space and time have "empirical reality."

Besides sensation and the real, the discussion in the second principle is about intensive magnitude. The distinction in the concept of magnitude between *quantum* and *quantitas* has already been discussed. If we speak about extensive magnitude, then magnitude is called *quantitas*, the measure of size (*Grössenmass*), and specifically that of an aggregate added piece by piece. The intensive, the *intensio*, is nothing else than the *quantitas* of a *qualitas*, or a real, e.g., the moon's shining surface. We apprehend the extensive magnitude of the object when we measure its spatial extension step by step. Its intensive magnitude, on the other hand, we apprehend when we do not attend to the extensive size, nor pay attention to the surface as surface, but the pure *what* of its shining, the "how great" of the shining, of the coloring. The *quantitas* of the *qualitas* is the intensity. Every magnitude as *quantitas* is the unity of a multiplicity; but extensive and intensive magnitude are this in different ways. In extensive magnitudes the unity is always apprehended only on the grounds of, and in the gathering together of, the many immediately posited parts. In contrast, intensive magnitude is immediately taken as a unity. The multiplicity which belongs to the intensity can be represented in it only in such a way that an intensity of negation down to zero is approached. The multiplicities of this unity do not lie spread out in it in such a way that this spreading yields a unity by adding together the many stretches and pieces. The single multiplicities of the intensive magnitude stem, rather, from the limitation of the unity of a *quale;* each of them, again, is a *quale,* they are many unities. Such unities are called degrees. A loud tone, for instance, is not composed of a determined number of these tones, but there is a gradation by degrees from soft to loud. The multiplicities of the unity of an intensity are many unities. The multiplicities of the unity of an extension are single units of a multiplicity. Both intensity and extension, however, permit themselves to be ordered as numerical quantities. But the degrees and steps of intensity do not thereby become a mere aggregate of parts.

e_3. Sensation in Kant, understood transcendentally; Proof of the second principle

Now we understand the principle in its general content: "The principle which anticipates all perceptions, as such, is as follows: In all appearances sensation, and the *real* which corresponds to it in the object (*realitas phaenomenon*), has an *intensive magnitude,* that is, a degree." (*A* 166, *N.K.S.,* p. 201.) In *B* 207 (*N.K.S.,* p. 201) this principle reads: "In all appearances, the real that is an object of sensation has intensive magnitude, that is, a degree."

We first grasp this principle, however, only on the basis of the proof which demonstrates wherein—as a principle of pure understanding—this principle grounds. The steps of proof are at the same time the interpretation of the principle. Only by mastering the proof shall we be in a position to evaluate the difference between versions *A* and *B* and decide about the superiority of the one over the other. It remains noteworthy that the principle says something about sensations, not on the basis of a psychological empirical description or even a physiological explanation of its formation and origin, but by way of a transcendental consideration. This means that sensation is taken in advance as something which comes into play within the relationship of a stepping over to the object and in the determination of its objectivity. The essence of sensation is delimited through its role within the transcendental relationship.

In this way Kant wins a different fundamental position within the inquiry about sensation and its function in the appearance of things. Sensation is not a thing for which causes are sought, but a given whose givenness is to be made understandable through the conditions of the possibility of experience.

These same circumstances also explain the designation of these principles as anticipations of perception.

The proof has the same form again even though the major and minor premises and conclusion are spread out over more sentences. The minor premise begins (*B* 208): "Now from empirical consciousness to pure . . ."; the *transition* to the conclusion begins: "Since, however, sensation is not in itself . . ."; the conclusion: "Its magnitude is not extensive. . . ."[37]

We will try to build up the proof in a simplified form so that the joints show up more distinctly. Since we have already conveyed the essential definitions of "sensation,"

---

[37] "Now from empirical consciousness to pure consciousness a graduated transition is possible, the real in the former completely vanishing and a merely formal *a priori* consciousness of the manifold in space and time remaining. Consequently there is also possible a synthesis in the process of generating the magnitude of a sensation from its beginning in pure intuition equals zero, up to any required magnitude. Since, however, sensation is not in itself an objective representation, and since neither the intuition of space nor that of time is to be met with in it, its magnitude is not extensive but *intensive*. This magnitude is generated in the act of apprehension whereby the empirical consciousness of it can in a certain time increase from nothing equals zero to the given measure. Corresponding to this intensity of sensation, an *intensive magnitude*, that is, a degree of influence on the senses (i.e., on the special sense involved), must be ascribed to all objects of perception, insofar as the perception contains sensation." (*B* 208, *N.K.S.*, pp. 201 f.) *Trans.*

"reality," and "intensive magnitude," no difficulty remains as to content. First we may be reminded again of the *probandum* of the proof. It is to be demonstrated that the pure concept of the understanding (here the category of quality) determines appearances in advance with respect to their *what*, their encountering aspect, that as a consequence of this quality of appearances a quantity (in the sense of intensity) is possible, thus warranting the application of number and mathematics. With this proof it is also demonstrated that an against cannot encounter at all without the presentation (*Vorhalt*) of a *what*, so that in any receiving there must already lie an anticipation of a what.

Major premise: All appearances in addition to the space-time determinations contain, as what shows itself in perception, that which makes an impression (Kant calls this the matter), what affects us, lies exposed and occupies the space-time domain.

Transition: Such an ex-posing and a present given (*Auf- und Vorliegendes*) (*positum*) can be perceivable as so lying before and occupying only by being represented in advance in the light of a *what-character*, in the opened range of the real in general. Only upon the open background of the *what*-like can sensibles become sensations. Such a reception of the what as it encounters is "momentary" (*augenblicklich*) and does not rest upon a consequence of an apprehension that puts together. The awareness of the real is a simple having-there (*Da-haben*), allowing it to be posited; it is the *positio* of a *positum*.

Minor premise: It is possible that in this open field of the real what occupies a place alternates between the extremity of full pressure and the void of the space-time domain. With respect to this range of the pressure there is in sensation a sizable that does not piece together an increasing aggregate, but always concerns the same *quale*, yet always of a varying so-large.

Transition: The how-large, the quantity of a *quale*, i.e., of something real, is, however, a definite degree of the same *what*. The magnitude of the real is an intensive magnitude.

Conclusion: Consequently what affects us in appearance, the sensible as real, has a degree. Insofar as the degree as quantity may be determined in number, and number is a positing in accord with the understanding of "how many times one," therefore what is sensed as an encountering *what* can be brought to a stand mathematically.

Therewith the principle has been proven. According to *B* 207 (*N.K.S.*, p. 201): "*In all appearances, the real that is an object of sensation has intensive magnitude,* that is, a degree." More exactly, the proposition ought to read: In all appearances, the real, which constitutes the constancy and the against-like (*das Gegenhafte-Ständige*) of sensations. . . . The proposition by no means asserts that the real has a degree because it is an object of sensation. Rather, because the impressing *what* of sensation is a reality for the representing which allows the standing against (*Entgegenstehenlassen*) and since the quantity of a reality is but the intensity, therefore sensation (as the something [*Sachheit*] of the object) has the objective character of an intensive magnitude.

On the other hand, the wording of the principle in *A* is subject to misunderstanding and nearly contrary to what is really meant. It suggests the misconception that sensation has, first of all, a degree and then in addition the reality which corresponds to it, differing from it in its thingness and standing behind it. But, the principle wants to assert that the real has first and properly as *quale* a quantity of degree—and therefore also does sensation, whose objective intensity rests upon the prior givenness of the reality character of what can be sensed. The wording of *A* is, therefore, to be modified in the following way: "In all appearances sensation, and that means first the real, which lets the sensation show itself *as* an objectivity, has an intensive magnitude."

It seems as though we have arbitrarily changed Kant's

text here. However, the different wordings of *A* and *B* demonstrate how much effort Kant himself expended to force his novel insight on the transcendental nature of sensation into the understandable form of a proposition.

e_4. What is strange about the anticipations. Reality and sensation

Just how new the principle was for Kant himself we easily recognize from the fact that he constantly wondered at the strangeness which the principle expresses. And what can be stranger than this, that even where we are dealing with such things as sensations, which assail us, which we only receive, that just in this "toward us" (*auf uns zu*) a reaching out and an anticipation by us is possible and necessary? At first glance, perception as pure reception and anticipation as a reaching and grasping beforehand (*entgegen-fassendes Vorgreifen*) are thoroughly contradictory. And yet it is only in the light of the reaching and anticipating presentation of reality that sensation becomes a receivable, encountering this and that.

On the one hand we believe that to sense or perceive something is the most ordinary and simplest thing in the world. We are sentient beings. Certainly! But no human being has ever sensed a "something" or a "what" alone. Through what sense organ could this ever take place? A "something" is neither seen, heard, smelled, tasted, nor felt. There is no sense organ for a "what" or for a "this" and "that." The *what*-character of what can be sensed must be pre-sented beforehand and anticipated in advance within the scope and as the scope of what can be received. Without reality there is no real; without a real, no sensibles. Since such an anticipating beforehand can be assumed least in the domain of receiving and perceiving, and to make this strangeness recognizable, Kant gives the name "anticipation" to the principle of perception. Seen in general, all principles in which the predetermination of the object is expressed are anticipations. Sometimes Kant uses this term alone in the wider sense.

Human perception is anticipating. An animal, too, has perceptions, i.e., sensations, but it does not anticipate. It does not permit the impressing to encounter in advance as a *what* that stands in itself, as the other which stands toward the animal as an other and thus shows itself as existing. Kant remarks in another place (*Religion Within the Limits of Reason Alone*) that no beast can ever say "I." This means that it cannot bring itself into a standpoint as that against which an objective other could stand. It must not be inferred from this that the animal has no relation to food, light, air, and other animals, and even in a very orderly fashion—we need only recall how animals play. But in all this there is no attitude toward what is any more than there is toward what is not. Their lives run their course on this side of the openness of being and nonbeing, though at this point the far-reaching question may arise as to how we know what is happening in the animal and what is not. We can never know it immediately, although mediately we can gain metaphysical certainty about being an animal.

Anticipation of the real in perception is strange not only by comparison with animals but equally in comparison with the traditional conception of knowledge. We are reminded of the "in advance" (*im vorhinein*) which at an earlier occasion was cited in the distinction between analytic and synthetic judgments. The synthetic judgment has the peculiarity that it must step out of the subject-predicate relationship to something wholly other, to the object. The first fundamental grasping-out (*Hinausgriff*) by representation in the direction of the having-there (*Dahaben*) an encountering "what" as such is the anticipation of the real, that synthesis, provision, in which a what sphere is represented at all, from which appearances are to be able to show themselves. Therefore, Kant says in the concluding sentence of his treatment of the anticipations

of perception: "But the real, which corresponds to sensations in general, as opposed to negation = 0, represents
only that something the very concept of which includes
being [i.e., presence of something][38] and signifies nothing
but the synthesis in an empirical consciousness in general." (A 175 f., B 217, N.K.S., p. 208.)

The anticipating representation of reality opens our
viewing for any being-what (*Was-seiendes*) in general
(here this means "being") and thus forms the relation
on the basis of which the empirical consciousness is at all
consciousness of something. The *what* in general is the
"transcendental matter" (A 143, B 182, N.K.S., pp. 183 f.)
the *what* which belongs in advance to the possibility of
an againstness (*Gegenhaften*) in the object.

Psychology may describe sensations in whatever ways;
physiology and neurology may explain sensations as
processes of stimulation, or however; physics may demonstrate the causes of sensations in ether waves and electric waves—all these are possible sorts of knowledge. But
they do concern the question of the objectivity of objects
and of our immediate relationship to these. Kant's discovery of the anticipations of the real in perception is especially astonishing if one considers that, on the one hand,
his esteem of Newtonian physics and, on the other, his
fundamental position in Descartes' concept of the subject
are not suited to promote the free view of this unusual
anticipation in the receptivity of perception.

e₅. Mathematical principles and the highest principle.
The circularity of the proofs

If we now take together both principles in a shortened
form, we can say that all appearances are extensive magnitudes as intuitions, and they are intensive magnitudes
as sensations: quantities. Such are possible only in

---

[38] Heidegger's interpolation. *Trans.*

quanta. All *quanta*, however, are *continua*. They have the feature that no separable part of them is ever the smallest possible. Therefore, all appearances, in the *what* of their encountering and in the *how* of their appearing, are constant. This character of appearances, the constancy, which concerns its extension as well as its intensity, is discussed by Kant in the section concerning the second principle for both principles together (*A* 169 ff., *B* 211 ff., *N.K.S.*, pp. 203 ff.). Thereby the axioms of intuition and anticipations are united together as mathematical principles, i.e., as those which metaphysically establish the possibility of an application of mathematics to objects.

The concept of magnitude—in the sense of quantity—finds its support in science and its meaning in numbers. Number represents quantities in their determinateness.

Because the appearances come to a stand as an against-ness (*Gegenhaftes*) in general and in advance only upon the ground of the anticipating collection, in the sense of the concepts of unity (categories), quantity and quality, therefore mathematics is applicable to objects. Therefore it is possible on the ground of a mathematical construction to meet with something corresponding in the object itself and to prove it by experiment. The conditions of the appearing of appearances, the particular quantitative determinateness of their form and matter, are at the same time the conditions of *standing-against* (*Gegenstehen*), the collectedness and constancy of the appearances.

Both principles of the extensive and intensive magnitude of all appearances enunciate (but in a particular respect) the highest principle of all synthetic judgments.

This fact must be observed if the character of the above proofs of the principles is to be comprehended. Apart from specific difficulties in content, there is something strange about these proofs. We seem constantly tempted to say that all thought processes move in a circle. This difficulty of the proofs needs no special pointing out. However, a clarification of the reason for the difficulty is necessary. This does not lie merely in the special content of the principles, but in their nature. The reason for the difficulty is a necessary one. The principles are to be proved to be those determinations which first make an experience of objects possible at all. How is something like that proven? By showing that the principles are themselves only possible on the basis of the unity and the belonging together of the pure concepts of the understanding with that which intuitively encounters.

This unity of intuition and thought is itself the nature of experience. Therefore, the proof consists in showing that the principles of pure understanding are made possible by that which they ought to make possible—experience. This is an obvious circle. Certainly, and for the understanding of the process of the proof and of the character of what we are discussing it is indispensable not only to suspect this circle and so to create doubts about the cleanness of the proof, but to recognize the circle clearly and to carry it out as such. Kant would have grasped little of his own task and intention if he had not been aware of the circular character of these proofs. His assertion that these propositions are principles, although, with all their certainty, never as obvious as $2 \times 2 = 4$, points this out. (*A* 733, *B* 761, *N.K.S.*, pp. 589 f.)

f. The Analogies of Experience

The principles are rules according to which the standing-against of the object forms itself for human pre-senting (*Vor-stellen*). The axioms of intuition and the anticipations of perception concern the againstness of an against from a double point of view: first, the wherein of what is against, and second, the *what*-character of the against.

The second group of principles, on the other hand, concerns (relative to the possibility of an object in general) the possibility of an object's standing, of its constancy, or, as Kant puts it, the existence (*"Dasein"*), "the actuality," of the object, or in our words, the being-present-at-hand (*Vorhandensein*).

The question arises why the analogies of experience do not belong to the principles of modality. The answer must be because *Dasein* is definable only as a relation of the states of appearances among themselves and never immediately as such.

An object stands first and is first disclosed as standing when it is determined in its independence of any accidental act of perception of it. "Independence from . . ." is, however, only a negative determination. It is not sufficient to establish in a positive way the standing of the object. This is obviously only possible by exposing the object in its relationship to other objects and if this relationship has the constancy and the unity of a self-subsisting connection within which particular objects stand. The constancy of the object is, therefore, grounded in the connection (*nexus*) of appearances—or, more exactly, in what makes such a connection possible in advance.

f₁. Analogy as correspondence, as the relation of relations, and as the determination of its being that (*Dass-seins*)

Connection (*nexus*), like *compositio*, is a mode of conjunction (*coniunctio*) (*B* 201, n.) and presupposes in itself the guiding representation of a unity. However, now it is not a question of those conjunctions, which set together the given, that which is encountered, in its *what*-content according to spatiality, reality, and their degrees; it is not a question of the conjunction of what is always of the same sort (homogeneous) in the *what*-content of appearance (*compositio*, i.e., aggregation and coalition). Rather, it is a question of a conjunction of appearances with respect to their sometime existence (*Dasein*), their presence. The appearances, however, change, occur at different moments with different durations, and hence differ from each other (heterogeneous) with respect to their existence (*Dasein*). Because it is now a matter of the determination of the constancy of the object, consequently upon its stand in the unity of its connection with the rest, and thus upon the determination of its existence (*Dasein*) in relation to the existence (*Dasein*) of the others, it is a matter of a conjunction of what is heterogeneous, a unified standing together in different time relationships. This standing together of the whole of appearances in the unity of the rules of its togetherness (*Zusammen*), i.e., according to laws, is, however, nothing other than nature. "By nature, in the empirical sense, we understand the connection of appearances as regards their existence according to necessary rules, that is, according to laws. There are certain laws which first make a nature possible, and these laws are *a priori*." (*A* 216, *B* 263, *N.K.S.*, p. 237.) For these "original laws," expressed in the principles, Kant reserves the heading "Analogies of Experience." It is not a question now—as in the preceding principles—of "intuition" and "perception," but of the whole of knowledge, wherein the totality of objects, nature as presence, is determined. It concerns experience. But why "Analogies"? What does "analogy" mean? We shall here try a reversed procedure. By clarifying the title we will prepare for an understanding of these principles.

First of all, let us again recall the contrast between these principles and the preceding ones. The mathematical principles concern those rules of the unity of conjoining according to which the object determines itself as an encountering *what* in its *what-content*. The possible forms of the encountering can be constructed in advance upon the ground of the rules of quantitative composition in the domain of the extension of space and the intensity of what is sensed. The mathematical construction of the whatness of appearances may be verified and proven from experience by examples (*A* 178, *B* 221, *N.K.S.*, p.

210). In the following principles it is not a question of the determination of what encounters in its whatness, but of the determination as to whether, how, and the fact that what encounters does encounter and does stand here, i.e., of the determination of the existence (*Dasein*) of the appearances within their connection (or context).

The existence (*Dasein*) of an object, whether and that it is present-at-hand, can never be immediately forced and brought before us *a priori* by a mere representation of its possible existence. We can only infer the existence of an object (that it must be here) from the relation of the object to others, not by immediately procuring the existence. We can look for this existence according to definite rules; we can even reckon it as necessary, but we cannot by this means conjure it up now or ever. It must first allow itself to be found. When it has been found, we can recognize it and "identify" it by certain marks as that for which we were seeking.

These rules for looking and finding the existential connection of appearances (*Daseinszusammenhang der Erscheinungen*)—the existence of the one non-given appearance in relation to the given existence of the others—these rules for the determination of the relations of existence of objects are the analogies of experience. Analogy means correspondence, a relation, namely, of "how ... so" (*Wie ... so*). What stands in this relation are again relations. Understood according to its original concept, analogy is a relation of relations. Mathematical and metaphysical analogies differ according to what stands in this relation. In mathematics the "how ... so" contains relationships, which, in short, are homogeneously construable: just how *a* is to *b*, so *c* is to *d*. If the relation of *a* and *b* is given, and *c* also, then, according to the analogy, *d* can be defined and construed, and can itself be provided by such a construction. In metaphysical analogy, on the other hand, it is not a question of purely quantitative relations, but of qualitative ones, relations between what is heterogeneous. Here the encountering of the real, its presence, does not depend on us, but we depend on it. In the domain of what encounters us, if a relation of two that encounter is given, as well as something that corresponds to one of the two givens, then the fourth itself cannot be inferred in such a way as though it were already present through such an inference. Moreover, according to the rule of correspondence, we can only conclude the *relation* of the third to the fourth. From the analogy we obtain only an indication about a relation of something given to something not given, i.e., an indication of how, from the given, we must look for the non-given and as what we must meet it when it shows itself.

Now it becomes clear why Kant can and must call the determining principles of relationship of the existence of appearances among themselves "analogies." Since it is a question of the determination of existence, that and whether something is, but since the existence of a third is never brought about *a priori*, but can only be encountered, and, indeed, in relation to something present-at-hand, the rules which are necessary here are always for a correspondence: analogies. There lies, therefore, in such rules an anticipation of a necessary connection of perceptions and appearances in general, i.e., of experience. The analogies are analogies of experience.

f₂. The analogies as rules of the universal time-determination

Therefore, the "principle" of the analogies of experience reads as follows in *B* 218 (*N.K.S.*, p. 208):

"*Experience is possible only through the representation of a necessary connection of perceptions.*" Or in more detail (*A* 176 f., *N.K.S.*, p. 208): "All appearances are, as regards their existence (*Dasein*) subject *a priori* to rules determining their relation to one another in one time."

The key word is "time," and it indicates the connection in which these principles as rules have their anticipatory power. Kant, therefore, expressly calls the analogies "rules of universal time-determination" (*A* 178, *B* 220). "Universal" time-determination designates that time-determination which is present in advance of all empirical time measurements in physics, and it is present in advance specifically as the ground of the possibility of such measurement. Since an object can stand in relation to time with respect to its duration and with respect to the sequence in which it occurs with other objects and with respect to its being at the same time another, Kant distinguishes "three rules of all relations of appearances in time" (*A* 177, *B* 219, *N.K.S.*, p. 209), that is, the existence of appearances in time with respect to their relation in time.

Up to now we have not directly discussed time. Why does the relation to time move into the foreground in the analogies of experience? What has time to do with what these principles regulate? The rules concern the relation of appearances among themselves in regard to their "existence" (*Dasein*), i.e., the constancy (*Ständigkeit*) of the object in the totality of what constitutes (*Bestand*) appearances. Constancy in one sense means that which stands here (*Dastehen*), the presence. But constancy also means continuance (*Fortwähren*), enduring (*Beharren*). In the term "constancy" we hear both in one. It suggests continuous presence, existence of the object. We can easily see that presence and presentness contain a relation to time just as do continuance and enduring. Principles which are concerned with the determination of the constancy of the object, therefore, necessarily and in an exceptional sense have to do with time. For us, the question is in what way. The answer presents itself when we think through one of the principles and run through its proof. We choose for this the first analogy. (*A* 182 ff., *B* 224 ff., *N.K.S.*, pp. 212 ff.)

By way of introduction we briefly point out how Kant circumscribes the nature of time. We restrict ourselves, thereby, to what is necessary for an understanding of these principles. Rightly seen, however, we first directly discover the essentials of Kant's concept of time only through the formation and proof of the analogies.

Until now time was discussed only in passing when the nature of space was being defined. There we attributed to time what corresponds to what was said of space. We also find that Kant introduces the discussion of time together with that of space in the transcendental aesthetic. We say "introduces" intentionally, because what is said there concerning time neither exhausts what Kant has to say nor is it the decisive part.

Corresponding to space and by the same fundamental proofs, time is first exhibited as pure intuition. Co-existence and succession are represented in advance. Only by this pre-senting-in-advance (*Voraus-vor-stellung*) can one represent to oneself that several encountering things are simultaneous or one after the other. ". . . Different times are not simultaneous but successive (just as different spaces are not successive but simultaneous)." (*A* 31, *B* 47, *N.K.S.*, p. 75.) Different times, however, are only parts of one and the same time. Different times are only as de-limited in one single whole time. Time is not first com-posed by a piecing together, but is unlimited, endless, not made by a composition, but *given*. The originally united, single totality of succession is represented immediately, in advance, i.e., time is an *a priori* intuition, a "pure in-tuition."

Space is the form wherein all outside appearances en-counter us. Time, however, is *not* limited to these; it is also the form of inner appearances, i.e., the appearing and succession of our modes of relation and experiences. For this reason time is the form of all appearances in general. "In it alone is actuality (i.e., existence, presence) of ap-pearances possible at all." (*A* 31, *B* 46, *N.K.S.*, p. 75.) The existence of each appearance, as existence, stands in a relationship to time. Time itself is "unchangeable and permanent," "it does not run out." ". . . Time itself does not alter, but only something which is in time." (*A* 41, *B* 58, *N.K.S.*, p. 82.) In each now time is the same now; time is constantly itself. Time is that enduring which always is. Time is pure remaining, and only insofar as it remains are succession and alteration possible. Although time has a now-character in each now, each now is unrepeatably this single now, and different from every other now. Accordingly, time itself permits different relations between appearances with regard to itself. What encounters can stand in different relations to time. If it is related to time as permanent, i.e., to time as *quantum*, as sizable, then existence is taken according to its time-magnitude and it is determinable in its duration, i.e., as to how much of time as a whole. Time itself is taken as a *magnitude*. If the appearing is related to time as the succession of nows, then it is taken as it is successively in time. If it is related to time as the sum total, then the appearing is taken just as it is now in time. Accordingly, Kant designates three modes of time: duration, succession, and co-existence. With regard to these three possible relations of the existence of appearances to time (the time-relations), there are three rules for their determination, three principles that have the character of analogies:

I. Analogy: Principle of Permanence.
II. Analogy: Principle of Succession in Time, in Accordance with the Law of Causality.
III. Analogy: Principle of Co-existence, in Accordance with the Law of Reciprocity or Community.

We shall try to grasp the first analogy, i.e., to follow its proof. Here it might be well to remember again the general nature of analogies. They are to be established as those rules which, in advance, determine the constancy (*Ständigkeit*) of the object (*Gegenstand*), the existence of the appearance, in their relation to one another. But because the existence of appearances cannot be at our disposal, this rule cannot present and produce existence through *a priori* construction. It only gives a direction for looking for relations along which we can infer from one existence to another. The proof of such rules has to demonstrate why these principles are necessary and wherein they are grounded.

f₃. The first analogy and its proof. Substance as a
time-determination

The principle of permanence reads: "All appearances contain the permanent (substance) as the object itself, and the transitory as its mere determination, that is, as a way in which the object exists." (*A* 182, *N.K.S.*, p. 212.) In order that this sentence may be read at once as an analogy, it is important to pay attention to the *"and,"* i.e., to the citing of the relation of permanence and the transitory. Kant points out that "at all times," not only in philosophy but also in common sense, something like substance, permanence in the change of appearances, is presupposed. The principle tacitly underlies all experience. "A philosopher, on being asked how much smoke weighs, made the reply: 'Subtract from the weight of the wood burnt the weight of the ashes which are left over, and you have the weight of smoke.' He thus presupposed as undeniable that even in fire the matter (substance) does not vanish, but only suffers an alteration of form." (*A* 185, *B* 228, *N.K.S.*, p. 215.) But Kant emphasizes that it is not enough for one only to "feel" the need for the principle of permanence as a basis. It must also be demonstrated: (1) that and why there is something permanent in all appearances; (2) that the changeable is nothing else than a mere determination of the permanent, i.e., something that stands in a time-relation to permanence as a time-determination.

Kant's proof is again presented in the form of a syllogism. The proof concerns rules for the determination of existence, but existence means "to be in a time," and, as Kant remarks, it is to be taken as a mode of time (*A* 179, *B* 222, *N.K.S.*, p. 210). Therefore, the hinge on which the proof turns must be time, in its peculiar nature in its relation to appearances. Since a proof in the form of a syllogism has its formal turning point in the minor premise, the decisive thing must be said in the minor premise, which mediates between the major premise and the conclusion.

Major premise: All appearances—i.e., all that which encounters us humans—encounter in time and, therefore, with respect to the unity of their connection, they stand in the unity of a time-determination. Time itself is the original enduring; original, because only as long as time endures is something enduring in time possible. Therefore, permanence as such is what faces us and underlies in advance all that encounters us: *the substratum.*

Minor premise: Time itself, as absolute, cannot be perceived as itself, i.e., the time wherein everything that encounters has its spot is not perceivable as such. If it were perceivable, the particular time-spots (*Zeitstellen*) of what encounters, and, therewith, what encounters in its time-spot could also be determined *a priori* in it. In contrast, time, as the permanent in all appearances, demands that all determining of the existence of appearances, i.e., their being-in-time (*In-der-Zeit-sein*), refer in advance and above all to this permanent.

Conclusion: Thus, first and above all the standing of the object must be conceived from out of permanence, i.e., the representation of enduring in change belongs in advance to the character (*Sachhaltigkeit*) of an object.

However, the representation of enduring in change is what is meant by "substance" in the pure concept of the understanding. Consequently, according to the necessity of this principle, the category of substance has objective reality. There is constant alteration in the object of experience, of nature. Constant alteration is that mode of existence which follows another mode of the existence of the same object. The determination of alterations, thus of natural events, presupposes permanence. Alteration is determinable only in relation to permanence, since only the permanent can be changed, while the transitory suffers no alteration (*Veränderung*), but only a change (*Wechsel*). The accidents by means of which the determinations of substance are grasped are, therefore, nothing other than various modes of permanence, i.e., of the existence of substance itself.

The whole of the constancy of objects is determined upon the ground of the relation of their alterations among one another. Alterations are modes of the presence of forces. For this reason the principles which concern the existence of objects are called dynamical. Alterations, however, are alterations of something permanent. Permanence must determine beforehand the horizon within which objects in their connection are constant. According to Kant, however, permanence as continual presence is the fundamental character of time. Time thus plays a decisive role in the determination of the constancy of objects.

In all the proofs of the dynamical principles this role of time comes to the fore through the decisive assertion about the nature of time which is brought to bear each time in the minor premise. Time, on the one hand, is the sum total within which all appearances encounter; within which, therefore, the standing of objects is determined in their relations of permanence, of succession, and of co-existence. On the other hand, as is always asserted in the minor premise, time itself cannot be perceived. With regard to the possible determination of the presence of objects at any time, this means nothing less than that the momentary position in time and time relation of an object can never be constructed *a priori* out of the pure running on of time as such, i.e., can never themselves be intuitively produced and presented *a priori*. What is actual of time, i.e., what is immediately present, is only the particular now. There remains only the possibility of determining the time character of a not immediately given but nevertheless real object, from out of what is just then present, thus determining it *a priori* in its possible time-relation to what is present; and thereby to gain a guideline for how the object is to be sought. The object's existence (*Dasein*) itself must always chance to occur in addition (*zu-fallen*). Accordingly, if the whole of appearances in its objectivity is to be capable of being experienced by us at all, then well-founded rules are required which would contain an indication of the time relations as such in which the encountering must stand, so that the unity of the existence of appearances, i.e., a nature, is possible. These transcendental time-determinations are the analogies of experience, the first of which we have been discussing.

The second analogy reads according to *B* 232:

"All alterations take place in conformity with the law of the connection of cause and effect"; while according to *A* 189: "Everything that happens, that is, begins to be, presupposes something upon which it follows *according to a rule*." (*N.K.S.*, p. 218.)

The proof of this principle presents for the first time the foundation of the law of causality as a law for the objects of experience.

The third analogy reads in *B* 256 as follows:

"All substances, in so far as they can be perceived to co-exist in space, are in thoroughgoing reciprocity"; while according to *A* 211: "All substances, so far as they coexist, stand in thoroughgoing community, that is, in mutual interaction." (*N.K.S.*, p. 233.)

This principle and its proof, aside from its content, is of special importance for Kant's argument with Leibniz, as all the "analogies" really throw a special light on the change in the fundamental position of the two thinkers.

In closing we refer to the second group of the dynamical principles, the last group in the whole system of principles.

g. The Postulates of Empirical Thought As Such

g₁. The objective reality of the categories. The modalities as subjective synthetic principles

We know that the system of principles of the pure understanding is ordered and divided according to the order and division of the table of categories. The categories are representations of unity which arise in the nature of the act of understanding itself, which serve as rules of judgmental connection, i.e., the determining of the encountering manifold in the object. The four titles for the four groups of categories are quantity, quality, relation, and modality. In retrospect we see more clearly:

In the axioms of intuition it is demonstrated in what sense quantity (as extensive magnitude) belongs necessarily to the nature of the object as something encountering.

In the anticipations of perception it is demonstrated how quality (reality) determines what encounters in advance as an encountering.

In the analogies, the principles of correspondence, of what-stands-in-relation and its determination, it is demonstrated in what sense the object with respect to its constancy can only be determined on the basis of a previous view of the relations in which what encounters (the appearances) stands. Since these relations must represent and include in advance all objects capable of coming to appearance in any way, they can only be relations of what is inclusive of all appearances—namely, relations of time. The three groups of principles corresponding to the categories of quantity, quality, and relation have this in common: they determine in advance what belongs to the factual nature of the object as something encountering and constant. With regard to these categories, these three groups of principles show that (and in what sense) the categories constitute in advance the factual nature of the object, its thinghood (*Sachheit*) as such and as a whole. These three categories are the realities of the nature of the object. The corresponding principles prove that these categories as these realities make the object (*Gegenstand*) possible and belong to an object (*Objekt*) as such. They show that the categories have objective reality.

The principles so far discussed constitute the foundation through which a horizon is first formed at all, within which this and that and many can encounter and stand in connection as something objective.

What more, then, is the fourth group of principles (the postulates of empirical thought) to accomplish? This group corresponds to the categories of modality. The term already indicates something characteristic. Modality: *modus*, mode, manner, a how—namely, in contrast to the *what*, to the real as such. Kant introduces the discussion of the fourth group of principles with the remark that the categories of modality have a "special" characteristic (*A* 219, *B* 266, *N.K.S.*, p. 239). The categories of modality (possibility, actuality or existence, necessity) do not belong to the factual content of the nature of an object. Whether, for instance, a table is possible, actual or necessary, does not touch on the thinghood (*Sachheit*) of "table." This remains always the same. Kant's way of expressing this is that the categories of modality are not *real* predicates of the object. Accordingly, neither do they belong to the content of (*sachhaltig*) the nature of objectivity at all, nor to the pure concept of that which delimits the nature of the object as such. Rather, they assert something of how the concept of the object is related to its existence and the modes of its existence, that is to say, according to which modes the existence of the object is to be determined.

The principles which say something about this cannot, therefore, like the foregoing, concern the question if and how the categories (possibility, actuality, necessity) have objective reality, since they do not belong at all to the reality of the object. Because the principles cannot assert anything like this, neither can they be demonstrated in this respect. There are, therefore, no proofs for these principles, but only elucidations and clarifications of their content.

g₂. The postulates correspond to the nature of experience. The modalities refer to experience and no longer to conceivability

The postulates of empirical thought as such indicate only what is required in order to define an object as possible, actual, or necessary. There also lies in these requirements ("postulates") the delimiting of the nature of possibility, actuality, and necessity. The postulates correspond to the nature of that through which objects are definable at all: the nature of experience.

The postulates are merely assertions of a requirement which lies in the nature of experience. This, therefore, comes into play as the standard by which the modes of existence and, therewith, the essence of being is measured. Accordingly, the postulates run as follows (A 218, B 265 f., N.K.S., p. 239):

"1. That which agrees with the formal conditions of experience, that is, with the conditions of intuition and of concepts, is *possible*."

Kant conceives of "possibility" as agreement with what regulates in advance the appearing of appearances: with space and time and their quantitative determination. The possibility of a representation can be decided only as the representation obeys what was said about the object in the first group of principles. Rational metaphysics, on the contrary, had until then defined possibility as non-contradiction. According to Kant, what does not contradict itself is indeed *thinkable*. However, nothing about the possibility of the existence of an object is settled by this possibility of thought. What cannot appear in space and time is an impossible object for us.

"2. That which is bound up with the material conditions of experience, that is, with sensation, is *actual*."

Kant conceives of actuality (*Wirklichkeit*) as connection with what shows us something real, having content (*Sachhaltiges*): with sensation. The actuality of an object can be decided only in that the representation obeys what is said about the object in the second group of principles. Rational metaphysics until then, on the contrary, formulated actuality only as a complement to possibility in the sense of conceivability: *existentia* as *complementum possibilitatis*. But with this nothing is settled about actuality itself. What could still be added to possibility within pure understanding is only the impossible, but not the actual. The meaning of actuality is fulfilled and borne out for us only in the relation between representing and the encountering of the real of sensation.

Here we are at the point at which the misunderstanding of the conception of reality begins. Because the real, specifically as a given, alone bears out the actuality of an object—people have wrongly identified reality (*Realität*) with actuality (*Wirklichkeit*). Reality, however, is only a condition for the givenness of an actuality, but not yet the actuality of the actual.

"3. That which in its connection with the actual is determined in accordance with universal conditions of experience is (that is, exists as) *necessary*."

Kant conceives of necessity as determination by that which, out of agreement with the unity of experience as such, establishes the connection with actuality. The necessity of an object can be decided only in that the representation obeys what is said in the third group of principles concerning the constancy of the object. Rational metaphysics, until then, on the contrary, understood necessity merely as what cannot not be. However, since existence is defined only as a complement of the possible and this only as what is conceivable, this definition of necessity also remained within the domain of conceivability. The necessary is what is unthinkable as non-existent (*unseiend*). However, what we have to think need not for this reason exist. We can never recognize the existence of an object in its necessity at all, but always only the existence of a state of an object in relation to another.

g₃. Being as the being of the objects of experience. Modalities in relation to the power of cognition

From this elucidation of the contents of the postulates, which is synonymous with the essential definition of the modalities, we gather that Kant, in defining the modes of being, at the same time delimited being to the being of the object of experience. The merely logical clarifications of possibility, actuality, necessity, as in rational metaphysics, are rejected. In short, being is no longer determined out of mere thought. From whence then? The recurring formula "what agrees with," "what is connected with," is striking in the postulates. Possibility, actuality, necessity are understood out of the relationship between our capacity to know (an intuiting determined in accordance with thought) and the conditions of the possibility of objects—conditions which lie in our knowing capacity itself.

The modalities (possibility, actuality, and necessity) add no content (*Sachhaltiges*) to the content (*Sachhaltigkeit*) of the object, and yet they are a synthesis. They put the object into a relationship to the conditions of its standing-against (*Gegen-stehen*). These conditions, however, are also those very ones of the letting-stand-against (*Gegenstehenlassen*) of experience, and, therefore, of the actions of the subject. The postulates, too, are synthetic principles, although not objective, but only subjectively synthetic. This is to say that they do not put together the content of the object, but they put the whole nature of the object as determined by the three first principles into its possible relations to the subject and to its modes of intuitively-thought representing. The modalities add to the concept of the object its relation to our cognitive faculty. (*A* 234, *B* 289, *N.K.S.*, pp. 251 f.) Therefore, also, the three modes of being correspond to the first three groups of principles. What is asserted in these presupposes the modalities. In this sense, the fourth group of synthetic principles of pure understanding remains superior in rank to the others. Conversely, the modalities are determined only in relation to what is posited in the preceding principles.

g₄. The circularity of the proofs and elucidations

Now it is clear that just like the proofs of the other principles, the elucidation of the postulates, too, moves in a circle. Why is there this circular movement, and what does it say?

The principles are to be proved as those propositions which establish the possibility of an experience of objects. How are these propositions proven? It is done by showing that these propositions themselves are possible only on the ground of the unity and agreement of the pure conceptions of the understanding with the forms of intuition, with space and time. The unity of thought and intuition is itself the essence of experience. The proof consists in showing that the principles of pure understanding are possible through that which they themselves make possible, through the nature of experience. This is an obvious circle, and indeed a necessary one. The principles are proved by recourse to that whose arising they make possible, because these propositions are to bring to light nothing else than this circularity itself; for this constitutes the essence of experience.

In the concluding part of his work Kant says of the principle of pure understanding that "it has the peculiar character that it makes possible the very experience which is its own ground of proof, and that in this experience it must always itself be presupposed" (*A* 737, *B* 765, *N.K.S.*, p. 592). The principles are such propositions which ground their ground of proof and transfer this grounding to the ground of proof. Expressed differently, the ground which they lay, the nature of experience, is not a thing present-at-hand, to which we return and upon which we then simply stand. Experience is in itself a circular happening through which what lies within the circle becomes exposed (*eröffnet*). This open (*Offene*), however, is nothing other than the between (*Zwischen*) —between us and the thing.

h. The Highest Principle of All Synthetic Judgments. The Between

What Kant hit upon and what he constantly tried to grasp anew as the fundamental happening is that we human beings have the power of knowing what is, which we ourselves are not, even though we did not ourselves make this what is. To be what is in the midst of an open *vis-à-vis* what is, that is constantly strange. In Kant's formulation this means to have objects standing against us as they themselves, even though the letting encounter (*das Begegnen-lassen*) happens through us. How is such possible? Only in such a way that the conditions of the possibility of experiencing (space and time as pure intuitions and the categories as pure concepts of the understanding) are at the same time the conditions of the standing-against of the objects of experience.

What is expressed in this way Kant has established as the highest principle of all synthetic judgments. It now becomes clear what the circularity in the proof of the principles means. It means nothing else than this: Fundamentally these principles always express only the highest principle, but in such a way that in their belonging together they explicitly cite all that which belongs to the full content of the nature of experience and the nature of an object.

The chief difficulty in understanding this basic section of the *Critique of Pure Reason* and the whole work lies in the fact that we approach it from our everyday or scientific mode of thinking and read it in that attitude. Our attention is directed either toward what is said of the object itself or toward what is explained about the mode in which it is experienced. What is decisive, however, is neither to pay attention only to the one nor only to the other, nor to both together, but to recognize and to know:

1. that we must always move in the *between*, between man and thing;

2. that this *between* exists only while we move in it;

3. that this *between* is not like a rope stretching from the thing to man, but that this *between* as an anticipation (*Vorgriff*) reaches beyond the thing and similarly back behind us. Reaching-before (*Vor-griff*) means thrown back (*Rück-wurf*).

Therefore, when, from the first sentence onward, we read the *Critique of Pure Reason* in this attitude, from the start everything moves into a different light.

Conclusion

We have sought to press forward to the doctrine of the principles, because in this center of the *Critique of Pure Reason* the question about the thing is newly put and answered. We said earlier that the question of the thing is a historical one; now we see more clearly in what sense this is the case. Kant's questioning about the thing asks about intuition and thought, about experience and its principles, i.e., it asks about man. The question "What is a thing?" is the question "Who is man?" That does not mean that things become a human product (*Gemächte*), but, on the contrary, it means that man is to be understood as he who always already leaps beyond things, but in such a way that this leaping-beyond is possible only while things encounter and so precisely remain themselves—while they send us back behind ourselves and our surface. A dimension is opened up in Kant's question about the thing which lies between the thing and man, which reaches out beyond things and back behind man.

ANALYSIS

In the pages to follow, four main topics will be discussed: (1) the sort of questions that are philosophical (to explain such questions as "What is a thing?"); (2) the text itself, dealing with sections A, in which the question "What is a thing?" is raised; B-I, which examines the basic assumption system involved in modern science; and B-II, which presents the way Kant fundamentally altered the grounds on which this scientific assumption system was based and the limits within which it can be valid; (3) the relationship of Heidegger to Kant; (4) the later Heidegger and future philosophy.

Heidegger's first section (A) is preparatory and is designed to give the reader a fresh start, freeing him from some of the preconceptions he is likely to have. Although written as a simple common-sense discussion, it contains all of Heidegger's major points. This analysis will attempt to relate these points as raised in section A with their carefully detailed analysis in sections B-I and B-II. However, before examining the text itself, we must discuss the meaning of the question "What is a thing?", and, as this question is one version of the sort of question philosophy always asks, we must briefly discuss what sort of questions are philosophical.

1. PHILOSOPHICAL QUESTIONS

The task of philosophy differs from that of science, for, unlike science, philosophy examines not our conclusions but the basic conceptual models we employ—the *kind* of concepts and ordering patterns we use. Philosophy concerns not the explanation of this or that but questions such as "What, really, is an explanation?"

For example, is something explained when it is divided into parts and if we can tell how the parts behave? This is but one type of explanation. It works fairly well for a car (although it does not tell what makes it run), less well for a biological cell (whose "parts" are not alive and do not explain its life), and very poorly for explaining personality (what are the "parts" of a person?). Or, choosing another of the many types, has something been explained when we feel that we "understand" it because we have been shown how it fits into some larger context or broader organization? These questions, philosophic questions, are not designed to determine the explanation of this or that, but to discover what an explanation is. Yet, as we have seen, there are many different kinds of explanations. In any one case, which shall we use? Or should we try to use them all, and, if so, when and with what advantages and pitfalls? How is our choice among these varied explanations to be made? Should it depend on the field in which we work, on what we want an explanation for, or on the style of the times?

When we ask questions of this sort, we seem to be talking about nothing in particular; as Heidegger points out, such philosophic issues at first seem to be empty. Yet, they very basically affect whatever we study, for, depending upon which mode of approach we use, different questions and hypotheses will be formulated, different experiments set up, different illustrations cited, different arguments held to be sound, and different conclusions reached. Much in our conclusions about anything comes not from the study of the things but from the philosophical decisions implicit in the way we start.

Ideally, a clear division could be made between what is asserted *of the things* and what is only characteristic of one's preferred *type of explaining*. But these two are so intermeshed and interdependent that the very research, findings, and objective results of one approach will seem to those holding another approach as completely irrelevant or poorly asked about and answered from start to finish. It would be convenient to be able to say, "These aspects I found by studying my subject matter, and about them you must accept what I say; whereas those other aspects of my results stem merely from the sort of approach I always use, from 'the way I slice things,' and so you needn't accept that side of my conclusions." But the effects of one's approach cannot be separated out. Even what we ask, the questions with which we begin (as well as every subsequent step and finding), is already a result of, and is formulated within, a certain context and a certain way of conceptualizing things.

Since it is philosophy's task to discuss, clarify, and decide about such choices, philosophy cannot be based on a study of how the things are in order to see what approach is most suitable. How we find the things to be already depends upon our approach. Thus, the question "What is a thing?" is one way of putting the basic question of approach.

The "thing," as we have things today, is a certain sort of explanatory scheme, a certain sort of approach to anything studied. Heidegger finds this approach current in both science and ordinary common sense. It is an approach that renders whatever we study as some thing in space, located over there, subsisting separate from and over against us and having certain properties of its own. It is as obvious as "that orange-colored chair over there," or "an atom," "a cell," "a self," "a sense datum," "a body."

Although Einstein's physics has changed this thing-model somewhat, Heidegger views Einstein's theory as a more complex modification of the same basic thing-model (20, *15*).* We assume the thing so naturally that only a far-reaching discussion such as Heidegger's can make us realize how constantly we approach everything in this way, how this approach came about, and how a different approach is possible. These are the sort of aims that are the task of philosophy.

Heidegger tells us that science begins and *can* begin without explicitly examining its basic approach. Science begins with contemporary problems, which arise in the context of how the people of the time approach things. Although philosophic questions are often decided in science, this occurs only implicitly. In proceeding further, science makes further decisions, but these are made through action.

Fashions in science change, and, therewith, much seemingly important work becomes irrelevant. But, since it is not the task of science to examine its implicit decisions directly, it can begin without preliminaries. Heidegger argues that philosophy, however, cannot simply begin. It asks a question "with which nothing can be started" (2, *2*). Therefore, the question of the thing is a question with which one cannot begin. Thus, we are faced with a dilemma: Since philosophy cannot simply start without abandoning its task, which is to examine how we are to begin, how we are to approach and conceptualize; *how, then, can philosophy ever begin and proceed at all?*

---

* In this analysis the first reference given will be to the English translation of *What Is A Thing?*, and the second, in italics, to the German text.

Another way to put this dilemma is to talk about "experience." People often say that they want their knowledge to fit (or to be based on) experience. But different modes of study involve different sorts of "experience." For instance, one might know something from reading a dial on a complex experimental apparatus, or one might know something from culturally learned common-sense observation. When these and other sorts of "experience" occur they *already* make sense, even before interpretations are formulated. The physicist's dial reading is obviously an "experience" into which much thought has already gone, and common-sense objects around us are also experienced only with interpretations already in them. What we appeal to, check against, and call "experience" is always already organized and cut up, defined and made. Thus, philosophy's problem is not solved by basing philosophy on experience. Once we have chosen how to have "experience" (and on what selected and shaped aspects of it our statements can be "based"), what philosophy must first examine has already been decided and concluded. Hence, the basic philosophical choices and decisions are already settled in any settled acceptance of "experience."

So far these have been presented as if they were quite free "choices," as if one could adopt any sort of method, type of concept, sense of explanation, form of thing, and type of "experience." But this is not so. In Heidegger's view we cannot today, for instance, ignore our mathematics and science and embark on some new beginning that bears no relation to science (95, 73). Nor can we ignore our common-sense perspective. One is always in a given situation, at a particular pass in history. The choices confronting us are choices *in our current historical context*.

Although a decision to assume our present context relieves us of what could otherwise seem an endless and arbitrary relativity of choices, Heidegger's decision to study this context is made in order to put it into question, to reopen questions that at present appear settled. In this examination Heidegger sees the answer to our dilemma of how philosophy can start at all without abandoning its basic task, how it can examine basic approach and not simply fall into the existing approach.

While we cannot accept our present approach unexamined, neither can we simply reject it, for in rejecting it we would still be standing in it and we would still be using it, constantly, implicitly, in spite of ourselves. We must, then, examine this approach as we have it, realizing that it has developed as a series of answers to a series of questions asked long ago, settled long ago, and now no longer asked. Our now unquestioned, implicit approach was once a new answer to a question that was then open. If we find our way back to those questions, we will not only see them as live questions and as they were answered at that time, but we will be, thereby, in a position to answer them differently. Regaining these questions as live and open is the only way to get behind our unexamined assumptions, to see how they are now our basis, and to change them (49–50, 38). Heidegger calls this "reopening" a question, or taking a question that is now "quiescent" and "setting [it] into motion" again (49, 38).

In order to move beyond the current context, the current way we see "things" and "experience," the way we have knowledge and questions, Heidegger presents the historical steps and philosophical decisions that brought us to the current approach. He reopens decisions that were made and are now implicit (are now "happening") in our assumed approach. Philosophy thus makes the current, implicit context *explicit* and thereby provides the opportunity to carry further, add to, or change "things" (49–50, 38)! Thus, Heidegger says that only philosophy builds the roads that create and alter what things are.

But does he not say that science and ordinary common-sense living in any culture do this also (65–66, 100; *50, 78*)? Yes, but they do it implicitly. Philosophy adds a different power in explicating implicit decisions, thereby reopening them and posing them for further decision (10, 41, 53–54; *8, 31, 41*).

Heidegger tries to reopen some of these crucial decisions that made things and experience as we now have them, decisions set by Plato and Aristotle, Galileo and Newton, Leibniz and Kant. The book reopens especially those basic cultural decisions that at first were involved chiefly in modern science, although they also came to determine how we now view and live with and in anything. Thus far we have seen what philosophy does and how, for Heidegger, it is possible only as it examines its own role in history.

But are we not today quite aware of the thing-model and its limitations? Is there now already a sufficiently widespread critical attitude of this sort? Since the publication of *Sein und Zeit* in 1927, an entire generation of thinkers—scientists, authors, artists—has lived and written in the climate that Heidegger (with Dilthey and Husserl just before him) helped create. Because of this intellectual climate, nearly all thinkers since the thirties have been at least indirectly influenced by Heidegger and his immediate predecessors. We owe to Heidegger much of current thought, with its emphasis on getting beyond mere models by appealing to the wider context of ordinary living.

In reading *What Is A Thing?* (which was first published in Germany in 1962, although it consists of lectures given in 1935),[1] we do much more than reinforce today's general attitude that science consists of man-made models within

---

[1] By 1935 Heidegger had already courageously withdrawn from support of Nazism, which had at first seemed to him a hopeful revolt against rationalized, technologized culture. He withdrew at a time when very few could see ahead, and his early support should not be remembered without also remembering his early withdrawal. On the other hand, why this type of philosophy was not a better guide for his political decisions and how this type of philosophy relates to political allegiance, are certainly questions to reopen!

a human world. We cannot remain content with this mere attitude, this implicit assumption about science. Only if we see an exact analysis of science in the human context, if that is spelled out, explicated, can we move further. We must go behind our own current climate of thought, which Heidegger helped to create, and examine Heidegger's exact analysis of the thing-model. The thing-model is, despite our current attitudes, still second nature to us.

In the following pages I will be more exact and will attempt to state some main points that should make the reading of Heidegger's book easier and more enjoyable (for the way in which the book reveals and delineates certain major aspects basic to our thinking is extremely enjoyable, once barriers to its understanding have been overcome).

2. THE TEXT

Section A

In citing the housemaid who laughed at the ancient philosopher Thales when he fell into the well while observing the stars, Heidegger agrees that philosophy can look like a laughable endeavor of no particular use; while searching for the ultimate grounds of things one can easily fall into a well, and in a well one falls a long time before hitting the ground. (We are searching for the "ground" or basis of how anything appears and is approached and studied.) Also, the maid is right in that it is best to look carefully at the ordinary things around us before looking far away.

As we shall see later, Heidegger goes beyond Kant and other philosophers, for he does begin with the ordinary things around us. To be more accurate, he begins with us *and* the things around us, as we are among them at this time in history. Kant does not do this, nor, in Heidegger's view, do the natural sciences. Throughout the book, therefore, Heidegger adds the larger human context to the discussion of Kant and of science.

We come today upon a scene in which "things" are held to be objects around us, separable and movable in space. But, already at the start of the discussion (4–6, 3–5), Heidegger prepares for his own larger context, which involves humans as well as things. Thus, he sets up three sorts of things: (1) the objects around us, (2) our human attitudes and procedures, and (3) the totality of these two in interdependence together. And, as he says later, the third is really first (16, 74; *12, 57*). *Within* this larger context, our inquiry here will center on the things we find around us. In order to grasp how these seemingly independent things come to be as we ordinarily find them around us we will have to concern ourselves also with our own human speech and attitudes and with the context that encompasses both us and them.

Heidegger uses such phrases as "the being of what is" or "the thingness of the thing," and means by that the basic way (model, approach, framework) in which we meet these things. This is not some mysterious, additional, floating "Being," for it is only the mode of being *of* these things around us, how *they* are (9, 7). But that involves more than they do. What they are also involves the context in which, together with us, they come to be the way they are for us.

Heidegger next discusses the difference between the things of common sense and those same things as rendered by science. Why does he discuss this difference here? He wants to make clear to us that the things we run into are not simply given, as they seem, but have always already involved a certain "approach," which could be different. Once we note these two very different ways in which we render things, we can no longer consider the things according to either as simply given, independent of us.

The ways in which science and everyday common sense present "things" are not at all the same. For example, in ordinary terms, the sun "rises" and "sets," while science says that it does not (13, *10*). What is the relation between these two things—the thing of science and the thing of common observation? Heidegger finds that an understanding of "an original reference to things is missing" these days between the things as rendered by science and the ordinary things around us (41, *31*). To relate these two current approaches of ours we would have to understand how *approaches* come to be. It is one of the tasks of this book to show this, and to show the common origin of these two.

Heidegger says that ordinary things are always particulars, this one or that one, whereas science studies only universalities (15, *11–12*). He asks: Does modern science drop out particularity? The common sense things around us are always this one or that one, but, for science, any specific thing or event must be "derivable" from general theories. We say that we lack an explanation (scientific account) of a thing as long as we cannot yet *derive* its nature and occurrence from universal, basic theoretical postulates (axioms, premises, principles, *Grundsätze*, postulates). This is the basic "axiomatic" character of modern science with which Heidegger deals in detail in the latter part of this book. In contrast, any ordinary thing is always this one, a singular, particular thing.

Heidegger next shows that the particularity of things seems to depend completely on their space and time, that each is here *or* there, now *or* then. If two things are alike (15–16, 23; *12, 17*), this one is different from that one only because it is here now, while the other is there, or is here later. It is space and time that make ordinary things particulars. Here he poses a question that he deals with only later: Scientific propositions, too, concern events in space and time, and not only generalizations. How does science use space and time so that events can be both specifically determined and derivable from universal theory (111, 129; *86, 101*)?

Kant assumed that human space and time are those of Newton's physics (77, *59*), and he showed how Newton's "absolute" space and time are really generated in the way man thinks about and perceives any lawful and specific object. (Later we shall see exactly how this is done.) While Heidegger's notion of man is fuller than Kant's Newtonian man, he, too, derives space and time in the same basic way as did Kant: *Space and time are generated* in the encounter between man and the things that humans point out, locate, and make specific.

But Heidegger asks: Is space really involved in the very make-up of specific things? Is not space merely a system of external relations obtaining between things? He shows (19, 198; *15, 153*) that even if we break a thing to get to the space "inside" we find external relations between its parts, bits, and pieces. Space seems to be not really "in" the thing but only the "possibility" of arrangements of its parts (in, out, next to, etc.). How does this possibility of spatial structuring come into what a thing is?

"Possibility" is an important concept in this book and always refers to how our basic approach first makes things: it is *our* possible mode of approach that makes it "possible" for things to be as they are encountered, located, and found by us (21, 189; *16, 148*). The thing is given there, over against us. This encounter's externality is an arranging that makes and gets into the thing. And just as we did not see space in the thing directly, we certainly never see or perceive time as such, or in things. Yet, only space and time are in the particularity of each thing.

To what does Heidegger trace this characteristic of things, that they are always "this one" or "that one" (and, thus, to what does he trace space and time, since space and time lend things their particularity)? He traces the thing's character of being always "this one" to the thing's relation to us or our relation to the thing. *We point at things* and so call them "this one" or "that one" (24–25, 202; *18–19, 157*).

Thus, again (as he did when he set up the three kinds of "things"), Heidegger invokes the larger, ordinary, human context in which we and things appear together. In that interplay between us and things, space and time are generated.

Heidegger argues that words such as "this" and "that," the demonstrative pronouns, should not be called "pro" nouns, that is, substitutes for nouns. The use of the words "this" and "that" is the most original and earliest mode of saying anything and thereby selecting and determining a thing (25, *19*). Only after our interplay with things do they come to have a resulting nature of their own. The noun becomes possible only on the basis of our pointing. Our demonstrative definitions precede more developed definitions, i.e., "things" arise only in the context of their relation to us and our pointing them out.

And so we arrive at what might be called the main theme of the book, the "between." Heidegger is not saying that a thing is something subjective. "What a 'this' is does not depend upon our caprice and our pleasure." What it is does depend upon us, but "it also equally depends upon the things" (26, *20*; *also* 243, *188*). This "between" is not as though first we and things could have existed separately and then interacted. Rather, what a person is is always already a having things given, and a thing is already something that encounters.

As we have seen, what a thing is (for instance, the sun) depends on whether we take the thing of science or the thing of common sense. As Heidegger phrases it, "The things stand in different truths (14, *11*)." What a thing is always depends on some interplay with us, upon some truth in which it stands.

But Heidegger never speaks of mere viewpoints concerning what things are. He is concerned with concrete situations, with things we run into, work on, and use (both the common sense things and the scientific airplanes we fly). That the airplanes we build actually fly is no mere viewpoint! It is through action in concrete situations that "things" come to be acted on and taken as of a certain character. The character of things is therefore no mere viewpoint, but is made in our actions and in the situations. With our approach we create. And by explicating the implicit approach, philosophy can reopen old decisions and make further crucial decisions that have equally concrete effects on what things are. Conversely, only in perceiving and acting on things do we constitute ourselves as humans, just as only thereby do the things become things.

Heidegger now illustrates this interplay "between" man and things with some examples from Hegel. Hegel showed that the seemingly obvious and solid things, "this here" and "this now," change constantly and are relative to us. Space and time are generated in the interplay between us and things. The "this here now" depends on me and is a different "this here now" when I turn. The mere "here now" is not enough to make a "thing." It lacks a lasting truth and is only its changing relation to us. Thus, the temporal and spatial aspects of this interplay "between" us and things is not alone sufficient to determine a thing. A second major consideration must be taken up (32, *24*).

This is our opportunity, therefore, to discuss the two major considerations along which everything in this book is divided: (a) sensation and (b) concepts, or, more basically, (a) givenness and (b) collection in a class, or (a) particulars and (b) universals: (a) the here-now "this one" and (b) "what it is."

What something is is always a universal (many other

things can be the same "what"). If we call "this one" here now a "cat," we thereby take and know it *as* the same as many other things not here now, which are also cats. "Cat" is thus a universal or a class. What is a cat? We can delineate the traits that make something a cat, and each of these traits is also a universal: many other things (other cats and still other things) are furry, or are animals, etc. These are "concepts" in Kant's sense of that word. For Kant (*A*320, *B*377), a concept is a "characteristic mark" that defines the members of a class. Concepts are commonalities; they are the same wherever and whenever they occur. A thing is a "this here now" that "bears" such universal "traits."

Heidegger calls time and space (as we just left them, above) the "realm" (32, *24*) in which things encounter us (now, and from over there), in which things can be "given" as over *against* us. Concepts, however, organize. They stabilize the flow of sentience; they make it into something. They bring it to a lasting *stand*. Only both make a thing. An object in German is a *Gegenstand*, literally, a standing-against (137, 140, 184, 190; *107–110, 144, 148*).

Both givenness and concepts are really interplays "between" us and things, for givenness is *their* mode of encountering *us*, and the concepts of traits are *our* way of determining and defining *them*. Thus, both givenness and concepts are our ways. And both are the thing's ways. Yet it is clear that both belong to us only in regard to how givenness and concepts make things, and belong to things only as encountering us.

But to what does Heidegger trace this conceptual trait-constitution of things? He traces it (37, *28*) to the structure of *our speaking* to each other about a situation (much as, earlier, he traced the time-space realm of the particularity of "this" or "that" thing to *our pointing* things out to each other).

Traditionally in philosophy, a sentence had been analyzed as a connection between a subject and a predicate. Heidegger puts the sentence into the larger context of a person's expressing himself to others about a situation in which facets of the situation are stated, and something (the predicate) is asserted about some facet (the subject). What is said, the predicate, becomes the "traits" of a "thing." The subject of the sentence is the thing, not as seen or perceived but as hypothesized as one "under" its many traits. The subject "bears" the traits. This ancient mode of the underlying subject, as familiar and pervasive as it is, seems foolish, and its widespread use must be puzzling unless it is seen in the light of its derivation from the context of uttering something in speech. Of course, once it is seen in this way, one is hardly inclined to assume that this model is simply a given thing that has this structure of its own accord and apart from us. In Heidegger's view, the underlying trait-bearing thing was modeled after the sentence.

Thus, we have the second of the two major considerations: the thing as bearer of traits (or classes), this, too, deriving from within an interplay "between" man and things.

It is vital that givenness and concepts are really seen as two *different* considerations. In modern times it is a Kantian contribution to insist upon the difference. Descartes, Leibniz, and many others before Kant did not view perception and thought as really different. Perception was viewed as still-unclarified thought. It could be *wholly* analyzed and reduced to thought units. But that meant that there was no realm of givenness of here-now "this one" and "that one." Hence, Leibniz had to hold the "principle of indiscernibles": Two things cannot be alike in every one of their conceptualizable traits. They would be only one thing (23, *17*). For Leibniz, only traits, not space and time, could distinguish two things. Why does this matter here? Because that view gave all power to axiomatic concepts and none to givenness. In that view, reason determines everything and depends only on itself (a rational, axiomatic, mathematical-physical system). That was the Renaissance way "things" were. Heidegger wants to show that it was this limitless power of *pure reason* that Kant "limits" in his *Critique*. Kant limits the rational by showing how concepts are only the ways in which sensory givens go into the make-up of the things we experience. These have been some of the main problems which Heidegger discusses in the first section and upon which he builds the latter sections of the book.

Even though it seems so "natural," the "thing" is a historical product (37, *28*). Things would not need to be as they are, over there, movable in space, lasting through time, each thing with its traits (universals) held, carried, and borne by an individuating space-time position.

"That orange chair over there" is a historical product. It is something made. A furniture manufacturer made it along certain lines of use and taste that a designer had before he designed the chair (71–72, *55*). And the "mere" observer is also a maker, but in a special, narrowed case that occurs in a setting of cultural making. As its character as a chair is made, so also are its general characteristics as a thing made, along the model of movable units in space and time, a model that the physicists first made, i.e., postulated axiomatically.

We might wish simply to reject this model of the thing because it is a "mechanistic," lifeless, rigid model. There is a current tendency among some groups to denigrate scientific conceptual methods without actually grasping their nature, and to reject pseudo-explanatory models altogether. In line with this tendency we might wish to reject the thing-model in favor of a simple appeal to the ordinary, or in favor of a reaffirmation of life and human creativity. But if we do only that we will fail to move beyond the thing-model, because *without examining it fully, we will not notice how it pervades the way we think,*

meet, and deal with almost any thing. Thus, we might reject the mechanistic, thinglike ways of thought where we
do see them clearly, and yet we will operate with them and
with nothing else in all we see and do. As Heidegger
argues, only by studying the model in depth, only by ap-
preciating the questions it answered (putting what it
decided into question anew) can we really get beyond it.

Heidegger gives some examples (51–52, *39*): We tend
to approach poems as things and thereby make the study
of poetry "dreary." We fail to understand plants and animals because we tend to approach them as "things," i.e.,
as movable bodies in space, as the orange chair over there.
We have become so accustomed to this "thing" that we
approach anything as a separable "thing" over there. A
plant is considered as a "living *thing*," as basically a
thing or body with mysterious added-on traits of life.
Works of art are considered "things" with aesthetic traits
somehow added on. Similarly, we often view personality,
and even ourselves, as a "personality structure," or a
"self" (as if it were a thing, inside), or as having "personality contents" or "personality traits"—as if a person
were a structure with parts, a container with things inside, or a subject bearing traits.

A thing has a separate location in space, and hence we
impute a separate location to anything we approach as
a thing. This model of the thing leads to a great many
separations: we separate subjects and objects, inside and
outside, feelings and situations, individuals and inter-
personal relationships, individual and community, the
time moment now and time a moment later, symbol and
knower, body and mind, etc. These many divisions are not
separate issues, since each involves the same type of conceptual construct of things, each as separately located, a
unit "thing" existing here now in a certain unit of space
and at a "moment," i.e., a unit bit of time. Time, too, is
conceived as made up of bit things, units, moments. Why?
It is not because we somehow perceive and study time and

find it to be such. One does not perceive time as such. We conceive time as moments because our approach is one of thing units.

Section B–I

Here, Heidegger traces the thing-model's history. We will likely take for granted that "space" is everywhere the same until we realize that the notion of such a space was lacking among the Greeks. Instead, they thought that each thing had its own proper *place*, and that the movement of a thing was always back to its proper place. Unless externally restrained, an earthen thing tended "downward" and a fiery one "upward." Each thing thus tended to move in a certain way of its own accord, and this was termed each thing's "internal principle of motion." Greek things were not mere bodies that had to be moved. If allowed to do so, they moved themselves back to their own places (83–84, *64–65*). Thus, there were different kinds of places in the Greek model. We realize that our own everywhere-uniform space, too, is very much a model, perhaps better than the Greek, perhaps not, but at any rate not self-evident.

In the Newtonian model, just as in the Greek, the nature of space is related to what thing and motion are. For us there is no "internal principle of motion" by which a body moves itself. Rather, bodies are moved, put into motion only by something else, and they remain in motion until stopped by something else. All our "principles of motion" are "outside principles": something else outside the body is always posited to explain why a body comes into motion. Our laws of motion are the same for all places, and, hence, there is "space," everywhere just the same. Of course the earthen things, when allowed to, can still be observed to move "downward" just as they did in ancient Greece. But how we grasp what things are differs. We posit gravitational attraction outside the thing to explain why it moves.

When the different motions of different things are explained by different outside causes, all "bodies" (things) are viewed as fundamentally the same in their basic nature. Of course they do not all look or act the same, but then we think of them as made up of little "things" (a few types, each always the same: atoms, electrons, protons), and we explain all differences as different arrangements of these same things. What, where, and when anything is or moves will always be derivable according to the same basic principles.

The world is conceived as made of arrangements of uniform units of matter and space (92–93, *71–72*). If two constellations are made of the same parts and in the same patterns, exactly the same events will occur. And if time and space do not make two otherwise identical constellations different (as for Leibniz they do not), such two things would really be only one thing.

Heidegger terms this aspect of the scientific approach its basic "mathematical" character. He calls modern science mathematical, not because it so widely employs mathematics but because this basic plan of uniform units makes it possible to quantify everything one studies. It makes everything amenable to mathematics.

Heidegger discusses two related reasons for calling the basic scientific approach "mathematical," i.e., two reasons for mathematics' becoming such an important tool in this approach: First, because it is a model of uniform units and hence makes uniform measurement possible everywhere, and, second, because it is "axiomatic"—that is it is posited (as an axiom in geometry). Furthermore, Heidegger argues that the model copies our own thought procedures. Its uniform units *are* uniform thought steps transformed into a ground plan postulated as the basic structure of things. Here these two lines of argument will be discussed in turn:

1) The approach to things as consisting of uniform units makes mathematics applicable to things: numbers are compositions of uniform units. Seventeen consists of

the same units as fourteen, only there are three more of them. Since the units are the same, it would not matter *which* three of the seventeen units were considered to be three more than fourteen. There is a serial procedure employed in counting. In this procedure we obtain various numbers because we always keep in mind the units already counted. Our counting "synthesizes" (puts together) fourteen and another, another, and another. We keep what we have with us as we add another same unit. Our own continuity as we count gets us to the higher number. As Kant phrased it, without the unity of the "I think," there would be only the one unit counted now, and no composition of numbers. We get from fourteen to seventeen by taking fourteen with us as we go on to add another, another, and another. Thus, our activity of thinking provides both the series of uniform steps and the uniting of them into quantities. These units and numbers are our own notches, our own "another," our own unity, and our own steps. Why do two plus two equal four? The steps are always the same; hence, the second two involves steps of the same sort as the first two, and both are the same uniform steps as counting to four. Thus, the basic mathematical composing gives science its uniform unitlike "things" and derivable compositions (70–71, *54*). Therefore, everything so viewed becomes amenable to mathematics (93–94, *72*).

2) But Heidegger terms the modern model of things "mathematical" (97, *74*) for a second reason. He argues that "mathematical" means "axiomatic": the basic nature of things has been posited as identical to the steps of *our own* proceeding, our own pure reasoning. The laws of things are the logical necessity of reason's own steps (102, *75*) posited as laws of nature. It is this that makes the model "mathematical" and explains why mathematics acquired such an important role. The everywhere-equal units of the space of uniform motion of basically uniform bodies are really only posited axioms. They are the uniform steps of pure, rational thought, put up as axioms

of nature. Descartes had said it at its "coldest" (101, 78) and most extreme: Only a method of reducing everything to the clear and distinct steps of rational thinking grasps nature.

Is not such an approach simply unfounded? Everything may follow from the starting assumptions, but what are *they* based upon? How can that be a valid method?

Heidegger says that the axiomatic method lays its own ground (98, 75). He thus gives the term "axiomatic" a meaning it does not always have: he makes it reflexive (as Descartes' method was). "Axiomatic" means not only to postulate axioms and then deduce from them; it does not refer to just any unfounded assumptions one might posit and deduce from. Rather, Heidegger emphasizes that the axioms that rational thought posits assert the nature of rational thought itself. Axiomatic thought posits *itself* as the world's outline. It is based on itself. It creates the model of the world, not only *by* but *as* its own steps of thought. As we have seen, it is rational thought that has uniform unit steps and their composits, logical necessity and so forth. The axiomatic ground-plan of nature is simply the plan of the nature of rational thought asserted of nature. This, then, is the basic "mathematical" character of modern science. It is founded on the "axiomatic" method of "pure reason," which, as we shall see, Kant retains but limits.

Heidegger now shows the extent to which science's axiomatic thought-plan had reigned. Even God was subject to it. Philosophically explicated (Descartes and Leibniz), the lawful character of nature meant that God's thinking (the thinking that creates nature) was axiomatic, logical thought. The power of axiomatic thought is thus limitless. It creates nature. And so it was held that God himself could not act otherwise than he does and that he is subservient to logical thought. Nature could not possibly be otherwise than along the lines of that which follows logically.

Heidegger recalls that medieval philosophy had be-

queathed three different main topics of philosophy: God
(theology), world (cosmology), and man (psychology)
(111, 86), which are similar to Heidegger's three sorts
of "things" (6, 5). All three now became determined by
man's axiomatic thought. There was thus a "rational
theology," a "rational psychology," and a "rational cosmology." Reason was limitless. Using pure reason, man
could conclude not only about man, world, and God but
about what was possible and impossible in any possible
reality. This unlimited power of pure reason leads to
Kant's task of setting its limits. We must notice, however,
not only the vast extent of this power and the evident
need to limit it but that this power is founded on the role
that thought has in generating the basic scientific ground-
plan, unity, and lawfulness of things! Kant limits the
power of reason only by showing more exactly how its
power *is* legitimately founded. He shows how thought
legitimately participates in the formation of anything we
experience. But first, Heidegger prepares for his discussion of Kant by reopening the question of the time: Why
is the axiomatic model applicable to nature? Heidegger
shows the vast role that came to be assigned to rational
thought. Then Kant limits it by showing the roles of
thinking in the experience of things, the generating of
space, time, units, the unity of anything, and the lawfulness of events.

We recall Heidegger's earlier discussion of the need for
the thing to be an *underlying* "bearer of traits." A person's
"this here now" is always changing. Something must stand
steady: it is the thing, which underlies all its visible and
changing traits. This view goes back to Aristotle, for
whom the thing was analogous to the subject of the
sentence and the traits were the predicates. The Greek
term for matter means "what underlies," and its Latin
translation is "subject." Thus, already for the Greeks, the
thing as the underlying matter was viewed in terms of
the subject *to which predicates are tied in thought.*

With the rise of modern science the axiomatic method of purely logical steps of thought has replaced the underlying matter that holds the traits together and explains how they change. (For instance, in Descartes' example (*Meditations*, II), a piece of wax is first white and then charred. The scientific explanation requires that the wax really be an underlying analytical framework. Both the perceived white and charred must be reduced to these underlying thought-dimensions.)

Heidegger points to the change in meaning that the word "subject" underwent from being "what underlies" as the subject of the sentence and the matter of the thing to its modern meaning as the "person" and "subjective" thought. The thing that underlies is now our own thought!

For Kant, too, the unity of things and of space and time (in fact, all necessary connective unity) comes from "I think." If there were not a single thinker and perceiver, thoughts and perceptions would be isolated: if you both saw and tasted a lump of sugar, it would be as though you saw white and someone else tasted sweet. The oneness of our thinking is "what underlies" (as, for example, when we count units we take them along and thereby unite them as we go on counting). Thus, the subject that "bears" the traits or predicates is the thought unity of the experiencer.

But this "I think" is not an object; it is only the unity of our process in knowing sensory objects. For Kant, rational logic is no longer valid independent of sensation. Sensation is no longer simply "confused" thought that must be reduced to analytic clarity derivable from axioms. Rather, the sensory given and rational thought are two different ingredients of any experience.

Kant's *Critique of Pure Reason* considers axiomatic thought to be only our human, finite thinking (rather than world-constituting rationality). This fundamentally alters the whole approach (135, *105–106*). As human and finite, our axiomatic thinking is limited to its roles in the make-up of sensory experience. Alone it does not constitute an object. Thereby, rational metaphysics comes to be seen as invalid speculation.

With Kant (and Heidegger), this valid, limited role of our thinking has always *already* occurred whenever we experience. It is not something we "get from" or "add to" experience. Thus, the mathematical aspects of nature are not some grid that we place over what we experience, but our approach to sensible things. Only with *some* approach does one encounter anything. Kant thought only the Newtonian approach was really basic to human experience; Heidegger views this as historically variable. But they agree that things are never experienced except as some approach has *already* played its role. Only then is anything such as "experience" rendered possible, for experience is always already organized (for example, laid out, sequential, quantifiable, predictable, and understood as whatever it is an experience of). We never experience something totally unrecognizable, unidentifiable, and out of context. Even if we were to have such an experience, we would identify it by time, place, and what led up to it. Thus, the Kantian *Critique*, and Heidegger too, will do nothing to overthrow those aspects of the axiomatic method that imply that *experience is made partly by thought*. The best example of this is the scientific experiment.

Heidegger argues that the basic character of modern science is missed if one says that it differs from earlier science by being experimental. For Heidegger, the fact that modern science is "experimental" is only another *result* of its being basically axiomatic: an experiment is no mere observing. An experiment in the modern sense always first sets up a hypothetical framework. We set up the conditions and procedures in advance; only within them is nature allowed to answer, and it can say only yes or no. It must respond within our framework (67–68, 93; 52, 72). (Bacon had said that it is not enough to observe nature. We must "torture" nature and see what then happens under the circumstances we set up and put into action. And Kant cites Bacon's point in his Preface.)[2]

Heidegger argues that objects in science are made in a way similar to the way we make tools. (Again, here he provides the broader, ordinary man-world context within which science and all else arise.) The use of a tool is known in advance and determines the structure we give it when we invent and make it (71–72, *55*). A context of culture and use is always already implicit when anything is made. As tools are made, the things of science and the results of experiments are also *made* and involve a prior cultural knowing—a pre-existing context of man and world in which the thing is made *as* (and can then be taken *as*) that kind of thing.

For the Greeks there was a basic difference between made things and things of nature (83, *63*). Only natural things had their own nature and internal origin of motion. Something artificially made had its being moved only from the outside, by being made. For axiomatic science all things are only as we mathematically "make" them.

Later in this analysis we will discuss Heidegger's attempts to move beyond the current technological situation, in which nature is something we make. Heidegger sees vast dangers in it, just as he criticizes the view of human nature, art, and life as "things." We have seen that the thing is made. Will man the maker reduce himself to an axiomatically made "nature" that can say only yes or no within a framework set in advance?

Of course this making of nature *works* only when nature says "yes" to the framework and apparatus we devise. But nature and reality are "working forces" (93, *72*). Nature "works" for us within the terms we pre-set. Thus, the experimental character of modern science is

---

[2] ". . . constraining nature to give answer to questions of reason's own determining" (B xii–xiii).

another aspect of its "axiomatic" character: *our deter-mining what things are.* As we will see now, Kant ex-plained and limited this puzzling fact.

Section B–II

Kant accepts the axiomatic character of thought (184, *144*), as can be seen from his own axiomatic way of pro-ceeding. He sets up a "system" and *derives* experience from the principles he sets up (122, *94–95*).

Kant also retains the mathematical approach to ex-perience: as we still often do, Kant views experience in terms of units. The mathematical method has been ap-plied to break things up into sense-data units—felt pres-sure sensations, heard bits of sounds, seen color bits, etc.—as if these were self-subsisting, separate unit-things (209, *162*). But for Kant these are not experience. Ex-perience is never had except as it involves much more than such unit sensations.

For example: I am hit on the arm by a rock. The sen-sations are the pressure, the sound thud, and the gray, etc. However, these sensations occur *here* (on my left arm), *now* (while the sun is shining), and at a certain, given, measurable intensity. For Kant, sensations never occur without being definitely located in space and time, nor do they occur without a certain intensity.[3] It is not

---

[3] These ways in which conceptual aspects participate in experi-ence to make up objects are ways in which objects become in-dividually and specifically "determined" (186, 202; *146, 157*). We must always see empirically just where and when something oc-curs, and with what intensity, and in which necessary explanatory connections. These specifications determine a specific thing. Any objective thing is necessarily determined along these respects, and as long as we do not know all these we have not determined the thing objectively.

Thus, explanatory concepts belong to the determinate charac-ter of any thing, as Leibniz held, but so do space and time loca-tions, as Newton held.

Leibniz argued, against Newton's absolute space, that space is

possible to have an experience of pressure such that I would not know where, or would not as yet know when, or not yet sense any degree of intensity. Finally, sensations are never experienced except as connected to other events. I would not consider it "possible" that I am being hit, but not by anything related to anything previous (if I had only this *momentary* appearance of pressure and a floating gray shape). If a rock hit me I would wonder who threw it. Someone "must have." Or it "must have" fallen from somewhere. It "could not" have popped out of nowhere just in front of my arm. Experience is only "possible" as a tissue of already connected events.

Of course we may not as yet know who threw it, or

---

only a system of relations between bodies. Thus, motion is always *only* relative. Motion is a change of location, but location for Leibniz was definable only relative to other bodies and not in an absolute space. If *this* body moves, one can just as well say that all others move in various ways with respect to it, and it is at rest. Things are real, but space is only their relation.

Newton, however, found that a body in motion develops centrifugal force. Yet nothing like this happens to the objects at rest, although they have motion with respect to the first body.

Thus, an object's spatial location (and change in location, which is motion) must somehow be absolute. The space system must be capable of determining *which* body is in motion, and not merely the spatial relations between them. In this context it is very important for Kant to show how spatial location has a determinative role in making up what the object is. Thus, for Kant, space and time are not concepts but (as Heidegger put it) "realms" in which anything encounters, or, in Kant's words, the form of anything sensorily given, i.e., outside us and sequentially. Kant thus showed both the quantitative idealization aspect of time and space, which has a conceptual origin, and the determinative role that space and time location must play in specifying any possible sensory object, this one rather than another one like it. (And thus, too, Leibniz's principle of indiscernibles comes to an end, precisely because it had been an expression of the limitless and sole power of axiomatic thought without its function in interplay with givenness.)

But, for Kant (*B*136 and 138), the united and uniform quantitative character of space is fundamentally organized only by the observer's thought connections. In this latter respect Kant anticipates Einstein, for whom also the measurer's framework is an inherent part of what space is and how it determines things.

even if it was a rock. If it looks very strange we may not yet know what it is. But we know it *cannot* be just a "sensory datum" of grayness and pressure, floating and unconnected to any other observable events.

Thus, the explanatory connective relations are always already necessarily involved in any sensory experience, and even if we do not yet know what they are we flatly insist that they are there and that we must study until we find them.

It may require long and highly specific empirical study to determine what the object is, i.e., what necessary relations actually obtain between this sensation and other sensations. (Say we eventually discover that it is a meteor, a leftover bit from a planetary explosion attracted to Earth by gravitation.) We do not just invent the specific conceptual relations that explain and tie together the appearances we sense. But *in advance* of determining what a given connection is, we already know and insist that *some necessary* objective connections do obtain. The general system of necessary relations is set in advance. Without it the pressure and gray shape could be purely floating appearances, but we consider that "impossible." The necessary relations are objectively there, they are already, in experience. We work until we discover them specifically.

Thus, in the scientific approach any experience always *already* involves definiteness in spatio-temporal quantitative and intensity respects, and necessary conceptual connections between events. The peculiar twist here is that it is just the *conceptual* connections (of thought) that make sensations into objects rather than mere subjective appearances.

This Kantian puzzle is resolved when we realize that "connections" are not possible without that which they connect. Therefore, these are valid thought-connections only as they are the connections *of* sensory givens. Kant begins with the interplay. "Experience" is an interplay.

Only within it are there a thinker and things. There is no human subject except as a receiver and thinker of experience. There are no things except as received and thought in experiencing.

As Heidegger views it, German nineteenth-century Idealism, although later than Kant, failed to absorb this insight of Kant's: that the whole experiential interplay is already involved in anything like a *self*. Similarly, Positivism failed to absorb Kant's insight: that the experiential interplay is already involved in anything like a separate *thing*. Therefore, in Heidegger's own historical sequence, Kant comes after German Idealism and Positivism. (Only as a result of the much later *neo*-Kantianism was Kant understood, says Heidegger (60, *46*). It was one hundred years late (57, *43*), as Kant himself predicted.)

How do conceptual connections function in given sensations?

An "object" is really *sensations*. But sensations have a definite size and duration in space and time (Categories, group I) and intensity (group II), and Kant calls such determinate sensations *appearances*. (Sensations never actually appear any other way.) And, when such determinate sensations are further determined by explanatory conceptual connections (group III) so that their occurrence follows from laws, Kant calls such sensations *objects*. (As unconnected, such appearances could only be subjective.) We really see only the gray shape, even when we see it now and here, so large and *as* a rock, which must have been thrown. Thus, objects *are* sensations, but the conceptual connectives have always already functioned in any actual experience.

Kant calls this conceptual tying together of sensations into objects "synthesis." But it is only *from* experience that we learn what specific connections do obtain between two events (and what space-time relations and what intensity obtain). Only the framework of the type of measures and questions is conceptual. It was in this same sense that we said earlier than an experiment poses the hypothetical framework in advance of the results, and only within this framework does the experiment have precise results. Only within the framework does it provide objective, empirical answers.

But such science raises the basic question: In what way does the given exert control over the specific conceptual connections? Thought steps such as in logic or counting must be such that sensory givens *can* control them! When and why?

Thus, Kant alters the basic view that until then had been held traditionally, concerning what such a thought step, a "judgment," is. As had been discussed by Descartes and Leibniz, a judgment was only a connection between two concepts (the subject and the predicate in a sentence). Heidegger's example, "The board is black" (155, *122*). A judgment was viewed as a connection between two *concepts,* a merely logical step from one to the other, tying the two. Now Kant shows that there is a type of thought step that connects not only concepts but, in the same act, connects the grid ("realm," *Bereich,* manifold) in which any possible sensations will occur.

Heidegger emphasizes that for Kant the view of judgments as mere connections between two concepts (Subject and Predicate) is insufficient. *Kant seeks the sort of connection between two concepts that simultaneously organizes whatever sensory givens can occur.* Kant calls such a connection "synthetic."

The question of judgment is now not "On what basis are a subject and a predicate tied together (S–P)?" Rather, the question is "How does an S–P tie go to make up (synthesize) an experience of an object (SP–O)?" It is not a thought coupled to another thought, but a thought-couple coupling all possible sensations, thereby making an object (157, *123*).

But there are four ways in which synthetic thought

connections work in an experience of objects. These are the four principles, the Kantian demonstrations, which Heidegger discusses in the last part of the book:

I.   For Kant, "two plus two equals four" is a "synthetic" judgment. By explaining his view on this, we can best shed light on the first role conceptual connections play in making up experience ("The Axioms of Intuition," 194, *151*).

Judgments are "analytic" when the subject already means the predicate. ("Bachelors are unmarried.") What Descartes said applies to such judgments: One need only avoid contradiction. Thus, the principle of non-contradiction is the "top principle of all analytic judgments." But, in opposition to Descartes, Kant holds that the principle of non-contradiction is not enough (173, 181–182; *135, 142*). Mathematics first involves a synthesis that is necessary for all experience.

Synthetic judgments involve a further *step of thought* not given by non-contradiction alone. But the "top principle of synthetic judgments" involves not merely the two concepts of this step of thought but also imagination and the unity of the thinker. "Two plus two," considered as mere concept, seems to give enough information to give us four, and thus seems analytic. But we are concerned with how the concepts are formed in the first place, and we are concerned with how, in being formed, they also synthesize the realm for all objects. In forming the concept of "two" and of "four" we must add, count, and keep or unify the steps to form the number. (Similarly, if we imagine drawing a line, we *keep* what we have imagined drawing as we draw further, or we would get no line, only momentary bits.) *The unity of one activity of thought provides the connective union.* Kant calls the judgment "synthetic" because in the connection of the steps of counting we generate the continuous quantifiable grid for all possible objects. We generate the quantifiable space (as we draw lines) and the sequence of *time* (as we count). Space and time are basically those of *imagined* drawing and counting units. Hence, the connections between our steps of thought "synthesize" the imagined "schemata" of space and time.

Thus, conceptual connections are involved in the generation of the continuous imagined grid of units of space and time, and anything ever sensed or imagined must appear within them.

Because of this synthesis or composition of units, we can also define the purely analytic relationships of the concepts. But, for Kant, the synthesis (the making) of concepts always *precedes* their analytic relationships. Concept *formation* precedes the analysis of already formed concepts. The origin of the connections in a concept must first be shown. And concept formation must be so accounted for that we can see how the experience of object is *thereby* patterned. In this instance we have seen the formation of numbers and the thought steps of counting in such a way that the uniform unit composition of experience in space and time was also shown.

Heidegger, too, shows how time, space, and unit things are generated in the interplay between man and thing. We are our concerns, fears, and hopes, and, because we are a projection into the future, we generate time. (Hence we must not think of ourselves as "things" present *in* time.) For Heidegger, we generate space in the context of pointing to and distancing objects as over there, plotting out a system of orientations in a social interaction with others amid things (25, *19*). But the uniform, quantitative grid of size and duration is only one of the ways that connections between conceptual steps also connect experience. Let us turn to a second.

II.   Quantitative measurement is applicable, not only to space and time locations and durations of sensations, but also to their intensity. Kant's "anticipations of perception" (206, *160*) concern this second and different way.

Space and time alone, only imagined, make geometry and arithmetic applicable to anything. Why is degree of intensity a different sort of thought connection? Because something actually sensed must appear. But even before it appears we know it must have a measurable "intensity." To color shades, light, intensity, degree of pressure, etc., the (conceptual) continuum of degrees and mathematical measurement is again applicable. This is the second way in which connections between concepts also thereby synthesize a connective continuum for sensory experience.

III. The first two have been Kant's "mathematical" principles. In these the thought steps and connections are inherent in the sensory appearance itself. In contrast, the third concerns connections *between different* occurrences of givens (224, *174*). Kant calls the third and fourth "dynamical." From something now given we can often infer that something else must soon happen. Let us say we know that the inferred always had happened whenever this sort of thing first happened. But our sequential memory alone cannot ensure that it *must* happen in the same sequence again. If we do not know *why* this always happens when that does, we may well be wrong or we may have neglected to account for some intervening change. At any rate, we did not yet have the objective connection. Only if we know *why* this makes that happen can we say that it "must" happen again. Thus, explanatory conceptual connections (just as Descartes said) provide the objective scientific connections of any possible appearances.

But, even so, we might be wrong. We are sure only that the general structure of experience is along these lines. There is *some* explanation connecting events. The specific explanations are constantly discovered, improved, and extended. They must be found from experience. When we find that we were wrong, we find that what we thought was an "objective" explanation really was not.

Thus, we experience "objects" only in terms of *necessary* connections between events, i.e., the explanatory relations we seek.

IV. Finally (236, *183*), since experience is possible only with us, not for objects apart from us, what can rational thought conclude in advance as to what is possible or impossible? For Kant, God, nature, and man are no longer subject to the logical laws of rational thought. Logical possibility is not *experiential* possibility. Only that is possible in experience which conforms to the above three groups of principles (I, II, III). Except as thought connections also synthesize actual sensory experience, thought alone is not decisive about what is possible or impossible.

In these four principles, Heidegger shows that Kant "demonstrates" the role of each conceptual principle in experience by a syllogistic sequence. The first (major) premise tells something that is the case in all experience. The second (minor) premise states that this aspect of experience is possible only as a certain conceptual connection has already participated. The principle Kant is proving then follows by logical necessity. But despite this elegant method of proof, the proofs are all "circular": the principle that is concluded (proven) is really merely shown to have been already involved in the first premise. In short, the demonstration shows how the principles are *already* involved in experience.

This "circle" (224, 241; *174, 187*) is of great importance to Heidegger and lies in the very nature of ontology (the study of how what is is constituted). Whatever is is always already patterned in interplay with us before we ever make explicit what and how it is. Our "understanding" prestructures everything in those respects we have outlined. We have always already been involved in anything we have experienced. Our approach has functioned already. To make it explicit is what Kant calls the "transcendental" task. We can show only circularly how we are always already involved. The human subject's process is always already involved implicitly and thought along with the thing when the thing is approached as a separate entity out there. Thus, the roles of thought in synthesizing what things are "leap ahead of" things in Heidegger's way of putting what Kant called "transcendental." Philosophy makes explicit how we have already approached and participated in the making of the thing (as well as, in the same process, in the making of ourselves as selves or subjects). But such explicating can alter (how we approach) things. Therein, Heidegger sees the power of philosophy.

3. HEIDEGGER AND KANT

One reason, among others, that it was necessary to go so exactly into Kant's approach is that Heidegger's philosophy follows Kant's in so many basic ways—with this difference: Heidegger begins with man in the context of the ordinary world rather than in the context of science. This difference gives a very different ring to everything Heidegger says. We will take up here how Kant's "transcendental" roles that *thought* plays (in what objects are) become Heidegger's "transcendence"—the way human beings' *feeling, explication, language, and action* "sketch" out the world, set up situations, and thereby partly create what the things are.

Heidegger, like Kant, views time's order as generated by us in our interplay with things. For Heidegger, however, this is not the linear time generated by mathematical thought but a time generated by the broader human process of "being-in-the-world," feeling, speaking, and acting in situations. Hence, it is a time in which the import of the past is being modified by how one is now concerned about what one is about to do.

Just as for Kant the human subject (the "I think" that provides the synthesizing and steps of thought) is not itself an object, so for Heidegger the human being is not a thing, but rather the process of approaching things. A human person is a being-in and a being-toward, always a caring for, worrying about, trying to avoid, striving for, being afraid of, hoping for, etc. Man *is* this projecting. (Heidegger calls it the care structure.) I am my being-in the situations (the sentence I am trying to write, the point I am getting at, the book I am finishing, the situation I am trying to create, the pitfalls I am trying to avoid, etc.).

Heidegger insists, as did Kant, that in any experience or situation the crucial ways we participate in creating things and situations have *already* functioned. Heidegger points out that apart from our own striving or fearing there cannot be a situation in the first place. A situation is not like given things in the room, but like my trying to find something, or get out, or in, or whatever I am trying to do there, perhaps what I wish I could and cannot. But there is no fact that I cannot do it until I first project it by wanting to do it, and this implies my purposes, fears, or concern.

Kant had shown that even for the things in the room to be given, thought has already functioned in constituting and objectively connecting sensations into objects. Thus, the role Kant assigned to scientific thought Heidegger assigns to the wider human feeling, living, and thinking.

For Heidegger, as for Kant, our transcending has always functioned in advance of (it "leaps ahead" and helps create) the facts we experience. But what for Kant was called "experience" (the connected system of experienced nature as rendered by science) becomes, for Heidegger, our always finding ourselves "thrown" into situations. Just as objects involve our being affected by sensations, so for Heidegger a situation is *my* situation because it can affect me (in terms of affect, feeling, *Befindlichkeit*). Like Kant, Heidegger asserts the partial independence of both the human role and the thing's role. We can define neither except as the interplay has already functioned, but what can be done with the things is not at all arbitrary, not just anything we like.

Kant derived the transcendental principles from "pure concepts" of the "*understanding*" (*Verstand*) (144, *112*). For Heidegger, how human feeling sets up situations is called "understanding" (*Verstehen*) and is pre-conceptual. A context of meaning is projected by the way we are feelingly in our situations. (Situations are made by our concerns in terms of which they are situations for us.) With words we can then explicate this "understanding" of our situations, which was already implicit in our felt being-in situations.

It is an error to consider feeling as something within us that could exist without constituting a situation, and to consider situations as external, apart from how we feel our thrownness and vulnerability. That view considers feelings along the thing-model as if they were little things located "inside" us. My fear *is* my vulnerability to being affected in the situation, and it constitutes the threat. The threat that could materialize or that I could avoid *is* my situation. What I feel is not my feeling but my situation. The situation is not physically defined facts but the significance and facts created by how I am and could be in them. Therefore, Heidegger says that man is his possibilities.

As for Kant, so for Heidegger: we do not "understand" relationships that are given in the facts except as we have already created those facts by how we have already functioned. And Heidegger is perfectly deliberate in so using the word "understanding" along Kant's lines, as creating ("synthetic") things and situations *before* we can explicate (Kant called it "analyze"). Here, too, and in the same sense, the synthesis of meanings precedes their analysis.

But, as we have seen, "explication" (*Auslegung*) for Heidegger is not merely conceptual and analytic, but is itself a further creative process. Thus, while the primary human "understanding" is a feeling process, the further human processes of explicating in language and thought are also "constitutive" of what man is. This means that what we are as humans and how we constitute situations and things is always partly and irreducibly linguistic. We have seen that Heidegger traces the metaphysical model of the thing as the "bearer of traits" back to modes of speech (the subject "bearing" predicates). Our approach to what is (the thing) was modeled on the nature of the proposition that, in turn, stems from the context of people's ordinary speaking to each other about facets of their situation (37, 64, 152–153; *27, 49, 119*). Explication and speech, as well as felt understanding, project possibilities and render things along certain lines. They are processes that transcend, sketch, and thus partly create what things are. Thus philosophy's power. Language and thought add their own structures and do not merely draw out the significances of feeling. They are of a different order. Explication must be based on what was already understood in feeling, but "based on" does not mean "equal." Rather, it means "hermeneutic," a process of further drawing out and further creating, which, when authentic, expresses my directly felt "thrownness" and creatively explicates what I am, i.e., my felt being-in my situations.

In keeping the role Kant gives to "understanding," but expanding it to be primarily feeling and only then explicative thought, Heidegger follows Schleiermacher and Dilthey. Dilthey had outlined a method of *Verstehen* in which one interpreted human products, institutions, and literary works as expressions of a felt experiential process that made its own sense. For Dilthey, mere logic uses only certain very thin derivatives from the felt continuity of human experiencing.

Of course for Kant too (and Descartes and others), logical relationships and logical necessity were derived from the continuity (Kant called it "unity") of human processes as, for example, the unity and continuity of the "I think" in counting units and keeping them so as to compose numbers. But to Dilthey this meant that logical relations were extremely thin derivatives from the broad lived and felt process of experiencing and its continuity. This continuity was the adaptive and historically elaborated process of the living human organism and was first of all felt. It made its own experiential sense and had its own experiential meanings in its organismic, structural, and functional context.

Thus, to attempt to explain something experiential by some logical construction was, for Dilthey, like explaining man by one of his own thinnest derivatives. Instead, Dilthey proposed viewing any human product as patterned by an experiential process with experiential significances. Thus, the felt "understanding" of the inquirer would parallel (and explicatively elaborate verbally) the "understanding" implicit in the felt experiential process itself.

Dilthey, too, was deliberate about the Kantian use of "understanding," and saw himself as providing a "critique of historical reason" to augment Kant's *Critique* of purely conceptual reason.

And, for Heidegger, history is always implicit in any man's ways of feelingly being-in and setting up his situations. The individual is a creative "repetition" of historical meanings in an always already historical context. I can attempt to live from out of my own authentically felt meanings, but I can do this only by explicating and elaborating the historically given meanings I actually already feel and live. Just as we said of philosophy in Heidegger's view, so also he views the individual as opening up new avenues, but only as he begins by feeling and explicating that which he already is. Nothing else is authentic. Nothing else can be creatively elaborated. To avoid what one authentically is leaves one totally alienated and at the mercy of routines and patterns given by others. Of course in such avoidance, when one is "fallen" into everydayness, one still has one's desire to maintain this avoiding, but one usually avoids explicating that as well. Explicating it would be one's most authentic move and would lead through everydayness beyond it. Therefore, in *Sein und Zeit* Heidegger begins precisely with "everydayness" and explicates its felt understanding.

One cannot authentically and creatively elaborate everything, nor would one want to. I must choose what shall be important to me. In some very few chosen respects I can attempt to work genuinely, creatively. In most respects each day I will remain more or less in everydayness. Either way I stand on and in a historically produced context and historical meanings.

Not only the other people of past history but the other people of now are already an inherent part of what a person is. One is always a being-with and a being-toward others, and human situations are not possible without this. Even being painfully lonely or needing to be alone is possible for human beings only because being-with is an inherent aspect of what they are. Chairs and tables neither feel lonely nor need to be alone.

Thus, Heidegger overcomes Husserl's problem of the existence of others by finding one's living with and toward others as already part of what it is to be a person. Again, here he follows Kant, who overcame the solipsistic problems left by Berkeley (for example, "Refutation of Idealism," *B*274), by not allowing the existence of subjects except as they are already a perceiving and thinking of objects. Heidegger, by widening "understanding" to the feeling and acting in situations, includes the others *as* they are for and to us in situations, that is to say, as humans whose concerns and cares are part of our situations. Thus, neither they nor I, as selves, are subjective things inside, but always already a feeling and living-in situations, and situations are partly created by our understandings. Just as Kant's "I think" is not an object but partly constitutes objects, so, for Heidegger, people are not objects but situation-constitutors. My being toward others is always already involved in any situation as I find myself thrown in one.[4]

Thus, both history and my being toward present other people are already involved in the felt understanding that has functioned to make me what I am, as I am a being-in the situations that are authentically situations for me.

4. THE LATER HEIDEGGER AND FUTURE PHILOSOPHY

Heidegger's emphasis in later years has been consistent with his earlier work, but in an important sense he has added something. He has made very clear exactly in what new sense one ought to interpret his earlier work. There

---

[4] The way in which being-toward others is inherent in what a person is cannot be split off from the person's living among things (as though *these* were our relations to other people and *those* were our relations to things). Rather, anything that encounters us is already the sort of thing it is (a door or a gun) by virtue of its having been made along lines of use and purpose by people, both historically in devising such a thing and currently as the makers of this thing. We have already seen what Heidegger does to the "understanding," to which Kant gave the role of partly constituting objects. Heidegger widens it to include human feeling and living. Hence, for Heidegger, a thing is no longer limited to its being a body in physics and chemistry, but also includes what it is as a use-object partly constituted by human situations. But in having that sort of being, every thing through and through involves the other people who made it and who are implied in it. Even the things of physics are humanly made and imply physicists and history, although such things involve narrowing the usual experience to a "mere" observing. We do not usually receive the pure sense of mere hearing. We do not usually hear "a sound"; we hear a door slamming downstairs. As Heidegger says (209, *162*), ordinarily experienced things must first be "broken up" into separate bits of "sense data," and only by this careful and deliberate process can we then have "sense data." A science that employs carefully narrowed perception and deliberate "mere looking" (as he says in *Sein und Zeit*) can have a perfectly legitimate place in Heidegger's view. But, it requires "a very complicated and artful focus" (209, *163*). It must be recognized as a narrowed focus within the wider human world and the wider human experiencing, which involves other people, history, and human making.

are two ways in which one could interpret all this insistance that things always already involve our making, defining, projecting, transcending, approaching. One might conclude that being is what we make it, what works for us, what we define and devise. But Heidegger denies precisely this view of being. A different interpretation is really intended in all his work: Heidegger has all along reminded us that what things are is made by our approach, but being is not the made things. Being is the possible interaction, a third which is first. It is not the things we made. Being is the whole context in which such making and defining *can* make, define, reveal, and bring forth. Being is predefined; it is the whole, infinite, as yet undisclosed richness of all possibilities, of all possible defining and making.

In this way arises Heidegger's great interest in the pre-Socratic philosophers, since they were concerned with predefined being, *"that in which* all defined things come to be and perish again."* It seems to Heidegger that this was lost with Socrates.

From Plato through Nietzsche, Heidegger sees one continuous development (with many decisive steps, some of which he traces in this book). From Plato on, being is taken as that which is clear, *already defined*, and constituted. Being is what is formed and what works. Modern technology is the ultimate development of this approach.

Heidegger terms the structure posited by technology a *"Gestell,"* which in German combines the meanings of "positing" and "structure," and also has the connotation of an apparatus or a contraption. As we look about us in the city today, we find ourselves surrounded by man-made things, by technologically determined routines and views. There has been a silencing of nature, including our own nature.

Heidegger sees vast danger in this way of construing being as something formed and made. That view is idolatry. It forgets our role in making anything formed. It misses being and may enslave us to what we have made.

Not only might man blow up the world with technology, technology has already gone far toward making man its appendage, making man into a thing whose nature can say only yes or no within the structuring of technological projecting. The danger is man (and being) as *made!*

Both "undisclosed" being and man must be grasped in their roles in the *making* of anything. "Being needs man," says Heidegger in *Die Technik und die Kehre*. To "rescue" ourselves from the danger of technology we must look precisely there "where the danger is." Technology shows us not just a few contraptions but a much larger fact—the interplay. Man is in danger of becoming something *made* of man and being. Instead, he must take himself as maker. So viewed, being is not what is *made*, but that vastly wider sense of being as the not yet made, in which we bring forth anything that is made.

Man's approach at a given historical time is a certain way, and hence things are a certain way. At another time the models are different, and so are things. Evidently, then, being can be defined *neither* by this nor by that model or approach. Rather, being is this whole condition in which different human approaches can differently determine what things are.

This is also what Heidegger means by overcoming metaphysics.[5] We must think beyond any one model, for any

---

[5] Kant had overcome the speculative metaphysics of his time. He showed that reason is valid only in its transcendental role of partly making experience. Kant was then able to show that apart from this experiential power the purely rational speculative schemes could be argued for or against equally well (Kant's antinomies).

Kant posited "things in themselves" as a limiting notion. We cannot know anything about things in themselves, for anything known is related to us, given to us, partly made by our reception. The notion of things in themselves allowed Kant to treat the things of experience *not* as things in themselves but as partly involving us. Heidegger puts being in relation to man, but, like Kant's things in themselves, being has no made form. It is that "in which" is formed anything we participate in forming. But Heidegger envisions the next development in man as going beyond this merely *made* and as approaching this being in another way.

model is still only that same approach that began with Plato and came to its height with Nietzsche and technology. A new approach to being is coming, says Heidegger. What is this new approach to being? He cannot tell us. It will be the work of an entire culture, not the work of one man (50, *38*).

No philosopher can "jump over his own shadow" (150–151, *118*). Heidegger means that no philosopher can jump over the historical context in which he works and which he alters. No one can get out of the limits of his own historical time to deal with the *further* changes that his own philosophical decisions have made necessary. (Only Hegel did it, but by "jumping into the sun," i.e., beyond history altogether, to the idea of an absolute end of all history. But that is purely theoretical. We are always still within history.)

And so Heidegger cannot jump over his own shadow. Each of his recent writings ends with his standing at the edge of an abyss, pointing into the fog of a coming new approach to what is.

Can we move beyond Heidegger's shadow?

On the one hand, we are not to fall back into models, metaphysics, this or that assumption system, which renders what is as merely these or those created things. On the other hand, an "approach" to being, as far as Heidegger has gone, always *is* a model, a framework, a sketching out of "things," be they similar to our things or different. Thus, the new approach he envisions poses a dilemma: It cannot be a new "approach"; it must be a different sort of thing altogether and, in fact, precisely not just a "thing."

In the first half of our century (and due partly to Heidegger and others) there has already occurred a fundamental split between models and concrete living. There is no longer a "thing," with a single inherent form seemingly of its own, nor does man view himself as having one given inherent human nature. That is exactly why we speak of "models" or "approaches"; these words indicate variety and relativity. The rigid bodies Newton located in absolute space have given way to Einstein's relativity to the measurer in physics. The cubists gave us things not from one but from many simultaneous perspectives. Pure form without representing anything permitted vast, wonderful, formal virtuosities, for example, in art and in logic and mathematics. Amazing achievements became possible with the variety that forms could have when freed from life. Non-Euclidian geometries, modern design, architecture in reinforced concrete, proliferations of specialized social roles—all these attest to the new power achieved with forms freed from what had been thought to be the constraints of their "natural" contents.

But whereas in the past man had lived and felt himself in his roles and definitions, now the relativity and contradictions of so many different forms do not permit that sort of inherent identification with a role or form. We are no longer any of the many roles, values, or forms of expression. Form split from living leaves living inchoate. Thus, living humanness has more and more expressed itself by inchoate protest against reason, against empty roles and forms. This protest has sometimes been beautiful and sometimes not.

How shall form (model, construct, "approach") and man come back together in a new way? It must be a *new way*, since there can no longer be a genuine restoration of some *one* model, form, metaphysics, value system, social role, or artistic style. "New way" does not mean the old imposition of some one model, but a method of using many models, a method of using this human modeling power rather than staying within some one model for a century or two. As I see it, the *process* of form*ing* must itself be the new type of "approach." What has happened occasionally and some centuries apart must now become routine for us. It is not this or that model, but the process of model-creating itself.

In modern life, to get through even one day an individual cannot depend solely on the models and interpretive patterns he is given by his culture. These contradict, they are too many, and often they do not solve the situation in which he finds himself. To deal with what he is up against they are too few. He *must* reinterpret, newly interpret, invent meaning, create myth, and generate new futures and new significances in order to mold the already given troubling meanings of his situation.

Recently, Kuhn's analysis[6] (highly consistent with Heidegger's analyses in this book) has clarified the basic difference between merely carrying out the implications of a given scientific model and creating a new one. Kuhn terms the creation of a new model a "scientific revolution." I have termed it the creation of meaning.[7]

The process (or doing) that creates and schematizes cannot itself be explained by some supposedly underlying or axiomatic model or scheme. In retrospect one finds that one's doing has set up a situation that is implicitly meaningful in ways that *can* be explicated. Such explication may look like a logical account of what occurred, but it is an error to view it as the cause of the process. The explication is a product of the process. It is a model or scheme created by the process, and we must see that the process as concrete doing is prior.

But is not such an approach to being—as the process of meaning making—really an invitation to arbitrariness? Is it not merely saying that there are no criteria, that you can have it any way you like? Anything you say or do is as good as anything else you might say or do; it all depends on your interpretation. Existentialism often

---

[6] Thomas S. Kuhn, *The Structure of Scientific Revolutions* (Chicago: University of Chicago Press, 1962).

[7] Eugene Gendlin, *Experiencing and the Creation of Meaning* (New York: The Free Press, 1962).

sounds like that.[8] But this is not at all the case! We know this from how difficult it is to devise courses of action and interpretations that take account of all in the situation and leave us feeling whole and unconflicted. That is why the situation in physics remained unresolved for so many years, and why Einstein worked for so many years. That is why we so often fail to devise any action or meaning that resolves "hang-ups." There are always plenty of easy alternatives for saying and doing something that fails to resolve anything.

To really resolve the "hang-ups" is a very different and far more difficult matter than just picking one or another of the many available schemes and actions that will not resolve anything. In practice we know the difference from the ease of one and the difficulty of the other, from our frequent failure to devise the latter, and from the unhappily unmistakable consequences of such failures. Thus, the use of this human power of defining is anything but arbitrary, anything but a choice from among many available alternatives. It is a highly controlled process of devising meanings that must take account of more facets than have ever yet been formulated.

Existentialism seemingly places a gap of arbitrariness between every moment and the next, just because existentialism denies the logical, deductive type of continuity. What sort of ethics, for example, can come from a view that rejects every statable criterion of value or rightness, and views it as created by, but not determining, human

---

[8] It is a question that besets the method of linguistic analysis also. The rules for the use of a word are not in the dictionary; they are implicit in our knowing how to speak. One explicates these rules, not by "leaning on a model," but by leaning directly on our knowing how to talk and act in situations. Current philosophy of both sorts is very much at the juncture at which Heidegger pictures it. There is a pre-conceptual court of appeal.

action? Must it not result in high-sounding rationaliza-
tions for doing absolutely anything one pleases? And,
similarly, how can there be a basis for discussing being or
science if one purports to explicate some not fully formulated "situation"? To say that it cannot be deduced or
checked against a scheme—how is that more than saying
that it must always remain unfounded?

Heidegger helped fight and win the battle against equat-
ing concrete living with a scheme, won the battle against
reading some theoretical scheme into things, and showed
that living humans are the reason for schemes and not
the reverse. Therefore, we must understand the seeming
gap as these oppositions to the earlier rationalistic and
logistic view.

We must reopen the question to which Heidegger's ap-
parent gap of arbitrariness is the answer. That question
was: Is there some rational or scientific thinglike defined order that determines world and man? His answer:
No.

Having seen the question to which Heidegger's "No" is
the answer, we can now separate out a different question
that is too often merged with the first. Our second question is: Are there other criteria, other ways we might
characterize and recognize an authentic, successful inventing and forming from those many, easily achieved
ways of interpreting, inventing, and forming that seem
to offer solutions but really leave us in pain, in conflict,
sick, or about to embark on something we will later say
we knew better than to do? Even if there is no logical or
rational scheme of things except one that is historically
derived and in the process of being changed—by us—
might there be a (nonschematic) way of recognizing
the scientific revolution and telling it apart from mere
nonsense or evil?

And, as Heidegger states so well, further reinterpre-
tations in life or philosophy are possible only on the
grounds of the ones we are already in, the given ones. We

cannot genuinely throw away our interpretations, values and reactions, problems and anomolies, no matter how emancipated we are in general, no matter how convinced we are in general that our values are "merely relative," that science uses "only models." In fact, they are not just "relative," they are "relative *to*" the situations in which they inhere, the problems they helped pose. Unless we carry all this *further* we cannot get out of it. Therefore, scientific revolutions and everyday problems are so difficult to solve adequately (and so easy to avoid or deny verbally in obviously futile and merely pained ways).

But is there nothing then that can be *said* to differentiate the authentically experienced, context-inclusive, unconflicted manner of meaning-making from an alienated, inauthentic, merely irresponsible manner of have it whatever way you like? In different kinds of situations there are different recognizable marks, some private and some observable (even in objective research). What basically sets the authentic manner of meaning-making apart is that it moves from the defined to the as yet undefined (the felt, concrete sense of the whole situation), and then from out of that to another, new or modified, more adequate form. This movement can apply to anything formed —things, words, art, ways of acting, or social roles.[9]

The next form is not just another model taking the place of the first; it is a "zag" in a continuing "zig-zag"

---

[9] On this and on the points made above, the reader may wish to examine my other writings: *Experiencing and the Creation of Meaning* (New York: The Free Press, 1962); "Experiential Explication and Truth," *Journal of Existentialism*, VI, (1966), 22; "A Theory of Personality Change," in *Personality Change*, ed. by Worchel and Byrne (New York: John Wiley & Sons, 1962); "Focusing Ability in Psychotherapy, Personality and Creativity," in *Research in Psychotherapy*, ed. by J. Shlien (Washington, D.C.: American Psychological Association, 1967), Vol. III; "What are the Grounds of Explication?", *The Monist*, XLIX (1965), 1; "Expressive Meanings," in *Invitation to Phenomenology*, ed. by J. Edie (Chicago: Quadrangle Books, 1965).

process between one's live sense and the realm of forms.

The next definition can change one's felt sense. To define a situation alters what one is about. Saying something in words has an effect on what one wants to say—it clarifies, intensifies, or shifts it. From such an "experiential shift" one can move to a further step of forming; one can suspend any given formulation and turn to the preconceptual, which always implicitly includes the whole complexity of which we are sensitive, and which develops further in interaction, and is carried forward in a zig-zag that is experientially (though not logically) continuous.

There are a number of different kinds of moving relationships between forms and concrete experiencing. I give experiencing the "ing" form because it is activity. In various distinguishable ways, experiencing lets us create an endlessly greater variety of relevant forms than the few rigid ones that culturally given perception and social roles hold steady for us. This experiential zig-zag movement is the approach that is more than an approach.

Eugene T. Gendlin

The University of Chicago

INDICES

Index of Names

Aristotle, 34, 35*n*., 40, 45, 49–50, 78, 80–83, 85, 106, 108, 112, 116, 118, 132, 153, 155, 172

Baliani, Giovanni Battista, 78
Baumgarten, Alexander, 112–15, 117, 121, 152, 155, 213
Bohr, Niels, 20, 67

Descartes, René, 17, 94, 98–106, 112
Democritus, 79–80, 208

Eberhard, Johann Augustus, 79, 131
Eckhart, Meister, 98
Eddington, Sir Arthur, 13
Eudoxus, 83

Fichte, Johann Gottlieb, 58
Frederick the Great, 112

Galileo Galilei, 66, 79–80, 88, 90–91, 116, 165
Goethe, Johann Wolfgang von, 58, 113
Gottsched, Johann Christoph, 113

Hegel, Georg Wilhelm, 28, 28*n*., 58, 113, 132, 134, 150–51, 191
Heisenberg, Werner, 67
Hume, David, 113

Kant, Immanuel, 5, 34, 55ff.
Knutzen, Martin, 113

Leibniz, Gottfried Wilhelm von, 23–24, 79, 94, 98, 108, 112, 121–22, 150, 166, 174, 191, 199, 235

Meier, Georg Friedrich, 154–55

Newton, Sir Isaac, 76–78, 80, 82, 85–88, 91, 94, 97, 126, 165, 199
Nietzsche, Friedrich, 43, 150

Plato, 2, 33, 40, 45–46, 49–50, 75, 82, 91, 112, 150, 208
Protagoras, 46

Schelling, Friedrich Wilhelm Joseph von, 58, 113, 134, 150
Schiller, Johann Christoph Friedrich von, 58, 113
Socrates, 73–74
Suárez, Francisco, 100

Thales, 3

Wolff, Christian von, 78, 87, 112, 152, 154–55, 172

INDEX OF GERMAN TERMS

Abzweckung (purpose), 149

Aktuellen (actual), 44

Anblickbar (capable of being viewed), 200

Angeschaut (something looked at), 197

Angeschautsein (being-intuited), 200

Anmessung (fitting), 35

Ansatz (approach), 28

An-schauen (looking at), 143

anschauen (looking at), 95*n*.; (intuiting), 198

Anschauung (intuition), 135, 197–98

an sich (in itself), 33

Anwesende (present), 63

Anwesenheit (presence), 64, 84

Aufhebung (being lifted up), 121

Aufklärung (enlightenment), 124

auf-und hingenommen (taken up and in), 142

Auf-und Vorliegendes (exposing and a present given), 218

auf uns zu (toward us), 220

augenblicklich (momentary), 218

Ausdruck (expression), 36

Ausgesagtheit (assertedness), 63

Auskunft (information), 36

Aussage (deposition), 37; (assertion), 62

Aussagen an, von, über (assertions of, about, to), 36

ausweisen (proven), 180

bedingen (to condition), 8

Bedingtsein (being conditioned), 48

Bedingung (condition), 47–48

Begegnen-lassen, das (the letting encounter), 242

Begriff (concept), 137

Begründung (foundation), 14, 55

Beharren (enduring), 229

Beistellung (putting-alongside), 181

Bekundung (manifestation), 128

Bericht (report), 37, 43

beständig (constant), 137

Bestand (what constitutes), 229

Bestandstücke (permanent elements), 139, 194

Bestimmungsstücke (determining elements), 157

Bewegtheit (being in motion), 86

Bewenden (point), 208

bloss (mere), 147

Dafürhalten (taking-for), 92

Dagegensprechen (speak against, contradict), 107

Da-haben (having-there), 218, 221

Dasein (existence), 41–42, 44, 49–50, 55, 65–66, 89, 96–98, 106, 113, 117, 191, 225–29, 235

Daseinszusammenhang (existential connection), 227

Ding, das (thing), 5, 15, 128

Dastehen (standing there), 194, 229

Ding an sich (thing-in-itself), 5, 128

Ding für uns (thing for us), 5

Dinghaftigkeit (thingness), 129

Dingheit (thingness), 7, 92

Dingsein (being-a-thing), 19

Dunst (illusion), 214

Ebene (level), 28

Eigenschaften (properties), 34

ein je dieses (one such this one), 15

ein räumen (to place space), 200

Einzelnheit (singleness), 49

Empfundene (what is sensed), 137

Entgegen (againstness), 158, 204

entgegen-fassendes Vorgreifen (reaching and grasping beforehand), 220

Entgegenstehen (standing-over-against), 158

Entgegenstehenlassen (allowing to stand against), 219

Entscheidung (decision), 9

Entwurf (project), 88–89, 92

Erfahrung (experience), 140; *anschauliche* (intuitive direct experience), 94

Erfahrungsurteil (experiential judgment), 139

Erkennbare (the knowable), 137

Erkennen (knowing), 137

Erkenntnisse (cognitions), 134

Erklärung (interpretation), 155

erläuternd (clarifying), 164

eröffnet (exposed), 242

Erscheinung (appearance), 128, 227

erweiternd (extending), 164

erzählen (tell), 37

etwas (something), 5–6

Faktis (facts), 121

Fehlen (privation), 213

Fortwähren (continuance), 229

Fragestellung (mode of questioning), 179

Fürwort (demonstrative pronoun), 25

Gebung (giving), 143

Gedachte, das (what is thought), 143

Gefüge (framework), 36

gegen (against), 137, 139–40, 184, 195, 205, 214

Gegenhaft (againstness), 222–23

Gegenhafte-Ständige, das (against-like constancy), 219

Gegenheit (againstness), 190

Gegenstand (object), 134, 137–40, 143, 181, 184, 190, 194, 205, 231, 237

Gegenständlichkeit (objectivity), 178

Gegenstehen (standing before), 188

Gegenstehenlassen (permitting a standing-against), 205, 241

Gegen-uns-stehenden (what stands-over-against-us), 202

Geistigen (spiritual), 51

Gemächte (product), 244

Gemeinsamkeit (sharing in common), 136

gerührt (stirred), 143

Gesammeltheit (collectedness), 203

Geschehen (happening), 48

Geschichte (history), 45

Geschichtlichkeit (historicity), 39

Grenzziehung (laying of limits), 120

Grösse (magnitude), 195

Grössenmass (measure of size), 215

Grosshafte (sizeable), 195

Grund (basis), 83; (principle), 148

Grundriss (blueprint), 91–92

Grundsätze (axioms), 124; (real principles), 193

Hervorgehens (emergence), 83

Hinausgriff (grasping-out), 221

Hinaus-zu (out-to), 199

Hin-nehmen (taking-in), 142

Ichheit (I-ness), 105

Identitäten (identities), 174

im vorhinein (in advance), 221

In-der-Zeit-sein (being-in-time), 233

inmitten des Seienden (in the midst of what is), 50

Insichgesammelt (what is collected in itself), 188

Insichstehende (what stands in itself), 188

je diese (just these), 15–18, 23

je diese Dinge (these things), 15

je dieses (this one), 15–18, 23–24, 28

Jediesheit (being-this-one), 14–15

je für sich (each-for-itself), 15

Jenseitige (ulterior), 25

jeweilig (particular), 30

Jeweiligkeit (particularity), 16

Kategorienlehre (theory of categories), 64

ledig (unencumbered), 147

Leitfaden (guideline), 64

Lichtung (illumination), 106

Logistic (symbolic logic), 156

Mannigfaltigkeit (manifoldness), 208

Menge (aggregate), 195; (multiplicity), 204

Mit-dazu-vorstellen (additional representation), 163

mitgesagt (co-asserted), 63

Mitteilung (communication), 36

Möglichkeit (possibility), 21

Natürding (natural thing), 127

natürliche Welt-ansicht (natural world-view), 40

neben (beside), 198

Nebeneinander (proximity), 198

Nichtauseinanderfahrende (what does not fall apart), 188

Objekt (object), 134, 139–40, 237

Offenbare, das (what is manifest), 141

Offene (open), 242

Ort (place), 16

physiologisch (physiological), 126

Präsenz (presence), 188

Prinzip (principle), 124, 193

Priorität (priority), 165

Raumhafte (the spatial), 196

Raum-Zeit-Bezug (space-time-relation), 19

Raum-Zeit-Stelle (space-time-position), 19

Realität (reality), 239

Richtigkeit (correctness), 45

Ruck (jolt), 2

Rückbesinnung (reflecting back), 207

Rück-wurf (thrown back), 243

Ruhe (quiescence), 44

Sache (fact), 126, 138; (a something), 212
Sachhaft (thinglike), 214
Sachhaltig (belonging to the content of), 239–40
Sachhaltigkeit (character), 233; (content), 240
Sachheit (something), 219; (thinghood), 213, 237
sachlich Vorgängige, das (what objectivily precedes), 166
Sammlung (gathering-together), 187
Satz (proposition), 36, 193
Satzaussage (assertion), 38
Satzgegenstand (object of a proposition), 38
Satz vom Grund (principle of sufficient reason), 108
Schauen (looking), 143
Schein (semblance), 12, 194, 214
schon Anwesende, das (the already present), 63
Seiender (one that is), 142
Sein des Seienden (the being of what is), 175
Seinsbestimmung (determination of being), 63
seinsmässige Herkunft (origin considered in terms of its mode of being), 105
Sich-Aussprechen (to declare oneself), 36
sich-im-Geiste-denken (to think in the mind), 91

Sich-richten (a directing-to), 35
Sich-selbst-eine-Kenntnis geben (giving-oneself-a-cognition), 91
Sich-zeigendes (what shows itself), 188, 200
Sinnlichkeit (sensibility), 143
sondern (to sort), 119
Spielraum (domain), 92
Spruch (saying), 171
Stammbegriffe (root concepts), 187
Stand (standing), 184, 190, 205
Ständigkeit (constancy), 229, 231
Stoffding (material thing), 51
Stofflichkeit (materiality), 213
Strecke (stretch), 56

Tatsachen (facts), 59
Träger (bearer), 34, 35*n*.
Tun (doing), 207

Übereinstimmung (correspondence), 36
überspringen (pass over, skip over), 8, 93, 151
Überstieg (passing over), 176
Über-weg (passing beyond), 176
umgänglich alltäglich Gegebene, das (the usual everyday given), 211
Um-uns-herum (round-about-us), 7
Unbedingt (unconditioned), 9, 47

unheimlicher (more un-canny), 44

unseiend (non-existent), 240

Unterlage (foundation), 34

Veränderung (alteration), 234

verbessern (reform), 10

Verbinden (connecting), 203

Verbindungswort (connec-tive), 38

Vergegenständlichung (ob-jectification), 141

Vernunft (reason), 64

verrücktes (deranged), 2

Verrückung (shifting), 2

Verschweigung (conceal-ment), 37

Verwandtschaft (relation), 136

Vorausgriff (anticipation), 92

Voraus-vor-stellung (pre-senting-in-advance), 230

vordeutende Erläuterung (preliminary elucidation), 61

Vordeutung (interpretation), 128

vor-gebildet (pre-formed), 201

vor-gefunden (found in ad-vance), 137

vor-gehalten (held-before), 200

Vorgreifen (beforehand), 220

Vor-griff (reaching-before), 243

Vorgriff (anticipation), 243

Vorhalt (presentation), 218

Vorhanden (the present-at-hand), 5, 11, 35, 52, 105, 199; (existing), 34

Vorhandensein (being-pres-ent-at-hand), 225

Vorherige, das (the preced-ing), 166, 168

Vorriss (outline), 121

Vor-stellen (pre-senting, rep-resenting), 200, 224

vor-stellend (pre-senting), 189

Vorstellung (conception), 32; (representation), 130, 136

Vor-uns-kommen (coming-before-us), 195

Vor-urteile (pre-judgments), 180

Wahrgenommene (what is perceived), 137

wahrhaft (true), 181

Wahrnehmungsurteil (per-ceptual judgment), 139

Was (what), 210, 213

Wasgehalt (what-content), 212, 214

was ist seiender (what more truly is), 210

Was-seiendes (being-what), 222

Wechsel (change), 234

Weg (path), 55–56

werfen (throw), 89n.

Wesensbau (essential struc-ture), 36

Wesensumgrenzung (essen-tial delineation), 161

wirklich (actual), 191

Wirklichkeit (actuality), 191, 239

wirkt (being effective), 191

Wissenschaften (sciences), 1

Womit (wherewith), 189

Worinnen (wherein), 194

Würdigen (evaluation), 92

würdigt (evaluated), 92

Zeichen (signs), 56

Zeitpunkte (time point), 21

Zeitraum (time-span), 16–17

Zeitstellen (time-spots), 233

Zensur (censor), 121

Zeugraum (equipment room), 21

zu-fallen (to occur in addition), 235

Zug (characteristic), 18

zu-gesagt (said of), 62; (attributed to), 63

zugleich (at the same time), 172

Zugrundeliegendes (something which underlies), 105

Zu-sagen (attribution), 62

Zusammen (together), 186; (togetherness), 226

Zusammensetzen (putting-together), 186

Zweifalt (doubleness), 135

Zwischen (the between), 242

Index of Latin Terms

accidens (accident), 34

actus mentis (action of the mind), 158

adaequatio (correspondence), 117

animal rationale (rational animal), 106

axiomata sive leges motus (principles or laws of motion), 77, 92

cogito (I think), 98, 104, 106–7

cognitio humana (what is knowable by man's pure reason), 116

commensuratio (fitting), 117

complementum possibilitatis (complement to possibility), 239

compositio (composition), 225

coniunctio (conjunction), 225

convenientia (agreement), 117

copula (bond), 156

cosmologia rationalis (rational cosmology), 110

determinatio (determinateness), 213

dynamis (force), 191

ens commune (things in general), 118

ens creatum (created thing), 47, 110

essentia (essence), 212

existentia (existence), 213, 239

experientia (experience), 93
experiri (to experience), 93

fundamentum (basis, ground), 104
fundamentum absolutum (absolute ground), 103

hic (this here), 24

ille (that far away), 25
inconcussum (unshakable), 103
iste (that there), 24
iudicium (judgment), 154

lex inertiae (law of inertia), 78

mathematica universalis (universal mathematics), 101
mathematica vulgaris (common mathematics), 101
mathesis universalis (universal teaching), 102
mente concipere (to conceive in the mind), 91–92, 116

metaphysica architectonica (architectonic metaphysics), 121
metaphysica generalis (general metaphysics), 111
metaphysica specialis (specialized metaphysics), 111
moto corporum, de (on the motion of bodies), 78
mundi systemate, de (on the system of the world), 78

systema mundi (system of the world), 126

theologia rationalis (rational theology), 109
transcendere (to pass over), 178
tribuere (to attribute), 154
tueor (to look, gaze), 95n.

veritas (truth), 117
vis centripeta (centripetal force), 77
vis impressa (impacted force), 88

INDEX OF GREEK TERMS

αἴσθησις (the sensible), 113; (sensibility, perception), 144

ἀλήθεια (truth), 46

ἅμα (at the same time), 172

ἀντωνυμία (pronoun), 25

ἀξιόω (evaluate), 92

ἀξιώματα (fundamental propositions, axioms), 92

ἁπλαί (simple movements), 84

ἀπόφασις (holding away), 154

ἀρχή (beginning), 83; ἀρχὴ κινήσεως (beginning of motion), 83

βίᾳ (by violence), 84, 88

διαίρεσις (taking apart, analysis), 160

δύναμις (force, power, capacity), 85

ἐκεῖ (that far away, there), 25

ἐπιστήμη (knowledge), 81

καθ' αὑτά (according to themselves), 83

καθόλου (in general, on the whole), 117

κατά (from above to below), 62

κατάφασις (assertion, attribution), 62, 107, 154

κατηγορία (category), 63

κίνησις εὐθεῖα (motion in a straight line), 84

κίνησις κατὰ τόπον (motion with respect to location), 83

κρίνειν (to sort, separate), 119

κύκλῳ (in a circle), 84

λέγειν (to address, assert as something), 64

λόγος (reason), 108, 145; (judgment), 144; (gathering together), 187; (assertion), 106, 108, 126, 152–53, 156, 178

τὰ μαθήματα (the mathematical, what can be learned), 69, 71, 73–74
μάθησις (mathematics, learning), 69, 71, 73, 75, 91
μανθάνειν (to learn), 69
μεταβολή (motion), 83
μικτή (mixture), 84
μέθοδος (method), 102

ποίησις (doing, making), 70
τὰ ποιούμενα (things made or done), 70, 81
τα πράγματα (things dealt with), 70
πρᾶξις (dealing with, doing, acting), 70
πρότερον φύσει (what is former in nature), 166

πρώτη φιλοσοφία (first philosophy, metaphysics), 64, 99
συμβεβηκός (chance, contingency), 34

τέλος (aim, end), 81
τόδε τι (this here, a particular), 49

ὑποκείμενον (what underlies, substance), 34, 62, 103, 105
ὕστερον πρὸς ἡμᾶς (what is later toward us), 166

τὰ φαινόμενον (that which makes itself manifest), 81
φάναι (to say), 62
φάσις (a saying), 62
φορά (being transported), 83, 86
τὰ φυσικά (things which come forth), 70, 81
φύσις (nature), 83, 126; παρὰ φύσιν (against nature), 84; κατὰ φύσιν (in accordance with nature), 84